Tongzhi Living

Men Attracted to Men
in Postsocialist China

Tiantian Zheng

University of Minnesota Press
Minneapolis • London

A different version of chapter 1 was previously published as "Contesting Heteronormality: Recasting Same-Sex Desire in China's Past and Present," *Wagadu: A Journal of Transnational Women's and Gender Studies* 12 (2014): 15–40; reprinted with permission of *Wagadu*. An earlier version of chapter 2 was published as "Masculinity in Crisis: Effeminate Men, Loss of Manhood, and the Nation-state in Postsocialist China," *Etnografica* (2015). Portions of chapter 4 were previously published in *Cultural Politics of Gender and Sexuality in Contemporary Asia*, edited by Tiantian Zheng (University of Hawai`i Press, 2015).

Published by the University of Minnesota Press
111 Third Avenue South, Suite 290
Minneapolis, MN 55401–2520
http://www.upress.umn.edu

Library of Congress Cataloging-in-Publication Data

Zheng, Tiantian.
Tongzhi living : men attracted to men in postsocialist China / Tiantian Zheng.
Includes bibliographical references and index.
ISBN 978-0-8166-9199-9 (hc)
ISBN 978-0-8166-9200-2 (pb)
1. Men—Sexual behavior—China.   2. Men—China—Attitudes.
3. Heterosexual men—China.   I. Title.
HQ1090.7.C6Z4734   2015
306.708110951—dc23   2014043038

Printed in the United States of America on acid-free paper

The University of Minnesota is an equal-opportunity educator and employer.

21 20 19 18 17 16 15   10 9 8 7 6 5 4 3 2 1

TONGZHI LIVING

I dedicate this book to Jack Wortman

Contents

A Walk in the Park

I t is 5:00 p.m. on a Friday afternoon. As part of our daily routine, twenty-four-year-old Tan and I walk to the park together. Soon his boyfriend, twenty-three-year-old Wang, joins us. We sit on one of the benches in the cruising spot and start chatting. This cruising spot is located in a corner of a major park in the center of the city, where about twenty to forty men gather and socialize every day. In addition to this park, two other major public parks in the center of the city have tongzhi cruising spots. (I explain the term "tongzhi," which is used for same-sex-attracted men, in detail later in the chapter.) The spot that I visit every day is furnished with eight benches, with four on each side facing each other separated by a small path. To the right of the eight benches are two large tables with seats around them, where tongzhi usually gather and play cards, while other tongzhi stand around the players and watch. Next to the two tables is an open space where tongzhi play a Chinese game called featherball with each other.[1] Once all the seats are occupied, the rest of the tongzhi have to stand around the benches and tables, conversing with each other. In front of the cruising spot are small woods, which some tongzhi enter at night to engage in sex. Behind the spot is a wall that separates the park from the city. On the right side, past the tables and the open space where the tongzhi play featherball, is the dead end of the park. On the left side is the area where female sex workers stand around soliciting customers, providing scenery as well as fodder for discussion for the tongzhi sitting on the benches.

The cruising spot is visited by tongzhi every day from morning until night, with most tongzhi visitors coming from 5:00 p.m. until 3:00 a.m. Tongzhi of all ages gather here not only for dates but also for relaxation where they can laugh, joke, and talk with each other about everything under the sun. The surrounding public park is frequented by all kinds of people from all walks of life. Loud music and dance noise arise from groups engaged in folk dance, modern dance, tai chi practice, chess playing, and card playing throughout the park. However, because this tongzhi cruising spot is in a dead end of the park, non-tongzhi rarely walk into this zone.

Sitting next to us is a man who first entered the tongzhi circle more than ten years ago. Still living with his parents, he says they keep him under constant watch. If he returns home late, they punish him. They are afraid that he is being influenced by immoral people.

As I sit in the cruising spot, I hear Tan ask people around us if they would marry their boyfriends if gay marriage were legalized. His question arises from my previous discussions with him about gay marriage. To his question, everyone looks startled and responds, "Of course not!" The man sitting next to us says, "No, this kind of thing cannot be brought into the daylight!" *(zhengda guangming)*. Another man says, "I haven't even thought [of marriage]. Two men together are just for play. It's different from the marriage between a male and a female. [The relationship] between two men is temporary and cannot be permanent." Tan adds, "If you get married, you'll be the focus of the world's attention as one of the few gay married couples—of course no one wants that! How shameful it would be!" *(duibu duiren a)*.

As we are talking, Wang, who is sitting next to me, suddenly grabs my arm and pulls me out of the cruising spot toward where an old man stands. I have no time to ask him what he is doing. As we walk toward the old man, Wang lets out three words: "That's my dad."

We stand right next to his father. With a stern expression, the old man asks Wang, "What were you doing over there?" I turn to look at Wang. His face is bright red and his whole body is shaking. He answers, "I was working with her trying to convince her to purchase a membership and get enlisted in our company." The old man looks at me suspiciously and asks, "Really?" I reply yes. My answer obviously eases the tension. The now-relaxed old man starts telling me about his company. He says this line of work is long term and can bring a substantial amount of money to the family. He continues to tout his product, an herbal substance, as good stuff and tells me that both he and his wife consume the product. "This is the best career because you'll be working for yourself and not for others," says Wang's father.

He stops, looks at me, and asks how old I am and what kind of work I do. Then he looks into me as if he can see through my soul and says, "Don't learn bad things. Don't go online and talk to people and learn to be bad and turn bad. Learn good things and walk on the right path." He turns to the cruising spot where a group of men sit and asks again, "What were you guys doing there?" Before I have a chance to answer, Wang jumps in, saying, "We were only talking about work."

The old man asks a few more questions and leaves, his doubts seemingly eliminated. After he leaves, Wang becomes restless. He keeps asking me to look and check if his father has really left. He says that if his father knew what he was doing, he would be caged in his house. He tells me that his first boyfriend came to live with him, and at first his father did not know that they were tongzhi. When he found out, his father smashed everything that belonged to his boyfriend into pieces. His grandmother learned about it and questioned him, "Why are you with men knowing that you cannot have children with them?" Seeing Wang laugh at her words, she turned anxious and raised her voice: "I'm serious!" Both his parents were so angry that they locked him in the house for three to four months and prohibited him from going anywhere, not even to work.

During this time Wang's parents kept urging him to get married. At the end of the fourth month he could not stand the isolation any longer. He asked his parents to find a woman for him to marry. They brought him their friend's daughter, whom he had grown up with and always treated as a little sister. Although he felt uncomfortable with her, he pretended that they were having a good time. After they got married, his parents loosened their tight control. However, his wife, his child, and he were still living with his parents, so he dared not return home late, because his parents would dress him down and would again ban him from leaving the house in the evening.

As disturbing as Wang's parents' response was to his sexual orientation, I discovered in the course of my research even harsher responses. While answering calls as a volunteer for a tongzhi hotline in a grassroots organization, I heard stories of parents who told their children that they would have aborted them had they known that they were going to be tongzhi. In one instance, the parents even encouraged the child to commit suicide, suggesting several methods in which he could bring about his own death. Tragically, this young man did commit suicide at the age of twenty-one.

TERMINOLOGY

Same-sex relationships have a long history in China. During the ancient and imperial period, there was a distinction between same-sex behavior and same-sex identity. Poetic metaphors such as *yu tao* (part of a peach that is not eaten) and *duan xiu* (passion of cut sleeve), derived from ancient same-sex love stories, were used to refer to same-sex actions, tendencies, and preferences rather than to an innate sexual essence (Hinsch 1992, 7). Therefore, neither metaphor was used to label a person. The term *"yu tao"* appeared in a traditional Chinese story in which Mizi Xia, the love of Duke Ling of Wei (534–493 B.C.), while strolling with the ruler in an orchard, bit into a peach and found it sweet. He stopped eating it and gave the remaining half to the ruler to enjoy. The term *"duan xiu"* came from a story in which Emperor Ai of Han (206 B.C. to A.D. 200) was sleeping in the daytime with his favorite Dong Xian, who was lying under his large sleeve. When the emperor wanted to get up, he cut off his own sleeve in order not to disturb the soundly sleeping Dong Xian. With these two well-known stories, *yu tao* and *duan xiu* came to signify same-sex love. Another category describing same-sex love invoked specific social roles such as "favorites," rather than sexual essence (Hinsch 1992).

At the turn of the twentieth century, Western scientific sexology was introduced into China; the Western terms "homosexuality" and "same-sex love" were translated as *tongxinglian* and *tongxing'ai*, respectively. With "a Westernization of Chinese sexual categories and a Westernization of the overall terms of discourse about homosexuality," Hinsch argues that the "fluid conceptions of sexuality of old, which assumed that an individual was capable of enjoying a range of sexual acts, were replaced with the ironclad Western dichotomy of heterosexual/homosexual" (Hinsch 1992, 169). As a result, instead of "passion of the cut sleeve" and other terms from history and literature, "Chinese now speak of 'homosexuality' (*tongxinglian* or *tongxing'ai*), a direct translation of the Western medical term that defines a small group of pathological individuals according to a concrete sexual essence" (169).[2]

Tongxinglian (homosexuality) has been the most commonly used term in Chinese scholarly writings (L. Chen 2003; Gao 2006; Y. Li 1998; Li and Wang 1992; D. Liu 2005; B. Zhang 1994; Zaizhou Zhang 2001). However, same-sex-attracted men rarely use it because it carries a pathologized and medicalized notion of homosexuality and has been used and represented in the media as an "abnormality" or a "perversion" *(biantai)* (Y. Li 2006; Micollier 2003). Moreover, the words "same sex" are included in the terms *"tongxinglian"* (homosexuality) and *"tongxing'ai"* (same-sex love), thereby exposing a homosexual identity and inviting the stigma attached to it.

Instead, same-sex-attracted men most frequently use the term "tong-zhi," translated as "comrade." Tongzhi is a Chinese translation of a Soviet Communist term referring to Communist revolutionaries who shared the same aspirations and comradeship in a classless egalitarian society. Since 1949, the word has evolved from a specific term for Communist Party members to a general form of address in everyday discourse. In 1989, it was first publicly deployed by Hong Kong organizers of the inaugural lesbian and gay film festival to refer to an indigenous Chinese same-sex identity distinct from a global gay identity (W.-S. Chou 2000; Y. Li 2006; Micollier 2003; H. Zhou 2000). The term then gained currency in mainland China in the 1990s.

In addition to tongzhi, the English word "gay" represents another elusive term denoting same-sex identity. Some of my respondents indicated to me that, because this English term is not well known to ordinary Chinese, they use it as a way to disguise their sexual identity. My respondents also perceived Western gay men as having achieved much greater progress, evidenced by the Stonewall movement in New York's Greenwich village in 1969 and legalized gay marriage. The appropriation of the English term "gay" seems to embody this hope for progress. My research shows that Chinese self-identified gay men imagine themselves as members of the global gay community as they aspire to contribute to the global gay cause (see also Ho 2009; Rofel 1999, 2007). Just as the imagined communities of the first European nation-state became possible because of print capitalism (Anderson 1983), Chinese tongzhi imagine themselves as part of the global gay community because of their shared gay identity and similar interests. Although they may have never met or known other members of the community face to face, they commemorate the Stonewall movement and call it "an important milestone for the tongzhi human rights movement, initiating the tradition that tongzhi around the world celebrate June as gay pride month" (Ga 2007, 2).[3] Activities were also organized annually around the international gay pride month of June, the international day of anti-homophobia on May 17, the AIDS Memorial Quilt, and International AIDS Day (Dai 2008; Hong 2007; W. Xi 2007).[4]

Although some Chinese same-sex-attracted men have appropriated the Western term "gay," anthropologists must be careful not to impose their terms and categories on the local same-sex-attracted population. Anthropologists have addressed the problems of using Eurocentric terms to refer to non-European local settings, making local sex and gender constructions invisible, "unidentified and unacknowledged" (Lewin and Leap 2002, 9; see also Boellstorff 2005; Manalansan 2003; Schmidt 2002). The Western terms "gay" and "lesbian" connote a fixed sexual identity, sexual practice, and sexual relationship that may not have similar meanings in other cultures and hence are not able to capture local nuances and diversities (see Rubin 2002).

In this book I refer to my research subjects as "tongzhi" (comrade), the term most commonly used by the men in my research to self-identify themselves in private. I also refer to my research subjects as "1s" and "0s," the terms they use to label themselves and others in the community. During my research, almost every man I spoke to identified himself as either a 0 or a 1. In our casual discussions, they often discussed the differences between 0s and 1s and instructed each other on strategies to help them resolve their differences. For instance, 0s shared with each other their difficulties in making 1s fall in love them and stay with them, as in their words, "It was in 1s' nature to only want sex rather than commitment." They advised each other to withhold sex from 1s for a month, so that the 1s would value and treasure them more.

Before entering the tongzhi community, same-sex-attracted men are not aware of the gender division between 1 and 0. On entry into the community, they find themselves overwhelmed by the question of whether they are 1s or 0s: 1, symbolizing the penis, is identified within the community as the male role, and 0, symbolizing the vagina, with the female role. Conversations on Internet chat rooms and at the tongzhi cruising areas often start with tongzhi introducing themselves as either 1s or 0s. Even registration forms on online friend-making websites for same-sex-attracted men require self-identification as 1s or 0s. New members in the community, who have no clue whether they are 1s or 0s, find themselves slowly socialized into these two categories. Some choose their own role, whereas others are assigned it through assuming a sexual position in their first sexual experience with someone who has already self-identified as a 0 or a 1. For instance, my informant Fan self-identified as a 0 and told everyone to call him by the name he had created for himself, "Flory Sister" *(huajie)*, because he said that he felt his personality fit the female role. My informant Deng was unsure about his role until he had the first sexual experience in which he was assigned the inserted position. After his first sexual experience, Deng acknowledged that he fit the female role and became more and more socialized into it.

Although their first sexual position can influence their future gender roles as 1s or 0s, ultimately, it is the gender roles—the cultural categorization of traits and characteristics as either masculine or feminine—that decide their self-identification as 1s or 0s. Although sex positions vary in a relationship, gender roles invariably determine whether one is a 1 or a 0; that is, even if a man has experienced the inserted position of 0 with the man he loves, he may still self-identify as a 1 because of his individual traits. Conversely, although a man may feel pleasure in the inserting role of 1 rather than the inserted role of 0, he may still choose to be the latter, self-identifying as a 0 because of his individual traits. As a result, as I was told by my informants, most 1s are able to choose the inserter's role to satisfy their physical needs, whereas most 0s are believed to endure the pain in their initial sexual experiences in order to satisfy their psychological needs (in my research, 0s discussed with me at length about how it usually took them a long time before finally becoming accustomed to, and even enjoying, the feeling). In other words, gender roles usually lead to sex roles. Through relationships and experiences, over time, tongzhi are formed into the identities of 1 or 0 according to the tacit rules and expectations shared in the community.

The 1/0 system is relatively pervasive among same-sex-attracted men, although it does not encompass every tongzhi's identity. In my research, two men identified themselves as 0.5, somewhere between 0 and 1. According to them, falling in love and one's increasing age may necessitate a change of roles, resulting in a flexible role as 0.5. Although these men cited Western models to question the 1/0 system, the presence of such a small number of voices has been unable to destabilize the system, which remains intact and hegemonic in the community.

The terms "1" and "0" may sound dehumanizing to Westerners, who may also find it problematic to assign 0 to the female role. However, as an anthropologist, I am obligated to use their terms and their categories to describe these same-sex-attracted men, just as I use "tongzhi"—their term—throughout the book, instead of "gay men," the Western term. It is the tongzhi community that uses the terms 1 and 0 to address and categorize each other and that assigns the female role to 0s and the masculine role to 1s. During my research, when my informants who self-identified as 1s talked about their "wives" as 0s, they said to me, "Both of you are the same—both of you are women." They see the 0s not as men, but as women, and they refer to them as women. In chapter 3, I point out that, in Chinese same-sex-attracted men's relationships, gender is pivotal and the members see each other as different even though both are biologically men, whereas in Western relationships, sexual orientation is key and there is no gender difference. The Chinese conception, in fact, resonates with the Thai lesbian relationship in which one person is labeled *tom* and assigned as the male, and the other is *dee* and is assigned as the female (Sinnott 2004).

In public, same-sex-attracted men in my research used ambiguous phrases such as "this kind of person" *(zhefangmian de ren)* or "not a good person" to refer to people like themselves. For instance, when I tagged along with my two key informants at a shopping mall, they constantly stopped and gauged whether a male passerby was a tongzhi. They either commented, "Do you think he is this kind of person?" or "This guy does not look like a good person." They consciously jettisoned labels that identified sexual identity in favor of vague phrases such as "this kind of person" and "not a good person" to refer to homosexuality, intending to elude the social stigma and prejudice attached to it (see also Miège 2009). Ironically, the very phrase they used—"not a good person"—itself embodied a discriminatory attitude toward homosexuality. As I explore in this book, this kind of self-criticism suggests their internalization of the dominant discourse. However, at the same time, tongzhi also used the phrase "not a good person" ironically, which even became a badge of honor as they reappropriated this discriminatory phrase in such a flirty and positive way that they resignified it as a powerful term of endearment.

SAME-SEX-ATTRACTED MEN IN POSTSOCIALIST CHINA

Although a homosocial and homoerotic culture was prevalent and relatively tolerated in imperial China, the imported Western pathologized model of homosexuality in the late nineteenth century ended this tradition (Y. Li 2006). Homosexuality itself was not illegal, but sodomy was considered a crime if it was nonconsensual or conducted with a minor. During the Maoist period, many same-sex-attracted people lived in terror and fear of persecution, including arbitrary penalties and Communist Party disciplinary sanctions (Y. Li 2006, 82). In 1997, sodomy was decriminalized. In the same year, the crime of hooliganism *(liumangzui)*, which was often invoked to penalize same-sex behaviors, was removed from the Criminal Law (p. 83). In 2001, the definition of homosexuality as a mental illness was withdrawn from Chinese psychiatric texts (83).

Economic reforms in the postsocialist era have led to the state's diminished control of the private sphere, a liberalizing attitude toward sexuality, a rise in individualism, and the emergence of new spaces in mass media and public culture where same-sex-attracted people can gather, meet, interact, share, chat, and develop a sense of identity through new media technologies such as Internet chat rooms, Twitter, and mobile phones (Kong 2010; S. Pan 1995, 1996, 1999; Y. Yan 2010; Zhang and Ong 2008; T. Zheng 2009a). China's economic and political liberalization in the 1980s and 1990s has resulted in tremendous growth in the number of self-identified gay individuals congregating in multiple venues such as online chat rooms, parks, bathhouses, bars, and public toilets (see Ho 2008; Rofel 1999, 2007). Yet, despite these social, cultural, and legal changes, especially the decriminalization of sodomy, the development of such liberal spaces continues to be restricted. Arbitrary arrests by the police and random hassles continue to make same-sex-attracted people feel unsafe and insecure in public places. All kinds of gatherings are still considered illegal unless they have been approved by the state. Civil law continues to prohibit the registration of nongovernmental organizations; they can only be registered as companies and are subsequently under constant state surveillance. Bathhouses, gay bars, and public parks are regularly raided, with same-sex-attracted people caught up in those raids being charged with a "violation of social order" or "prostitution."

It is in this historical period of change, characterized by increasing freedom but continuing surveillance and repression, that this book situates and examines the lives of same-sex-attracted men. It probes the question of how these men are affected and shaped by the rapid social, cultural, and economic transformations in postsocialist China. By investigating and exploring the rarely seen lives and lived experiences of tongzhi, this book sheds light on this marginalized population that has forged distinctive gendered and sexual identities, developed coping mechanisms to survive in a hostile cultural environment, staged a special form of health and social activism, and shaped new social inequalities and class differences in the midst of rapid social and economic transformation in the postsocialist Chinese cultural milieu.

The book is based on eleven months of ethnographic fieldwork conducted in the metropolitan city of Dalian from 2005 to 2013, phone and e-mail contacts with research subjects from 2005 to the present, and archival data of online postings from gay-related Internet websites, LGBTQ and tongzhi (gay men) e-mail lists, and newspaper and magazine articles. My ethnographic fieldwork involved interactions and in-depth interviews with self-identified gay men in cruising places such as parks, gay bars, and bathhouses; participant observation as a volunteer in two local grassroots AIDS organizations whose members were exclusively self-identified gay men; and interviews with health officials and local residents. In the grassroots AIDS organizations, I attended myriad social events, meetings, and lectures.

BEYOND LOCAL ESSENTIALISM AND WESTERN HOMOGENIZATION

Recent studies of the globalization of gay and lesbian identities engage in the debate between "local essentialism" and "Western homogenization." Drawing on ethnographic and historical sources, the first view argues that non-Western societies have distinctive local sexual identities at each time and place or have "indigenized" Western discourses to fit the local cultural constructions of multiple gender identities (Jackson 1999; see also Plummer 1992; Lim 2005). The second view contends that Western-style lesbian and gay identities outside of the Western world are indicative of Westernization on a global scale.

Stephen Murray (1992) theorizes Western homogenization as a neo-evolutionary process toward a universal, egalitarian, Western gayness. He maps out an evolutionary model of homosexuality from unequal relations based on age (ancient Greece), gender roles (modern Mesoamerica), and class (early capitalism) to equal relations. In Murray's evolutionary model, an increasingly strong gay and lesbian culture, identity, and politics have been diffused little by little throughout the Western world. Eventually this Western model will be what other countries and cultures will follow.

Dennis Altman (1996a, 1996b, 1997) also contends that the global trend is moving from gender-based identities to Western egalitarian sexual identities that are not rigidly tied to a particular gender identity. He argues that, through the vehicles of global media, entertainment, and tourism, Euro-American experiences and notions of sexuality are becoming increasingly globalized and widespread: A "global queering" process is taking place through the influence of Western concepts of sexual identity.

The two views—the Eurocentric and universalizing perspective versus the reification of the local and tribal—are mired in the "West (global)–Rest (local)" dichotomy. It assumes the centrality of the West and deems the global as tantamount to the West, which is appropriated, imitated, or resisted by the Rest (see also Martin et al. 2008; Plummer 1992). Moreover, the universalizing perspective generalizes same-sex experiences as sharing a common meaning that is identifiable and coherent across time and cultures. This standpoint is untenable given the diverse meanings and contexts of same-sex practices, such as the ritual of oral insemination of young Sambian boys by Sambian men to ensure their maturation into men (Herdt 1994; see also Rubin 2002), a point I return to in the next section.

Rather than these polarized views, a more complex, nuanced, and critical theoretical framework is needed to examine same-sex experiences. Lenore Manderson and Margaret Jolly (1997) caution us to avoid simplistic assumptions of sameness or difference in relation to the West when studying gender and sexuality in different regions, because "local" and "global," and "traditional" and "modern," are not mutually exclusive categories. Plummer observes that "same-sex experience moves in fits and starts along diverse paths to disparate becomings. It is . . . part of a historical dialectic. . . . Same-sex experiences have become increasingly fashioned through the interconnectedness of the world" (1992, 17).

This book employs a framework that decenters the West and contends that the categories of Western and non-Western cultures of gender and sexuality have never been isolated and discrete entities. They are, and continue to be, the products of mutual borrowing and mutual transformation through interactions and encounters (see also Martin et al. 2008).

This book thus complicates the dichotomy of West vs. the Rest and argues that the Chinese tongzhi is not a category nor a structure, but rather a complex, dialectic process of making and remaking through continuous interactions, integrations, and reworkings based on interregional influences and global interconnectedness. Imagining themselves as a part of the global gay community, the Chinese tongzhi have forged identities based on a wide array of factors that include their knowledge about the rights discourse and gay movements in the international gay community, Chinese state politics, their economic conditions, cultural moral discourses, nationalist sentiments, and their entrenchment in family politics, especially the pressure to marry women. The interplay between their understandings of the global and the complexities of local cultural politics and their own economic status embodies neither a traditional nor a Western mode of being or living.

GENDER, SEXUALITY, AND THE NATION

As illustrated, the universalizing perspective holds that same-sex practices exhibit a unified meaning that is independent of culture. This emphasis on sexual acts as the determining factor in identifying a person as homosexual eschews "the cultural contexts that gave rise to particular sexual practices" (Rubin 2002, 80). It fails to recognize the cultural meanings associated with sexual practices. As mentioned, in Herdt's study (1994), Sambia boys go through the initiation ritual of ingesting the semen of older men for years to build their masculinity and mature into men. Engaging in these same-sex acts does not warrant assigning them a label of "homosexual"—a personal and social identity with a particular history within the Western cultural context—but must be understood in Sambia's cultural context. These same-sex acts are cultural practices that are informed and constituted by gender ideologies of antagonism and by cultural beliefs in the finiteness of men's seminal essence and the role of its ingestion in boys' maturation into men.

This book contributes to the literature on sexuality in two ways. First, it underscores the linkage between gender, sexuality, and the nation by exploring the ways in which distinctive gender roles are construed as crucial in safeguarding the security of the nation in postsocialist China. As shown in the book, gender is used to control sexuality as gender deviance is governed and controlled to prevent and control sexual deviance. At the same time, homosexuality has become a scapegoat onto which anxiety over current social problems such as dissolved marriages is displaced. It is seen not only as a public menace but also a metaphor for passive masculinity and the national crisis. Homosexuality is considered a peril to the security of the nation because it reflects powerlessness, inferiority, feminized passivity, and social deterioration—and is thereby reminiscent of the colonial past when China was defeated by the colonizing West and plagued by its image as the "Sick Man of East Asia." It is believed that reviving and strengthening the nation require building a strong manhood and sharpening male gender roles.

Second, this book highlights the intersection between sexuality and gender by emphasizing the role that gender plays in constructing men's same-sex identities. It builds on the work of feminist anthropologists who have asserted the relationship of gender and sexuality; that is, sexuality is mutually constituted by gender, and "gender had to be taken into account in understanding sexuality" (Rubin 2002, 82).

In China, gender has undergone enormous transformations since the Maoist era. Then, to tap into women's energy to support the state project of nation building, the slogan, "Women hold up half the sky," was propagated, and the objectives of women's liberation and gender equality were broadcast ubiquitously in the media. Men and women wore unisex clothing, and femininity was rejected as bourgeois. In Mayfair Yang's words, there was an "erasure of gender" (1999). In the 1990s, this ascetic policy of effacing gender difference began to be reversed to emphasize salient categories of gender difference.

Economic and political liberalization occurring since the reforms in the 1980s has unleashed expressions of gender differences by reconstituting a feminine identity for women. Market reform and consumerism have produced flourishing images of sexualized and hyperfeminine women. Media images, social roles, and cultural expectations have not only demarcated but also dramatized gender differences.

This book foregrounds this new cultural system of gender and power to better understand Chinese tongzhi's sexuality, everyday life, and intimate relations. As described earlier, tongzhi categorize themselves in the female role of penetrated, referred to as 0, and the male role of penetrator, referred to as 1. This book illustrates how 1s and 0s are inextricably linked with and engage in cultural constructions and cultural understandings of gender. Within the tongzhi community, 1s and 0s usually do not share a common identity based on shared sexual orientation, but are distinguished from each other based on gender difference. The dominant cultural discourse that constructs binaries of feminine versus masculine becomes the available framework within which tongzhi understand themselves and construct their own identities. As Plummer observes, "in a polarized and fixed gender structure that hinders the emergence of alternative models of identities for individuals, homosexuals are left with nothing but clearly defined gender roles" (1992, 45).

This book probes the ways in which sexuality is culturally structured and answers the following questions. How do gender norms structure and shape the lives of the Chinese tongzhi? How do the Chinese tongzhi negotiate, rework, and recast hegemonic codes of masculinity and femininity in their relationships and create unique forms of engagements with gender? How do 0s, identified with the female role and adopting certain female traits, contribute to "strengthening of the myth of masculinity as well as to ridiculing of it" (Plummer 1992, 46)? Why do 0s simultaneously appropriate and downplay masculinity, and embody and reject femininity?

POLITICAL ECONOMY AND SEXUALITY

Sexuality not only is linked to culture and gender but also intersects with power and political economy. In *Discipline and Punish,* Foucault (1977) traces a shift in the eighteenth and nineteenth centuries in the technologies of control brought about by the rise of surveillance techniques and the construction of the subject by scientific and expert discourse. In the neoliberal era, this technology of control involves a form of domination in which the delineation of normal and abnormal replaces violence as a technique of power and power is maintained through a normalizing process in which "the whole indefinite domain of the non-conforming is punishable" (Foucault 1977, 178). Hence Foucault treats the pressure for conformity as a technique of power. Certain groups and behaviors are deemed abnormal through labeling and through systematically organized stigmatization. In contrast to the previous era in which the dominator was visible and oppression was institutionalized in the form of direct violence or force, in the neoliberal era, the dominator has become increasingly abstracted, disembodied, and invisible, and domination is exercised through the dominated themselves. In the absence of a physical mechanism of control and punishment, through the technique of the self, individuals alter themselves using an internalized disciplinary gaze to escape the peril of being excluded as abnormal.

In postsocialist China, the neoliberal technology of control is realized through labeling normal as not only being heterosexual but also being wealthy and living a high-consumption lifestyle. Economic reforms and a transition from a socialist planned economy to a market mechanism in postsocialist China have reshaped state operations and brought about profound social and cultural transformations. The state uses different techniques to legitimize its rule in the postsocialist stage—managing to maintain its control and power at a distance by not only freeing up a space for people to exercise a plethora of choices but also by maximizing its economic gains by allowing individuals to fully pursue their self-interests and accumulate individual profits. The state operates in a seemingly nonpolitical way through the vehicle of the market, thereby masking state control and preventing people from recognizing and thus criticizing state power, in a process that Li Zhang and Aihwa Ong term as "socialism from afar" (2008, 2; see also M. Yang 1999[5]).

This new technology of governance produces, and relies on, the new subjects who self-manage and self-govern while desiring and pursuing economic wealth. This "enterprising and desiring" subject—the new moral individual, as characterized by researchers such as Rofel (2007) and Kleinman et al. (2011)—results from the new moral context created by the values implicit in the market reforms. In the past, personhood was embedded in the family network, social relations, and political control (Y. Yan 2010). Since the 1980s, state policies of decollectivization, privatization, and marketization of institutions, such as education, health care, and housing, have created this new "enterprising and desiring" personhood by imposing new responsibilities on individuals to compete in the market economy, maximize self-interest, and fulfill their material, sexual, and emotional desires (Kleinman et al. 2011).

Ironically, desires for this new self or personhood cohere with loyalty to the Party and the state, so that the new self is simultaneously individualistic, nationalistic, and patriotic while still adhering to authority (Kleinman et al. 2011, 9). This new technology of governance causes individuals to fall into a state of false consciousness, not realizing that their choices are in fact regulated and controlled by the state within the context of private enterprise, consumption, and employment; in other words, there is market individualism rather than political individualism. Thus their seemingly self-interested pursuits are in fact aligned with, rather than opposed to, state interests (see also Kleinman et al. 2011).

This book unravels the ways in which this technique of power influences and shapes the everyday lives, identities, activism, and intimacies of the Chinese tongzhi. I discuss how the Chinese tongzhi forge a collective identity based on this abnormal, deviant, and derogatory label and, at the same time, engage in a technology of the self and internalize the disciplinary gaze to manage the self. As Foucault observes, seeing the self as an entrepreneur renders the self both the object and subject of change (1977, 170). In envisioning the self as the ultimate opponent, tongzhi in my research engage in self-criticism and self-censorship, rather than social criticism or a desire for social change. In so doing, they channel agency inward toward the self to ensure self-transformation, rather than outward to ensure social change.

I also explore the complicated intersection between sexuality and class by explaining the internal differentiation and class structure among the Chinese tongzhi and the ways in which money, wealth, consumerism, and class affect and impinge on their romances and intimacies and certain tongzhi's choice to work as money boys (male sex workers, usually rural migrant men around seventeen to twenty-six years old who provide same-sex sexual services). Illustrating their desire and pursuit of material wealth to become "normal" postsocialist subjects, I argue that this politics of what I call "economic normalization" falls short of a political strategy by perpetuating a market personhood, rather than a political subject pursuing the recognition of same-sex-attracted people's rights. In linking sexuality with power and political economy, this book demonstrates that the Chinese tongzhi are caught in a constant tension—both contesting and embracing normality while negotiating and carving out a legitimate space for themselves in the rapid social and economic transformations taking place in postsocialist China.

QUEER STUDIES AND CHINESE TONGZHI

This book not only challenges the Euro-American purview of queer studies with an ethnographically grounded case study of China (see Boellstorff 2007a; Manalansan 2003); it also contributes to queer studies by presenting a political economic analysis of how economic differences, social stratifications, and political discourse produce and are reproduced and legitimated by divergent same-sex practices and the experiences of Chinese tongzhi in the process of their negotiations with the dominant state discourse.

Queer studies critiques the process of governance informed and shaped by heteronormativity and destabilizes the notions of "normal" by embracing all-encompassing non-normative sex acts and sexualities categorized as queer and renouncing the monolithic and restrictive terms of lesbian/gay or LGBT[6] (Boellstorff 2007a, 2007b; Freccero 2006; Sedgwick 1990). It rejects and transcends the binary of heterosexual/homosexual or heterosexual/LGBT by incorporating all non-normative sex acts and sexualities beyond the binary, such as the intersexed, transgendered, pansexual, *kinksters, tombois,* leatherfolk, tom, *dee, waria, mahu, mak nyahs, travesti, bakla, hijra, kothi, jankhas,* and *panthi* (Besnier 2002; Blackwood 1998, 2005; Blackwood and Wieringa 1999; L. Cohen 1995; Elliston 1999; Graham 2003; Johnson 1997; Kulick 1998; Manalansan 2003; Prieur 1998; Reddy 2005; Schifter 1999; Sinnott 2004; Teh 2002; Weiss 2011; Young 2000). In the homosexuality literature, some theorists argue that homosexuality is an essence that is determined by genetic disposition, whereas others contend that it is a label that is socially constructed at a historical time and applied to individuals (Dynes and Donaldson 1992; Epstein 1987). Queer studies jettisons elements of the literature of homosexuality that identify homosexuality as a defining trait for the group and debate whether this trait is natural/biological or social. It also refutes the unified, minority-focus, and Eurocentric notion of homosexual identity implied in this literature and argues that this notion is a result of the normalization process created by the heterosexual/homosexual binary (Butler 1990; Fuss 1989; Lauretis 1991; Martin 1997; Sedgwick 1990; Warner 1993).

My contribution to queer studies is twofold. First, whereas queer studies scholars have resorted to cultural analysis and literary criticism to destabilize heteronormativity and crystallize the normalization process (Boellstorff 2007a; Kong 2002; Manalansan 2003), this book contributes to the literature through an ethnographic account of Chinese tongzhi's lived experiences. I eschew a unitary and monolithic category of Chinese tongzhi and argue that this group, rather than being a static category, is a dynamic process whereby tongzhi negotiate with the state, the tongzhi community, and society to create multilayered and multifaceted identities that are in constant flux. In this process, tongzhi not only share certain experiences such as the 1/0 system but also exhibit differences and disparities in the configuration of class.[7] This book spells out these contradictions by fleshing out both the universal and the variegated, diverse experiences that are shaped by social class and economic hierarchies in the socially stratified Chinese postsocialist society.

Second, this book contributes to queer studies by highlighting the politics of difference elucidated in feminist works and by providing a political economic analysis of sexuality. Sexuality, as scholars have contended, links individuals to socioeconomics, relations of inequality, and social hierarchies (A. Murray 2001; Weinberg 1994; Weiss 2011). For instance, Weiss (2011) argues that sexual cultures such as BDSM (an overlapping abbreviation of bondage and discipline [BD], dominance and submission [DS], and sadism and masochism [SM]) are structured by social inequalities and reproduce social hierarchies and neoliberal capitalism. Murray (2001) shows how social class marks the main divisions among Jakarta's lesbians. D'Emilio (1983) argues that historically capitalism created and structured lesbian and gay identity and communities. In linking sexuality with socioeconomics and politics, scholars such as Chasin (2001), Dean (2009), Halperin and Traub (2010), Mitchell (2011), Puar (2007), and Warner (1999) have also critiqued the surrender of the gay rights movement to consumerism, advertising, sponsors, and homonormative politics (including an overemphasis on marriage).[8]

My political economic analysis of sexuality continues this line of analytical inquiry and highlights the relationships among state polity, socioeconomics, and cultural practice by illuminating the ways in which sexual practices are simultaneously produced by and reproduce social inequality, economic stratification, and the legitimacy of the Chinese state. It goes beyond the purview of recent Chinese studies that focus on one class category of tongzhi (see Ho 2009; Jeffreys 2007; Kong 2011b; Rofel 2007, 2010) and explores a wide array of hierarchies and status differentials within Chinese tongzhi. In so doing, it enriches our understanding of the contemporary dynamics of Chinese tongzhi at different class positions in the rapid social and cultural transformations in postsocialist China.

FIELDWORK

In 2005, when I was conducting research on condom use and HIV/AIDS in the sex industry for my second ethnography, I visited the local Center for Disease Control (CDC), local Red Cross, and local AIDS organizations. It was in these local AIDS organizations that I first encountered and later befriended a community of tongzhi. I was surprised to learn that all the members were tongzhi, because the name of the organizations—AIDS Work Groups—gave no indication of the sexual orientation of their members. Later I learned from the local CDC and local Red Cross that they would not work with these organizations if their name contained any reference to tongzhi.

During my fieldwork, I served as a volunteer at two AIDS organizations. I was even given the formal title of "international counselor" by one of them. In the organizations, I participated in training sessions, such as a two-day session on drug abuse; heard lectures by invited scholars from around the country; took part in activities such as peer education with college students and outreach work at bathhouses, parks, and bars; and joined in social events such as outings, excursions, and cruising in the park. The leaders, male staff members, and male volunteers in these organizations were known to each other only via their fake names. Most held regular jobs, but the job types and companies were unknown to all.

When I began my volunteer work in the organizations in 2005 and explained my project to the members, some warned me not to work with well-known activists and not to mention anything about human rights. To quote their words, "The Party targets activists. If you help those activists, the Party will target you too. Don't mention a single word about human rights. Otherwise you'll invite fire onto your body. You know what'll happen to you if you work against the Party." To me, these words were indicative of their attitude toward their work in the organization and society as a whole. For example, one of the organization leaders opened a tongzhi bar, but the police closed it. The disillusioned leader left the organization and became a monk at a temple in South China. The leader who succeeded him opened a tongzhi bathhouse that was also closed down by the police. After police crackdowns on unreported gathering and tongzhi-related websites, the new leader terminated all events and activities of the organization.

Political sensitivity to my project was one of the main impediments to my fieldwork. For instance, one afternoon, I was invited by the aforementioned organization leader to meet the director of the local CDC at her office. He knew the director, but I had never met her. As soon as I told her my name, the director responded coldly, "Yes, I know who you are, *Xiao Jie* (hostess). What do you want, *Xiao Jie*?" I was taken aback by her words. How did she know me? Why did she call me *Xiao Jie*? Although the term *"Xiao Jie"* indicates both a hostess and a general term of address, her deliberately lengthened and emphasized tone in enunciating that word seemed to be asserting something. What was that something she was asserting? My first two ethnographies about sex work and HIV/AIDS in the city in which she worked immediately came to mind.

I started explaining my new project to her and the fact that I had been working as a volunteer at local AIDS organizations. I asked very politely if she could spare a few minutes to talk to me about the local CDC's HIV/AIDS intervention work in the city. To my shock, she immediately raised her voice and yelled at me, as if she and I were embroiled in a vicious verbal fight: "What information do you want?! Why would I give you any information?! Why should I report to you this kind of work?! These are all secrets!! I can't give you secretive information because I don't know what you're going to do with it!! Why do you volunteer with these organizations? What is your real motive?" She ranted for about ten minutes. I stood there because she did not invite me to sit down, completely astounded. Why did she chastise me with these ruthless and rude questions? I could feel my heart pounding, and I could not move. Once again, after calming down, I explained to her about my project and my collaboration with local organizations, but in the middle of a sentence, she showed me the door and asked me to leave: "Leave this office, *Xiao Jie* (hostess)! Leave!!"

It was a profoundly humiliating experience. On the way back to the organization, sitting on the bus and looking out of the window, I played the entire scenario again and again in my head, trying to figure out what went wrong. In the end, the only explanation I could find was that my published books on sex work and HIV/AIDS in the city must have either infuriated her or alerted government officials who had warned her against working with me.

Later that day I called the leader and told him what happened at the CDC. He said that the director had called him that afternoon and told him not to work with me or tell me any secrets because I would "do bad things and write bad things about China." He said, "She told me to keep a distance from you and not to let my guard down because you may be an American spy. She also warned me not to release any data or information to you because you intended to do harm to the CDC, and you would publish harmful data in America and hurt the reputation of our city." Because his local organization could not survive without funding from the CDC, he told me he had to follow her instructions.

This leader later proved to me that he would carry out her words to the letter. On one occasion, after I sent an e-mail to the Chinese tongzhi e-mail list applying to resubscribe, he sent out a public response to all the subscribers on the list, questioning the ulterior motives of my request and asserting that his organization rejected my application. In his e-mail, he described my background. Emphasizing my American citizenship, he questioned the motive of "a foreign citizen" who was interested in the Chinese homosexual community. He wrote, "Tiantian Zheng is not a homosexual. She told me herself. She is an American—a sufficient reason for us to suspect that her research and her data are not friendly to China. In view of the fact that she is not a homosexual and her long-term job is in a foreign institute, we are very suspicious of her motives in joining the Chinese tongzhi e-mail list. We reject her application to join our e-mail list." I then wrote a response explaining my research and the discipline of anthropology. After deliberation, the organizer of the e-mail list approved my subscription to the list.

An awkwardness permeated my interactions with this organization leader. Learning that I was an American citizen, he demanded we speak English so he could improve his English skills, not only privately but also in front of others. For instance, when we took a taxi to a tongzhi bar, he told the taxi driver that I was an American college professor. He then conversed with me in English in front of the taxi driver and another tongzhi, which made me feel quite uneasy. When I accompanied one of my key informants, who had just tested HIV positive, to the leader's office to ask for advice, he drew a diagram on a piece of paper and in the middle of explaining the virus and CD-4 cells, he switched from Chinese to English and asked me whether certain English expressions were correct. Then he started speaking English to me, ignoring my friend who had just heard the worst possible news about his HIV status. These situations made me feel embarrassed and awkward, because neither the taxi driver nor the key informants knew much English. The leader also asked me to invite him to lecture at my university in the United States and provide free room and board accommodations for two weeks. Despite these uncomfortable moments and his increasing demands, I tried my best to accommodate his requests. I hope these stories can give the readers a glimpse of the kinds of predicaments I encountered in conducting my fieldwork.

In addition to these obstacles, my entry to tongzhi bars and tongzhi bathhouses was never easy; each time a long negotiation process was required as my key informants tirelessly explained to the proprietors that I was not a civilian-clothed police officer but a researcher and that I would not harm their business. When my informants and I visited tongzhi bathhouses, the customers took me as a man in drag, one of a group of people in the community who often performed drag shows at tongzhi bars and bathhouses.

Through volunteering in the AIDS organizations, I made friends with more than fifty tongzhi. I followed them to tongzhi cruising areas such as tongzhi bars and parks. I also visited some of their families, workplaces, and living places. In our spare time, we went to shopping malls together and enjoyed recreational activities such as singing at karaoke bars and dining at nice restaurants. As time went by, they came to address me as "elder sister" or "younger sister," depending on our age difference. My key informants introduced me to their boyfriends, money boys, bar and bathhouse owners, and madams of brothels. They told me their life stories and their painstaking struggles with parents, boyfriends, girlfriends, and wives.

Because I visited the cruising spot in the park every day, all the regulars knew me and were friendly to me. At times they were too friendly. Indeed, I received quite a few sexual requests. I either extricated myself from those awkward situations by leaving the area or dissolved the tension by tapping into the techniques I had learned from my previous research on clients and sex workers, such as using jokes and diverting their attention. Direct sexual requests were commonplace from both money boys and men whom I presume were bisexual. They first tried to impress me with stories about how great their sexual techniques were and how they made other women reach their climaxes so intensely that these women kept on looking for them for sex afterward. Uncomfortable as these stories made me, I always remained calm and diplomatic, while asserting to them that I was not interested. Some money boys told me that because they had very few sexual encounters with women, they yearned for sexual experiences with women. Despite my empathy toward some of them, I firmly declined their requests.

I also received marriage proposals and direct sexual advances. For instance, a man who was a veterinarian proposed marriage to me, asking me to marry him the very next day. He also talked about taking me to see his parents because they were waiting for him to bring a girlfriend home. To his marriage proposal, I simply told him that I already had a boyfriend. In another situation, a married man with a child told me that he wanted to divorce his wife and marry me because of the way I talked, the bone structure of my body, and my beauty. As he was talking, he walked toward me, taking first one of my hands and then the other, and then he stepped toward me, attempting to embrace me. At that point I got very scared; I broke off and walked away.

Despite these episodes, cruising with tongzhi earned me many close friends. According to my informants such as Chan and Tang, who were a couple, I was a "bridge connecting them." We hung out on a daily basis. We sang karaoke, shopped, and went on other recreational excursions together. I visited their workplaces, their homes, and their families. When I was with them, they said they felt free and unleashed, not worrying about others and society. Once when we were walking on the street, Chan and Tang played around with each other. At one point, Chan put Tang on his back and carried him across the street. After we crossed the street, Chan still carried Tang on his back. A male pedestrian who was walking toward us stopped. Looking baffled, he turned to Chan and me while pointing at Tang and asking, "Is he drunk? Is he sick? He's a grown man but you're carrying him—he must be drunk, right?" Chan and I immediately responded yes. The pedestrian shook his head, murmured something, and walked past us. We looked at each other and burst into laughter.

Couples such as Chan and Tang liked having me around not only because I was their "attention-diverter from others" but also because I assuaged tension between them and served as a social lubricant. For instance, when I was around Chan and Tang, they got along perfectly fine, laughing and telling jokes to each other. When I was not around them, however, they quarreled, had physical brawls, and then called me for urgent help. After every fight I spent a lot of time talking to each of them on the phone, analyzing the issues, giving them my advice, and reminding them of their love for each other. After I talked to both of them, I arranged a time and place for the three of us to meet. At every arranged meeting, they immediately got back together and were lovebirds again.

I kept close contact with all my key informants via phone and e-mail while I was in the United States. Couples such as Chan and Tang continued to relate to me their skirmishes and fights, and I continued my attempts to resolve them through phone conversations with each of them. Over the years I grew so close to them that it changed our relationship from researcher-subject to a sister-brother relationship. They regarded me as their sister, soliciting my help and advice about their job choices and relationships with colleagues, girlfriends, wives, and parents. Every time when I left China for the United States, my key informants went with me to the airport to see me off. While I was away, I also mailed them Christmas gifts such as brand-name sweatshirts that they liked.

DIFFERENT SEXUAL ORIENTATION, SHARED CULTURE

At the beginning of my research, I was apprehensive about conducting research on male tongzhi because I am a heterosexual woman. I was afraid that these men would feel nothing in common with me or that they would have an aversion to women. I was worried that nobody would want to talk to me. Initially, I was very cautious, testing the water to see how these tongzhi reacted toward me. As time went on, I was pleasantly surprised to find out that they not only saw no barriers between us but also opened up to me and told me their life stories. This was the opposite of my previous research experience in which, during my first encounter with hostesses, when I initiated a conversation with a hostess sitting next to me, she stood up and left me in the cold. Compared with hostesses who did not accept me until I started working with them and living among them, male tongzhi were more willing to talk to me and share their stories.

Although I am not a homosexual, because I am Chinese I share with tongzhi a filial attitude toward parents. Also, as did the tongzhi, I experienced parental disapproval of my choices of romantic partners, albeit for different reasons. For the tongzhi in my research, this disapproval was due to their sexual orientation; for me, it was due to class differences. Like the tongzhi encountered in my research, throughout my life, I have been caught between personal desires and cultural constraints. Unlike the tongzhi who were able to find their own kind and gain a sense of reprieve in a community, I had to wrestle with the conflict between my individual happiness and cultural filiality on my own while consumed by an overwhelming sense of shame and guilt.

As a child in China, I learned and subsequently believed steadfastly that a daughter should live for the honor of her parents. As a daughter, I believed that my life was fulfilled when I could bring honor and pride to my parents. My parents to me were everything; it was my goal to please them at the expense of everything, including my individual happiness.

I grew up as an obedient child and a subservient daughter. I had internalized the cultural ideal so much that, on becoming aware of any acts of disobedience, I would be besieged by a sense of shame. I believed that my parents were always correct, and therefore I should always follow their lead. Just as chastity became part and parcel of my identity as a woman, submission to parental power and authority became an integral part of my identity as a daughter.

In high school, I followed my parents' wishes to take the TOEFL—Test of English as a Foreign Language—and to apply for universities in the United States. My parents wanted me to study there, and determined to fulfill their dream, I achieved a high score on this entrance test. However, although I was accepted by several schools, I was refused a visa five times. The refusals were heartbreaking and devastating. Ultimately I had to abandon my parents' wish for me to study abroad.

At the end of my sophomore year in college, I started dating. The dating experience offered me a sense of autonomy that I had never experienced. When I told my parents about this burgeoning relationship, they were so enraged that they ordered me to end it and pounded into me that my real devotion should be my studies. When I continued dating despite their admonitions, they told me they had deposited 6,000 yuan[9] under my name in the bank. If I chose to continue dating the boy, they said that this small amount of money would be all they would leave for me. They told me to take the money and remember never to enter their home again.

My parents' outrage and scathing criticisms induced an insurmountable shame in me for having feelings for that boy and forgetting my real mission. I anguished over their reaction, believing that I had become so deranged and so corrupted by my emotions that I had ceased to be an obedient, asexual daughter. I ended the relationship. I chose my parents over my personal happiness, as an obedient daughter should.

For many years, I viewed this incident as a detour that had derailed my devotion to my parents and my study. After the detour, in my junior year of college, I followed my parents' instructions and took both the GRE test for American graduate schools and the entrance exams for a Chinese graduate school. Throughout the remaining two years of college, I did nothing but study. I not only received a high grade on the GRE but also ranked in the top three among those applying to a key Chinese graduate school. My success in my studies reaffirmed my belief in my parents.

In my second year at the Chinese graduate school, at the age of twenty-two, I started dating again. When I told my parents about it, once again, I received a response of outrage and disapproval, but this time for a different reason. They wanted me to find someone who had acquired the same educational level and had a family with a sound financial condition. The man I dated did not satisfy either of these two requirements. Once again, I was forced to undergo a fierce inner struggle to choose between my parents and my boyfriend. Meanwhile my parents were active in introducing me to men of whom they approved. Although I resisted their introductions and continued dating the disapproved man behind their back, subconsciously I never ceased feeling guilty and shameful for doing the wrong thing, as if I was committing a crime simply because my parents did not approve of him. As a result, my relationship was severely disrupted; it was ultimately destroyed by my unyielding suspicion that my parents might be right in their judgment of him and by my lack of trust in my own instincts.

After receiving a master's degree, I was accepted to and chose to study in a Ph.D. program at Yale University. During my studies there, more than a year after coming to the United States, I received a letter from my mother expressing her concerns for my emotional life. She wrote, "Do not think that now that you are at Yale, you do not need my instructions any more. You need to deal with your emotions better. Do not let them get in the way of your study. Do not be led astray by your emotional life and let it ruin your professional life." The letter reminded me of all the shame and guilt that I had felt when I had "gone astray" and had not been an obedient daughter and a good student. After receiving the letter, it took me several days to calm down.

I had been told that marriage was about the merging of two families and not about love or individual happiness. I had been told stories of other women whose husbands bought them houses and brought them stable financial conditions. In my fifth year of teaching as an associate professor in the United States, my mother commented in front of me, "What's wrong with you? Why is it the case that other women can find husbands to buy houses for them, whereas you cannot find anyone to do it for you? Look, you have to buy a house for yourself! Why are you only able to get along with men of the lowest class?"

Although I was living in the United States, I still carried the cultural ideal that an obedient daughter should always fulfill her parents' dreams and trust their judgments above her own. My parents' questions made me confused and lost, and I started questioning myself. Really, was there something wrong with me? Why couldn't I find someone my parents approved of? Was I really so low and so debased, just as my mother always said, that a "classy boy" of whom my parents would approve would never find me attractive?

These questions continued to plague me. They made me suspect my judgment of men and ultimately feel inadequate as a woman. Meanwhile, I had internalized my parents' cultural lens and was never satisfied with the men I dated who did not have a respectable academic degree or a good financial condition. Furthermore, it deeply bothered me whenever I would find myself happy with a man whom my parents would categorize as lower class.

I spent years of my life in the United States wrestling with this issue. How I wished I could satisfy my parents by being with the kind of men of whom they approved. Constantly I felt a painful, irresolvable tension between my wish to fulfill my parents' demands and my own feelings.

This tension eventually subsided when I came to grips with the crux of the issue. I came to understand that the source of the tension was my internalized cultural ideal of an obedient daughter. I came to understand that it was time for me to reexamine and qualify this cultural ideal that I had been holding so dear to my heart that it had become the core of my identity.

Little by little, I began to question the cultural ideal of womanhood in which I had been mired. I came to realize that I should not feel ashamed of my feelings simply because my parents disapproved of them. I also came to realize that I was a different person from my parents. Therefore, they should not expect me to follow their directions forever and live my life according to their standards.[10]

My own struggle immensely enhanced my ability to comprehend the tumultuous lives of tongzhi who, like me, are living through the fierce personal struggle between individual happiness and cultural constraints. Like tongzhi who are trapped in making a choice between parents, society, and their own individual happiness, I too have many times extinguished my personal happiness in deference to cultural and social approval. Being an anthropologist in this foreign culture of the United States has given me an outsider's lens through which to scrutinize and reevaluate my entrenched cultural roots. With the advantage of a foreign cultural lens and an education in anthropology, to some degree I was able to rise above the conflict and unfetter myself from my cultural shackles; tongzhi, not having my advantages, are still engulfed in their internal struggles.

This break from my past is undoubtedly less complete than my narrative suggests. Understanding my plight intellectually has not entirely freed me from deeply ingrained feelings; still it has allowed me to begin the process of change. As I worked with the tongzhi every day, I felt great empathy for the trap they are in, perhaps because I had only partially escaped from this trap and continue to experience the tug of war between my personal needs and the demands of Chinese society.

OUTLINE OF THE BOOK

The introduction casts my research in the broader context of gender politics and political economy that are inherent in the formation of tongzhi identities in postsocialist China. In linking sexuality with culture, gender, the political economy of class, economics, and state power, this book not only unravels the process of making tongzhi identities in an era of rapid social transformations but also highlights the formation of new social inequalities in postsocialist China.

By elucidating the historic continuities of diverse, malleable, ambiguous, and fluid sexual imaginations in China, chapter 1 critiques the postsocialist construction of heteronormativity and the portrayal of homosexuality as a representation of a decadent lifestyle imported from the West. It argues that recasting the past and linking the past to the present can enrich our understanding of the present and challenge the current discourse. During the ancient and imperial periods in China, same-sex desires were deemed normal and were enjoyed by many emperors and upper-class scholars and bureaucrats. There was never a fixed or reified sexual identity linked to a certain sexual preference. Sexual fantasies during these many centuries in China were fluid, diverse, and in constant flux. At the turn of the twentieth century, the onslaught of Western medical knowledge changed this cultural tradition and indoctrinated in society heteronormativity and a pathologized and vilified vision of homosexuality. This inaugurated the repression of same-sex-attracted people during the Communist era. The normalizing of heterosexuality and disavowing of China's past continued in the postsocialist era.

Chapter 2 combines ethnographic research and archival research to capture current social attitudes toward homosexuality in postsocialist China. A scrutiny of the cultural milieu can help us understand the kind of environment that structures the everyday lives of Chinese tongzhi. Through an analysis of interviews and media coverage, this chapter argues that social attitudes toward homosexuality are not as open and tolerant as previous researchers have ascertained. My interviews with civilians and my analysis of media coverage suggest a common understanding of homosexuality as a perversion, deviation, and abnormality often caused by poor parenting, mistakes in child-rearing techniques, traumatizing experiences with the opposite sex, and misidentification of gender roles. As this chapter shows, homosexuality has become a scapegoat on which is displaced anxiety over current social problems such as dissolved marriages and the AIDS epidemic. Although a dissolved family is pinpointed as one of the key factors that can lead to a child's homosexuality, the media also portray homosexuality not only as a public menace and a threat to the family but also as a metaphor for passive masculinity and a national crisis. Homosexuality is considered a peril to the security of the nation because it reflects powerlessness, inferiority, feminized passivity, and social deterioration, reminiscent of the colonial past when China was defeated by the colonizing West and plagued by its image as the Sick Man of East Asia. It is believed that building a strong manhood and sharpening proper male gender roles are required to revive and strengthen the nation.

Chapter 3 unravels the gender roles and gender dynamics in tongzhi relationships. More specifically, it explores the ways in which tongzhi negotiate, rework, and recast hegemonic codes of masculinity and femininity in their relationships and create unique forms of engagements with gender. Through foregrounding the relationships between 1 (penetrator) and 0 (penetrated), this chapter argues that these relationships and identities are constructed and shaped within the hegemonic gender norms that dictate gender roles, such as female sexual faithfulness as the object of control and male sexual promiscuity as the master of control. After entering the tongzhi community, as a result of his first sexual experience, which involves either penetrating or being penetrated, each man is often defined as either 1 or 0 and expected to assume either a masculine or a feminine role. These roles are not mere replications of dominant gender hegemonies, but are creative reworkings and recastings of hegemonic codes. In this community, men learn how to be 1s and 0s through their experiences, and often their challenges and manipulations manifest the unstable and contentious nature of gender roles. Although these creative aberrations and appropriations of hegemonic gender norms allow for the individual pursuit of sexual pleasure and a certain degree of freedom, they continue to be self-contradictory and subject to intense contention.

Chapter 4 unravels tongzhi's negotiations and interactions with the dominant discourse of the "normal" postsocialist person and the impact this discourse has on the class structure, career, and romantic relationships among tongzhi. Although class structure among Chinese tongzhi is largely shaped by wealth, higher-class tongzhi can practice what I call "covert gayness" because they can afford to eat and drink and congregate in more secretive places, such as high-cost bars. Lower-class tongzhi are compelled to practice more "overt gayness" because they tend to cruise in free, open spaces, such as parks and public bathrooms. The dominant discourse of the normal person also impinges on the intimacies of romantic relationships and career choices of some rural migrant men who work as money boys in hopes of accumulating enough money to catapult themselves to a higher class, such as businessmen. Wealth and class are implicated in the selection of partners and in the intimacy of romantic relationships. This chapter argues that tongzhi embrace the dominant discourse in order to pronounce themselves as normal postsocialist persons. In so doing, they paradoxically are co-opted by the state apparatus, thereby legitimizing and perpetuating state power.

Chapter 5 discusses the underlying complexities of the tongzhi's health and social activism. It illustrates the community building in AIDS organizations, the goals and strategies for promoting health and social activism by these AIDS organizations, and the effectiveness and outcome of their activism. Some researchers predict that AIDS activism could lead to an unintended consequence of the growth of a homosexual movement in big cities in China, However, this chapter highlights the mutual constitution and dynamic interactions between tongzhi and the state, as well as with the dominant cultural order, which challenge the assumption that dichotomizes them as polarized entities. In this activism, Chinese tongzhi purport to work in collaboration with, rather than against, the state. Deploying and appropriating the state-endorsed AIDS cause, they draw on the dominant moral order as a legitimate resource to infuse tongzhi activism while still seeking legitimacy in the mainstream culture. By declaring that elimination of homophobia is essential to curbing AIDS transmission, they turn AIDS activism into a protection that provides legitimacy for their tongzhi activism. The fact that they rely on state-regulated funding systems and government organizations to exist legally shapes their tactics, forces them to mask their tongzhi identity in public, and impedes the extent to which they can infuse tongzhi activism into their HIV/AIDS cause. Their collaboration with the state mitigates their tongzhi activism, leaves the social norm unchallenged, and allows further stigmatization of their tongzhi identity. Thus AIDS politics—although serving as an important tool and opportunity for the tongzhi to advance tongzhi politics, albeit in a limited scope—paradoxically reinforces the association between tongzhi and AIDS and perpetuates the stigma that AIDS is a tongzhi problem.

Chapter 6 discusses the ways in which tongzhi in my research cover up their sexual identities and fail to formulate an open-identity social activist group. Indeed, the power of postsocialist heteronormativity seeps into the everyday realities of their lives, overshadowing transnational media about gay rights and thwarting potential collective actions. It is through tongzhi's erasure of their own identity because of their desire to be normal and their ambivalence toward their own group that this power of the postsocialist heteronormativity predominates. Although tongzhi congregate in cruising areas and work at local AIDS organizations, they keep their real names, home addresses, and workplace information confidential from each other. They are cautious and discreet for fear of possible blackmail or disclosure of their tongzhi identity to their family and colleagues. Relationships are usually superficial. The weak ties and lack of solidarity among them have engendered an environment that is not conducive to organized protests. Aspiration for membership in the dominant culture has also weakened their solidarity. Self-shame and self-negation lead to an ambivalent attitude toward the group, which undercuts their collective solidarity. This ambivalence is conducive to the oscillation of "affiliation cycles" in tongzhi's identification with and participation in the tongzhi community. Tongzhi feel torn between their attachment to their own group and to the mainstream world. When tongzhi's self-criticisms coalesce with their acceptance of the heteronormative discourse, it marks a decline in their identification with the tongzhi community and an increase in their identification with the mainstream. When tongzhi offer each other advice on how to cope with romantic relationships and how to fend off parents' pressure to marry, it marks an increase in their identification with the tongzhi community and a decline in their identification with the mainstream. In a nutshell, they fluctuate between their affiliation and identification with their own group and the mainstream.

Chapter 7 explores popular sexual practices among tongzhi, including group sex, threesomes, and one-night stands, and the ways in which political, social, and cultural factors play a critical role in shaping tongzhi's high-risk sexual behaviors and susceptibility to HIV and sexually transmitted infections. Political factors such as police harassment, police arrests, and a hostile environment fuel high-risk sexual behaviors and inhibit condom use. The gender dynamics between 0 (female role) and 1 (male role) often give 1s the power as the decision maker about condom use. Sociocultural factors such as the symbol of condoms as promiscuity, infidelity, and an antithesis to love also curtail their use in sexual encounters. Condom use is further impeded by the belief in the Taoist ideology and Chinese traditional medicine and by drug use. Thus this chapter investigates the underlying complexities and nuances that are implicated in tongzhi's decisions about condom use in the era of HIV/AIDS in postsocialist China.

The conclusion summarizes the current situation of the tongzhi, reiterates the main themes of the book, and offers speculations about the possible future course of tongzhi in China.

CHAPTER 1

A Cultural History of Same-Sex Desire in China

In this chapter I chronicle changing meanings of homoerotic romance in the cultural history of same-sex desires in China in the imperial period, the Republican era (1912–49), Maoist times (1949–77), and the postsocialist era. During the imperial period in China, same-sex desires were deemed normal and were enjoyed not only by many emperors, scholars, and bureaucrats but also by common people of all social classes. At that time there was no fixed or reified sexual identity linked to a certain sexual preference. Sexual fantasies during this vast historic time in China were fluid, diverse, and in constant flux.

At the turn of the twentieth century, the onslaught of Western medical knowledge changed this cultural tradition and indoctrinated in society heteronormativity and a pathologized and vilified vision of homosexuality. Whereas people during the imperial period were able to indulge in an unlimited range of sexual expression, the Western influence caused more rigid and clear lines to be drawn between heterosexuals and homosexuals, defining a person in terms of his or her preference for one or the other sex. This inaugurated the repression of same-sex-attracted people during the Communist era. The postsocialist era continued normalizing heterosexuality and disavowing China's rich sexual past. This chapter contends that reclaiming the past and linking the past to the present can enrich our understanding of the present and contest the current discourse.

IMPERIAL CHINA

The tradition of homoerotic relationships in China is as ancient as the history of Chinese culture (Bullough 1976; E. Chou 1971; Hinsch 1992; Ruan 1991, 1997; Ruan and Tsai 1987; Van Gulik 1961). Homoerotic relationships were considered natural, were common, and were widely accepted in Chinese society during the imperial period (Vitiello 2011). To Westerners at that time, influenced by the condemnation of homosexuality by Christianity, this phenomenon constituted evidence of Oriental moral degeneracy (Hinsch 1992, 4).

Classical Chinese medicine did not view the human body in binary terms as either male or female (Barlow 1994); every individual contained elements of both female and male gender, as represented by the symbols of yin and yang. Hence representations of sex and gender were unfixed and indefinite (Mann 2011; Yi-Li Wu 2010). In her essay on gender boundaries and biological aberration in Chinese medical history, Charlotte Furth (1988) discusses gender categories of "false males" and "false females" that denoted certain men and women's inability to conceive. However, a same-sex-attracted male or female was not categorized as a kind of "false male" or "false female." Indeed, there was no category of "perversion" in Chinese medicine and medical literature, and the Chinese tradition viewed homoerotic relationships in a positive light. The Western concepts of "unnatural" sexual acts, perversion, and psychologically deviant personality were not associated with same-sex acts.

It is important to note that the classical Chinese language had no term to denote a person who engaged in same-sex acts. Nor was there any identification of a particular sexual identity, sexual essence, or sexual orientation. The language distinguished same-sex behavior from same-sex identity, using poetic metaphors based on ancient same-sex love stories to refer to same-sex actions, tendencies, and preferences rather than to an innate sexual essence (Hinsch 1992, 7). As described in the Introduction, the phrases *yu tao* and *duan xiu* came to signify same-sex love. Another category describing same-sex love invoked specific social roles such as "favorites," rather than sexual essence (Hinsch 1992).[1]

The earliest recorded homoerotic relationships between emperors and their male favorites are from the Zhou Dynasty (1122–256 B.C.). Open expressions of same-sex affections were common (Hinsch 1992), as exemplified by the story of Mizi Xia. Men were free to admire other men and engage in homoerotic relationships. In addition, extramarital heterosexual relationships for men were also accepted.

In the Western Han (187–180 B.C.), ten of the eleven emperors either had at least one male favorite or had homoerotic relationships with palace eunuchs (Ruan 1991). In fact, these favorites were often seen as threatening the political order by profiteering from the emperor's love (Hinsch

1992). Folk songs, poetry, tales, and art recounted stories of homoerotic relationships in the imperial court and among scholars and officials in the Han and later dynasties.[2] For instance, *History of Han Dynasty* records a story in which a male favorite, Deng Tung, used his mouth to drain the liquid from the skin blisters on the Han emperor's body (Han Shu).[3] *The Book of Poetry* includes homoerotic poems written for a famous male beauty. *Spring-Autumn Annals* reveals the jealousy of rival male beauties, stories of homoerotic love in the royal court, favorites' fears of being replaced, and the successful use of homoerotic seduction as a political and military weapon (Ruan 1991). These latter two books were both required readings by Confucius.

By the late Ming era (1368–1644), we have records that show that homoerotic relationships had become a popular vogue. The late Ming "libertinism" gave rise to more widespread and less bounded sexual expression that included homoerotic sentiments, which epitomized the newfound sexual pleasure among men of every social class (Vitiello 1992, 1996, 2000; C. Wu 2004). With material prosperity, the literati heralded a libertine ideology of following the heart and pursuing homoerotic pleasures as one of the many vehicles to seek adventure and cultural refinement (C. Wu 2004).[4] Indeed, in the late Ming period a "homoerotic fashion" was cultivated, pursued, and followed throughout society (Vitiello 2000). A literature on homoerotic themes and pornographic materials emerged and flourished (Vitiello 2011) thanks to the liberal atmosphere in Ming society. A review of this literature suggests that homoerotic relationships influenced society beyond a small circle of elite males, across all social classes (Vitiello 2000).

Many literati were so swept away by the romantic images of homoerotic love that a vogue developed in which elite men patronized boy actors as male prostitutes (catamites) and household entertainers (C. Wu 2004). As young men served elite males as entertainers, servants, and male prostitutes, long-term romantic relationships often formed that consolidated the elite men's status, power, and cultural taste. Most young catamites were owned by elite men as part of household music troupes.[5] Young boys became an indispensable spectacle at parties and gatherings in the houses of the elite men where they entertained guests; their presence was emblematic of the hosts' wealth, prestige, status, and aesthetic taste. Scholars bragged about their enjoyment of catamites in their writings;

thus homoerotic expressions were not only popular but also served as a focus of public admiration, envy, and excitement.

In the Qing Dynasty (1368–1911), homoerotic sentiments developed into a cultural, aesthetic taste, a status symbol, and "an extreme form of romantic idealism," especially in Beijing (C. Wu 2004, 61). These sentiments had enormous social importance and were celebrated in both literature and the social realm (25). For instance, homoerotic themes are elaborated in classic novels such as *Dream of the Red Chamber (hong lou meng)*, *The Golden Lotus (Jinping Mei)*, and *Mirror of Theatrical life (Pinhus baojian)*. Historical records also recounted stories of the homoerotic relationships of Qing emperors Chien Lung (1736–95), Hisen Fong (1851–61), and Tung Chih (1862–74) with their male subordinates (E. Chou 1971).[6]

The intensely patriarchal quality of the Qing Dynasty reinforced the flourishing same-sex sentiment. Homoerotic practices received even more widespread acceptance and enjoyed "a more central and stable role in cultural life" because the larger social environment held men who had relationships with other men in high esteem (C. Wu 2004, 26). Men interacted with each other in their social circles, exchanging ideas and appreciation of art and cultural tastes. Such social relationships among men were a fundamental part of the social and cultural life in the Qing Dynasty.

Same-sex erotic sentiments came to dominate cities such as Beijing not only because of the homosocial environment in the Qing Dynasty but also because of the patriarchal ideal (C. Wu 2004). The sexual ideal was embodied by young, often feminine, male bodies. Appreciation of the beauty of young catamites abounded in the literature of the time. The following account is one such example:

> Across tens of thousands of miles, through five thousand years of history, nothing and nobody is better than a catamite. Those who do not love a catamite should not be taken seriously. Elegant flowers, beautiful women, the shining moon, rare books, and grand paintings, all those supreme beauties are appreciated by everyone. However, these beauties often are not in one place. Catamites are different. They are like elegant flowers and not grass or trees; they are like beautiful women who do not need make-up; they are like a shining moon or tender cloud, yet they can be touched and played with; they are like rare books and grand paintings, and yet they can talk and converse; they are beautiful and playful and yet they also

are full of change and surprise. The loss of a catamite cannot be compensated. (Ruan 1991, 118)

It was the feminine, delicate appearance of a young boy that was most admired and appreciated by the literati (C. Wu 2004), who selected the most feminine boys as their favorites. They enjoyed the young boys' loyalty, beauty, emotionality, and also their abilities to perform art, write poetry, and paint. Some writings implied that a "male femininity" was superior to female femininity. *woman, but better o bc actually men!*

Continuing the practice began in the late Ming era, the predominant type of same-sex relationship occurred between elite men (literati, officials, merchants) and boy actors (*dan*; C. Wu 2004); its prevalence and social influence were unmatched by any other form of same-sex relationship. On stage, boy actors played young female roles in traditional theater such as Beijing opera. Offstage, they usually performed the role of catamites, tantamount to that of female courtesans. This aesthetic pursuit of boy actors became a vogue. Guidebooks flourished that instructed leading patrons how to locate famous boy-actor beauties at the entertainment quarters and nightclubs.[7] For instance, an earlier catalog of female courtesans was replaced by one showing male beauties exclusively.

In Beijing, a romantic obsession with a boy actor signified a patron's social status, taste, and connoisseurship of male beauty (C. Wu 2004). In contrast, obsession with a female prostitute signified a lack of taste. In the south, another type of male prostitution took place in the Taoist temple Chao Than Gong in Nanjing, which became famous for providing young monks to entertain elite men for a high fee (Ruan 1991). However, the taste for boy actors and boy prostitutes did not prevail in the Yangtze delta region, where female courtesans dominated the entertainment scene (C. Wu 2004).

Another common form of same-sex relationship throughout Chinese history was between affluent men and boy servants (C. Wu 2004). Boy servants and boy actors were sometimes one and the same when affluent men purchased boy actors from music trainers and turned them into boy servants or when boy servants were sold into the opera business. Although this kind of homoerotic romance was widespread in the Qing Dynasty, the literati often construed it as a crass form of lust and a reflection of a lack of cultural taste.

Homoerotic romance between men who shared equal status and similar age was a marginal form of same-sex relationship, although it was present across class in late imperial China (C. Wu 2004). For instance, in Fujian, male-to-male marriages, called "contract brothers" *(qi xiongdi)*, were endorsed by their parents, relatives, and friends. The marriages traditionally lasted until the age of thirty, when the men left their male partners and married female brides. However, outside of Fujian this form of relationship was often perceived as an aberration.

During the Qing Dynasty, although same-sex relationships were culturally acceptable, there was legal bias toward homoerotic romance between equals, but rarely toward same-sex relationships between men of different classes (C. Wu 2004). More particularly, legal statutes targeted relationships between lower-class men. Legal documents reflected the belief that an equal-status same-sex relationship was impossible because a power hierarchy was at the core of the relationship between the penetrator and the penetrated (Sommer 2002; C. Wu 2004).

Although some scholars (Geyer 2002; V. Ng 1987) assert that the Qing 1740 rape law had the effect of suppressing the same-sex behavior that was popular during the Ming Dynasty, others (D. Wang 1997; C. Wu 2004) claim that the law targeted nonconsensual sexual practices between equals. Given that a hierarchical sexual relationship between two different classes was socially accepted, the 1740 rape law was mainly concerned with sexual violations or transgressions of a person's will in either same-sex or heterosexual practices between equals (C. Wu 2004). Indeed, in spite of this rape law and the ban on officials visiting male or female prostitutes, it was heterosexual eroticism that was under rigorous and strict moral scrutiny (D. Wang 1997; C. Wu 2004). More specifically, regulation of widow marriage and female chastity was at its height during this time, whereas same-sex practices were unlicensed and continued to flourish and prevail during the Qing Dynasty. Some even argue that the male courtesan culture supplanted the suppressed female straight courtesan culture (D. Wang 1997).

As long as same-sex relationships observed the order of social hierarchy, they were perceived to be aligned with the Confucian moral system. It was passion or love in both heterosexual and homoerotic relationships that was construed as threatening and transgressive to social hierarchy and social order (Vitiello 2001). Same-sex relationships were usually structured according to gender, age, and status (Hinsch 1992; C. Wu 2004); these features determined the dominant and submissive roles in hierarchical homoerotic relationships. As we have seen, younger men's age and poor economic status relegated them to the inferior female role—confirming their passive, penetrated sexual roles and making them yield to the mature elite men who took on active, penetrating sexual roles as a result of their greater wealth, age, or education.

Sexuality was believed to be malleable, and variegated sexual behaviors were accepted as long as family responsibilities were fulfilled. The vast majority of the elite men in homoerotic relationships were married, fulfilled their family responsibilities, and played the penetrating role in the same-sex liaisons. Indeed, Chinese records showed that both heterosexual and homoerotic relationships were equally practiced in society. As we have seen in this section, homoerotic romance not only evinced elite male power and status but also expressed elite men's aesthetic cultural taste, economic status, and political roles (C. Wu 2004).

REPUBLICAN CHINA (1912–49)

The national crisis and the determination to modernize China prompted intellectuals to translate and introduce Western knowledge into China, including Western concepts of homosexuality (G. Pan 1946).[8] The direct translation of the term "homosexuality"—*tongxinglian*—emerged in the Chinese language in the 1930s. The Western pathologized view of homosexuality came into China along with the translation and spawned a reconfigured interpretation of homoerotic relationships as immoral, deviant, decadent, and, ultimately, the cause of a weak nation. As we see in the next chapter, this Western view of homosexuality has become the dominant medical discourse about homosexuality in China and continues to shape the current era's cultural understanding of homosexuality.

At the turn of the twentieth century, what was once an emblem of aesthetic culture and social status was transformed into a reprehensible and disgraceful practice that came to be seen as one of many causes of a weak nation. Following the Western intrusion into China and the colonizing countries' treatment of the Chinese as second-class citizens, the national crisis brought forth several popular movements—the May Fourth Movement, the Self-Strengthening Movement, and the New Culture Movement—that offered a scathing cultural critique on which to build a modern, strong nation. This cultural critique attacked male homoeroticism as the epitome of the many fundamental flaws in Chinese culture.

This critique deployed gender as an allegory for the nation, attacking Chinese men as weak and sick, leading to a sick nation. Constructions of gender and sexuality were inextricably connected to the construction of a nation. Chen Duxiu, for instance, described Chinese men in the following way:

> They lack the strength to tie up a chicken in their hand, and they do not have the courage to be a man in their mind. Their faces are pale, and their bodies are as delicate as women's. As fragile as sick men, they can endure neither heat nor cold. How could a national group with such a weak body and mind shoulder a heavy burden? (Kang 2009, 5)

Aspiring to emulate what was conceived as the Western modern concept of gender identity, Chinese intellectuals asserted heterosexual masculinity as a means to empower and strengthen the nation. According to them, men should represent the strength, domination, and civilization of a nation. They relegated men in homoerotic relationships to the status of women, weak and feeble. To build a strong nation, intellectuals needed to turn the female-role actors from emasculated victims to heterosexual men so they could reclaim their masculinity.   ugh

As part of this reconstruction of gender and sexuality to build a strong nation, sexual desires were strictly regulated (Dikotter 1995). Individuals were called upon to discipline their sexual desires. Prostitution and pornography were denounced and attacked, along with sexual practices such as premarital and extramarital sex, masturbation, and same-sex practices.

What was once glorified as a romantic relationship between actors and patrons was condemned at this time as a form of exploitation. The critique of homoerotic behaviors was part of Chinese intellectuals' critique of the decadent Chinese tradition. Ba Jin and Lao She's stories about boy actors came to be seen as depicting not romance and love but sexual and economic exploitation in the opera theaters. Indeed, beginning in 1912, many actors staged protests against the master-servant system for its forced prostitution, and the catamite houses were abolished around this time (Kang 2009). To correct the perceived flaws of the Chinese opera, new roles for older male *(lao sheng)* and female performers were on the rise during this time (J. Goldstein 2007; J. Jiang 2009).

That same-sex practices and sexual meanings took on different political and cultural meanings at this time—changing from a symbol of status and taste for elite men to a symbol of a weak nation—once again reveals that they are shaped and produced by the cultural and political context instead of by biology. During the first half of the twentieth century, the colonizing threat and national crisis led Chinese intellectuals to modernize China with imported Western knowledge. Men in homoerotic relationships were highly vilified and stigmatized as sick, weak, and destructive to the nation's survival.

MAOIST PERIOD (1949–77)

The Maoist era enforced a heterosexual, marital, and reproductive sex model wherein sex was only legitimate for reproductive purposes within marriage (see Evans 1993; Honig 2003; T. Zheng 2009a, 2009b). Family was emphasized as the basic cell of society, and marriage was highlighted as a social cause and the fulfillment of a social responsibility to produce children for the Communist state. Those who did not marry, did not have children, or divorced were condemned as socially irresponsible and harmful to the socialist state.

Sex for reasons other than reproduction was deemed deviant and abominable and so needed to be policed and regulated. These forms of sex included premarital sex, extramarital sex, prostitution, and same-sex acts. Sexual desires were demonized as lowly, corrupt, decadent, and incompatible with the state, because sex was believed to weaken, sap, and debilitate people's energy that should be devoted to building the state. Sexual desires, according to the Maoist state, should be sublimated to the purposes of constructing socialism and contributing to the state. Self-restraint and self-discipline were emphasized as imperative in marital sex that would produce the next generation for society.

Regulation of the "corrupt" forms of sex such as same-sex acts relied on arbitrary administrative punishment. During the Maoist period, administrative and disciplinary sanctions were a vehicle of social control. The Chinese Communist Party replaced the Qing criminal code with a system of administrative and Party sanctions, which were then replaced by a new system of criminal laws during the economic reform period (1978 to present). Forced sodomy and sodomy with a minor continued to be treated as a crime (Y. Li 2006).

In the absence of laws against consensual same-sex acts, same-sex acts were subject to a wide array of administrative and disciplinary sanctions under the charge of "hooliganism" (Y. Li 2006). Hooliganism was a general term that encompassed myriad forms of offenses and was often invoked to punish same-sex-attracted individuals. It was reported that many men were charged with the crime of hooliganism during the Maoist era. However, at times, a hospital certificate of a diagnosis of same-sex love illness could potentially lift the criminal charge.

During the Cultural Revolution (1966–76), same-sex-attracted people were classified as "bad elements" under the "five black categories," along with landlords, rich peasants, counterrevolutionaries, and rightists (Geyer 2002). On discovery of their same-sex acts, individuals received harsh criticisms, interrogation, and penalties. Some were beaten to death, and others were driven to commit suicide. Administrative punishments included harassing, detaining, persecuting, and reforming individuals through education or labor, whereas disciplinary sanctions often meant withholding wages and suspending Party membership (Y. Li 2006).

Because of the stringent control and regulation of same-sex acts, same-sex-attracted people usually dreaded public exposure and arbitrary penalties. They chose to conceal their sexual identity and marry opposite-sex partners to fulfill their family obligations.

POSTSOCIALIST ERA (1978–PRESENT)

The Maoist era's model of sex for reproduction was superseded by a postsocialist model of sex for pleasure within marriage. One of the unintended consequences of the one-child policy implemented in 1980 was to acknowledge sexual pleasure between married couples after the birth of one child (S. Pan 2006; E. Zhang 2011). The postsocialist era recognizes the importance of sexual pleasure *within* marriage because it maintains marital harmony and thwarts extramarital affairs; harmonious conjugal families are critical to secure social stability and state control (Sigley 2001; T. Zheng 2009b).

The reconfigured sexual meanings, sexual revolution, and the state's loosening control led to growth in the number of self-identified gay men who gathered at parks, street corners, bathhouses, bars, and toilets. It was reported that such gatherings started as early as 1978 and 1979 at certain places such as Xidan Park in Beijing (Geyer 2002). In 1992, a forum titled Men's World Salon focusing on same-sex topics also emerged in Beijing, but it was short-lived and closed by the police (Geyer 2002).

Bowing to the pressure to marry and produce progeny, more than 90 percent of same-sex-attracted people in China are estimated to choose to marry opposite-sex partners and form heterosexual families with children (Liu and Lu 2005; X. Xuan 2010). Young people were usually able to engage in same-sex relationships because the market economy provided them with an opportunity to delay marriages until their late twenties and mid-thirties. However, these relationships were difficult to sustain because both parties were aware that they would eventually forsake the other to marry an opposite-sex partner and bear a child. A novel that reflected the author's lived experience (Yang Mu 2011) depicted a story where two young men were passionately in love with each other but were forced to end their loving relationship of six years when their parents coerced them into marriage. Broken-hearted, one of them committed suicide, and the other one followed a year later. The secret nature of same-sex relationships that continued outside of a heterosexual marriage usually made them vulnerable and short-lived.

Despite the market reform and rule of law, the Chinese police continued to apprehend, interrogate, and detain people for engaging in same-sex acts (Y. Li 2006). Crackdown campaigns targeted same-sex behaviors and centered on places where same-sex-attracted people tended to congregate, such as public parks and toilets. Stories circulated among same-sex-attracted people about police brutality, including vicious beatings, humiliations, threats of public exposure, and deliberate intimidation. The 1996 film *East Palace, West Palace* (Yuan Zhang 1996) vividly captured police harassment and brutality toward same-sex-attracted men who congregated in public toilets. Indeed, the lack of specific laws and regulations relating to same-sex acts continued to result in arbitrary administrative penalties (Y. Li 2006).

State censorship of movie contents has impeded the dissemination of knowledge about same-sex-attracted people. Zhang Yuan, the director of *East Palace, West Palace,* had his passport revoked by the police and was banned from making movies in China. Cui Zi'en, another film director making films about same-sex-attracted people, was banned from teaching for twenty years. For eight years, Cui was followed, monitored, and spied on by the Security Council; both his cell phone and home phone were tapped. Film activities have also been curtailed. For instance, in 2004, before the opening ceremony of the Gay and Lesbian Film Festival in

Beijing University, the police broke in and ordered the students to leave and cancel the event.[9]

Scholarly works about homosexuality started emerging during the 1980s and 1990s, but the major concern of many books was to cure and treat homosexuality. For instance, Chinese sexologist and sociologist Liu Dalin and his collaborator published a book in 2005 titled *A Study of Chinese Homosexuals*, which had an entire chapter devoted to the social causes of homosexuality, its different categories, and its prevention and cure (Liu and Lu 2005). Another sociologist, Fang Gang (1995), published his study on homosexuality in China in 1995, which discussed how he posed as a physician and persuaded same-sex-attracted men to accept his antidote for homosexuality, in his attempt to procure information from them. On the one hand, these works broke the taboo on discussing this topic and made the public aware that same-sex attraction existed in Chinese society. On the other hand, they were harmful in ascribing attributes of illness and deviance to same-sex-attracted people (see also Geyer 2002).

Indeed, as the next chapter illustrates, the police, state, popular media, and many academic works continued to pathologize same-sex-attracted people and regulate same-sex acts. As Li Yinhe points out, "The continued use of administrative sanctions denies homosexuals equality before the law, including the right to equal employment and opportunities for promotion" (Y. Li 2006, 94). In the current era, same-sex-attracted people still masquerade their sexual identity for fear of social, cultural, and administrative consequences.

CONCLUSION

Through a critical analysis of the cultural history of homoerotic romance in China, this chapter not only refutes and discredits the postsocialist naturalization of heteronormativity but also reveals the plasticity and contingency of sexual meanings and sexual practices, which are defined by the cultural and political context.

Before Western intrusion, same-sex-attracted people in China were not categorized by their sexual essence, but by their particular social roles. Homoerotic romance was an integral part of society and spanned social classes from imperial emperors and government officials to working-class laborers. It was not only widely accepted but also respected and admired as a form of cultural capital indicative of a person's social status, artistic creativity, and economic class.

Homoerotic romance was by no means construed as antithetical to Confucian family ethics. Rather, it was considered to adhere to Confucian family ethics, because it did not conflict with heterosexual marriage and child-rearing responsibilities. As we have seen, mature men who were involved in homoerotic romance had already fulfilled their family obligations by marrying wives and producing progenies. Marriage was envisioned as a social structure with its specific social functions being to bring together two lineage groups and consolidate status and class. The social functions of marriage determined that it was devoid of romance and love, which could be pursued and obtained outside of marriage. Social ethics did not see any conflict between intramarital responsibilities and extramarital pleasures from homoerotic romance. Indeed, as long as marriage continued to be viewed as a vehicle to fulfill social functions rather than individual happiness, a convergence of heterosexual marriage and extramarital homoerotic romance would persist.

The onslaught of Western ideas at the turn of the twentieth century overturned the fluid and indeterminate representation of sex and gender in classical Chinese medicine. Sexuality had never been central to the notion of gender before this time. It was the family structure and social roles on which gender was anchored. In the early twentieth century, gender differences, for the first time in Chinese history, were defined in biological terms. The biological and unitary category of women—*nuxing* (female sex)—was created during the May Fourth Movement in 1919. For the first time in Chinese history, there was a word meaning biological woman (Barlow 1994). The creation of this word not only facilitated the nationalists' attack on the Confucian family but also opened a new space to discuss gender and sexuality.[10]

Acceptance of Western concepts ended the Chinese cultural context that had spawned the acceptance and admiration of homoerotic romance. Chinese intellectuals imported and accepted a scientific discourse of biological determinism that pathologized and demonized nonreproductive sexuality, including same-sex acts. The category of "homosexuality" was created during this time, and it was vilified and demonized as detrimental to health and the social order. New concepts of "normal" sex deemed homosexuality a deviance, and therefore a crime, and blamed it as the very source of a weak nation in crisis.

This transition from a family-based gender difference to an essential-ized, naturalized view of sexual difference with a biological basis (Fou-cault 1978)[11] led to virulent regulations, surveillance, and even punishment of same-sex acts by the state, especially by the Maoist state. The Maoist state's denunciation of sexual pleasures prompted the state to "penetrate private bodies" "in an increasingly detailed way" (Foucault 1978, 106–7).

The Maoist state restricted sex to reproduction, which it deemed beneficial for society and state building. It castigated sexual pleasure as a feature of the decadent and degenerate capitalist lifestyle. The state was intent on policing, disciplining, and penalizing same-sex acts and other nonprocreative sexual activities that were perceived as criminal and deviant.

This historical account of same-sex relationships in China's past and present should help debunk the myth that was spread during the postsocialist era that same-sex romance was a decadent, corrupt lifestyle imported from the West and was therefore alien and foreign to Chinese culture (Jones 1999). As we will see in the next chapter, in continuing to revile and punish same-sex-attracted people as deviant criminals and a threat to the social order, the postsocialist era disavowed China's past and dismissed the long tradition of homoerotic romance prior to the Western assault.

CHAPTER 2

Popular Perceptions of Homosexuality in Postsocialist China

> Homosexuality is an impediment *(zhang ai).* Homosexual men are afraid of women and have had unhappy experiences with women. I feel disgusted by them. It's natural to have a male and a female together, otherwise it's unnatural and pathological. They may have experienced sexual abuse or something that made them go astray. Our country should make them illegal. Our country should imprison them and attack them. They are abnormal.

This quote is representative of local people's attitudes toward homosexuality in my interviews. As I demonstrate in this chapter, such attitudes dovetail with media representations of homosexuality in postsocialist China. Based on around sixty interviews and research analysis of coverage in the media including newspapers, magazines, TV shows, and online articles, this chapter scrutinizes the cultural milieu that structures the everyday lives of Chinese tongzhi.

In China studies, researchers such as Li Yinhe (2008) have argued that social attitudes toward homosexuality have become increasingly open and tolerant in postsocialist China (see also E. Zhang 2011). Li (2008) claims that this accepting attitude stems partly from China's homoerotic tradition; she also attributes her survey results, which demonstrate that the Chinese public's tolerance toward homosexuals is higher than in the United States, to China's not sharing the Western Christian prejudice against homosexuality. Li's survey includes questions about whether a person would like to make friends with a homosexual, whether a homosexual should be allowed to be a teacher, whether a homosexual should have equal employment opportunities, and how a homosexual should be treated by family members. Li concludes that her findings of a positive attitude are very inspiring and portend a future where homosexuals will enjoy improved equal rights and minimal prejudice (see also Z. Pan 2011).

To argue that Chinese society has become as open or more open to homosexuals than American society is certainly wrong and misses several critical changes that have happened in the United States. President Barak Obama has spoken out in favor of gay marriage, and it is now legal in thirty-six states; its status is currently being considered by the Supreme Court. But even before these developments, there was a strong gay political action movement gaining support within the Democratic Party and influencing legislative as well as judicial decisions. Perhaps more significantly, American media have produced sitcoms such as *Modern Family,* which has done for the gay community what the *The Cosby Show* did for African Americans; that is, portray them as sympathetic and normal human beings. There is no equivalent phenomenon in China. For instance, when *Sex and the City* came to China, the dialogue of "I am a lesbian" was translated into "I hate men." Recent polls in the United States reflect the impact of political actions and media portrayals, showing that a significant majority of Americans are now accepting of homosexuality.

It is true that both Catholic and fundamentalist religious groups condemn homosexuality, but to argue that the absence of these religions in China has made China less homophobic is to ignore the twentieth-century history of China. Although homosexual practices were common among upper-class males in China, the New Culture Movement in the early twentieth century vehemently rejected homosexuality as part of the decadence of traditional Chinese culture. My extensive interviews of local people and my survey of Chinese media make it clear that this point of view continues to be dominant in contemporary China.

Through an analysis of interviews and media coverage, this chapter argues that social attitudes toward homosexuality are not as open and tolerant as previous researchers have claimed. Rather, interviews with civilians and media coverage depict homosexuality as a perversion and abnormality often caused by poor parenting, mistakes in child-rearing techniques, traumatic experiences with the opposite sex, and misidentification of gender roles. The media portrayal not only influences local people's opinions about homosexuality but also reinforces the borders of mainstream heterosexual culture and perpetuates a heteronormative paradigm in framing homosexuality as distasteful and deviant.

DISCOURSE AND REPRESENTATIONS

Unpacking media representation is vital because the media not only shape social reality (e.g., the cultural meaning of homosexuals) but also are a powerful mechanism through which common stereotypes and understanding of social groups are inscribed and constructed. The power of discourse in knowledge production has been argued by many theorists.

Power, originally theorized by Parsons (1963) as the influence of one person's actions on another, is expanded on by Foucault in the first volume of his *History of Sexuality* (1978). Foucault defines power as the will to knowledge produced from multiple discourses. Power is ubiquitous, without which neither history nor culture can be understood. It is initiated and perpetuated by different forms of institutionalized knowledge, discourse, and representation. In his works, Foucault exposes the ways in which subjects are constituted through institutionalized knowledge in clinics, prisons, asylums, and so on, as power. Power is thus an instituted and reproducible relationship of force. Foucault's close scrutiny of the micro-politics of power relations in different localities, contexts, and social situations leads him to conclude that there is an intimate relation between the systems of knowledge (discourses) and of domination within localized contexts.

As such, Foucault and other French poststructuralists such as Lacan and Derrida articulate that subjects are constructed and constrained by the power of discourse—a "discourse regime" of signification, through the historical process of "reiteration and citation" (Derrida's term is later used by Butler 1993). According to them, the development of self and self-awareness is both discursively and practically produced and maintained (Bourdieu 1977, 1990).[1] Discourse, as Butler notes, has the power to call a subject into being and ascribe identities and characteristics to a subject. In other words, the subject does not come into being until repetitively "being called, named, interpellated, and addressed" (Butler 1993, 225; see also Gupta and Ferguson 1997).[2]

The repeated naming process in the discourse fixes values to social groups and reifies, materializes, legitimates, and congeals the group as a natural sort of being (Butler 1999). As Stein and Plummer note, "Modern sexuality is a product of modern discourses of sexuality. Knowledge about sexuality . . . constitutes that sexuality itself" (Stein and Plummer

1994, 183). This politics of knowledge production about homosexuals through discourse has been rendered the root of oppression of minority sexualities (Butler 1990; Gamson 1995; Sedgwick 1990; Seidman 1996; Warner 1993; Wilson 2007).

Appadurai contends that our lives "are inextricably linked with representations" (1996, 64). In attributing values and characteristics to certain groups and bodies, representations can be diffused into the social milieu and accepted as reflections of authentic, real people and groups. A symbolic violence can result from the deleterious effect of representations in constituting and imposing a social reality that devalues and demonizes certain social groups. As shown in this chapter, there is a convergence between local people's attitudes toward homosexuality and the media construction of homosexuals, accentuating the pernicious reach and impact of the latter. In this chapter I unpack such media representations.

HIGH-RISK GROUP OF HIV/AIDS

Although homosexuality was virtually silenced in the public discourse during the Maoist era and the early 1990s, the years since have witnessed an increase in media coverage of homosexuality. China's HIV/AIDS epidemic has constituted a platform and catalyst for the mediation of knowledge by naming homosexuals as a high-risk group.

At the beginning of the AIDS epidemic, homosexuality was portrayed as a corrupt Western import that was alien and foreign to Chinese culture (Jones 1999). Officials insisted that the low figure of only 5 percent of the total reported infections in 1997 and 1998 was due to homosexual transmission indicated that homosexuality was not widely practiced in China (China Ministry of Health and UNAIDS 1997, cited in Jones 1999).

In recent years, HIV/AIDS prevalence has acted as a catalyst for knowledge production within the cultural environment. The growing public discussion about the HIV/AIDS epidemic was seized on to underscore the intrinsic tie between homosexuality and this disease. Homosexuals were depicted as a high-risk group transmitting the HIV/AIDS virus to the "general public" (Bai 2001; Z. Ji 2006; K. Xing 2005; Zhang and Yu 2009). Since 2000, it has been ubiquitously reported that homosexuals belonged to the second highest risk group for HIV/AIDS, after drug users but higher than prostitutes, and had the fastest-growing HIV infection rate (Chai 2005; F. Chen 2008; N. Ji 2011; Z. Ji 2006; Wei 2009; S. Yi 2007; Zhuang 2008).[3]

News articles contended that because the HIV infection rate through male homosexual contact was twenty times higher than through hetero-sexual contact, it was easier for male homosexuals to get HIV/AIDS (Ru 2001; Yan Wu 2007; K. Xing 2005; Zhang and Yu 2009). It was highlighted that the first AIDS patient in China had many same-sex sexual relation-ships and that 48 percent of Beijing AIDS patients in 1996 were male homosexuals (K. Xing 2005). Details of the lives of homosexual AIDS pa-tients were also shared in the media (Bing 2006).

Media coverage reflected a shift from a denial of the existence of ho-mosexuality in China to a campaign to demonize homosexuality. News articles highlighted the association between homosexuality and male pros-titution, promiscuity, and HIV/AIDS, interpreting HIV/AIDS as rooted in a promiscuous and perilous homosexual desire (Ai 2007; Lao 2007; P. Xia 2008). Many articles portrayed homosexuals as male prostitutes (Shuai 2005; P. Xia 2008); for example, a news report titled "A Scan of Shanghai Homosexuals: The Lives of Three Boy Prostitutes" equated homosexuals with prostitutes (Shuai 2005).

Homosexuals were thus portrayed as promiscuous, and this promis-cuity—particularly, illicit homosexual behavior in prostitution—was viewed as the connecting link with HIV/AIDS. Homosexuality was linked not only with the promiscuity of prostitution but also with extramarital sex, rape, incest, and sex abuse as crucial factors leading to transmission of HIV and other sexually transmitted diseases (STDs) (Jiu 2008). In turn, it was reported that promiscuity led to violent and harsh sex that could destroy membranes and cause abrasions, torn issues, and bleeding (W. You 2012). Because few people belonged to this "pervert group," as noted by media articles, HIV/AIDS was transmitted faster within this limited circle and infected more people than did heterosexual sex (Fi 2007; W. You 2012).

Media reports also associated homosexuality with multiple, indiscrim-inate sexual partners, one-night stands, higher sexual frequency, and or-gies, thus making homosexuality synonymous with both immorality and HIV/AIDS (Ai 2007; Bai 2001; Fi 2007; Z. Ji 2006; D. Nan 2011; K. Xing 2005; M. You 2005).[4] One media report publicized a study in a college that showed 90 percent of male homosexuals engaged in one-night stands (Fi 2007). Other media reports noted that homosexuals were satisfied with sex with strangers in unsafe, filthy environments (X. Wang 2006; Zhang and Yu 2009). Because these journalists also reported that most Chinese

homosexuals married, the implication was that their promiscuous behaviors could transmit the virus to their wives (Shi 2007; X. Wang 2006).
This led some commentators to characterize homosexuals as lustful, immoral, and perverse as opposed to heterosexuals who were portrayed as
pure, moral, and responsible (Bai 2001; Z. Ji 2006; K. Xing 2005).

AIDS was appropriated as a proof of the danger of homosexuality. The
media construction centered on the causality between sexual promiscuity and disease, thus making promiscuity the defining property of homosexuality. Headlines and news stories dramatized the dangers of casual
sex among homosexuals and the existence of homosexual AIDS patients,
rendering homosexuals a public health threat (Bing 2006).

DEVIANT BEHAVIOR

I interviewed sixty randomly selected, self-identified straight people from
all walks of life in Dalian whom I met via different venues through informants and friends during my fieldwork. They included taxi drivers, busi-
nesspeople, office and business employees, hotel workers, college professors,
and government officials. My interviews showed that the most common
perception was that homosexuals were deviant; their deviance was believed to be caused by pressures in life, influences of the West, or negative
experiences with women. In each interview, words such as "sick," "disgusting," "sickening," "abnormal," "freak," and "not moral" were invariably invoked by interviewees in discussions about homosexuals.

One local man in his forties said, "They are sick. I am extremely disgusted by homosexuals. They make me want to vomit. How do they even
do it? I think they masturbate for each other? That sounds really dull and
no fun at all." When I asked an interviewee if he was accepting of homosexuals, he answered, "Accepting them? Are you kidding me? They make
me vomit the food that I ate ten years ago! Disgusting! Terrifying! Sickening! How do they even do it? I can't understand." Others made comments such as the following: "They are abnormal freaks (*ji xing*) and not
moral. I feel extremely disgusted by them. If they were my friends or part
of my family, I would not accept them." "Our ancestors told us that males
should repel males and males and females should attract each other. Homosexuals run against this ancient truth. They are disgusting, stupid, and
have psychological problems. Women are so pretty and beautiful—why

are they not interested in them? How can they like men? How do they even have sex? These people are abnormal! People these years are turning crazy."

One interviewee said that he had been chatting online with a male friend for a while but did not know he was a homosexual until he disclosed his sexual identity. He said, "Hearing that he was a homosexual, I terminated the chat immediately. I was so terrified that every hair on my head stood up straight because of the fear. I got rid of him as a friend after that."

One female interviewee who practiced Buddhism and Taoism categorized homosexuality as one of the fifty-one evils *(mo)* that stem from a person's corrupt, insidious heart and lead one to be possessed by the devil *(xinshu buzheng, zouhuo rumo)*. According to her, to counteract evil forces in the universe, you needed an upright and righteous spirit or a strong physical body so that evil forces would not be able to affect you. A strong physical body could house the spirit securely so that the spirit was safe and would not be disrupted by the evil forces. The ideal state of harmony between the body and soul would guard against the infringing evil forces.

My interview results dovetailed with the harsh online comments found attached to articles about homosexuality (S. Bao 2008; M. Da 2008; C. Qiao 2005; Tang 2007).[5] For instance, one comment read, "Homosexuals are worse than pigs and dogs! Even pigs and dogs distinguish females from males when mating. We despise mentally perverted people" (Junyong Wang 2008). "A normal man should kick a homosexual couple in the park into the lake and a homosexual couple in the bus off the bus. . . . Those who have money can solve the problem with transgendered surgeries and those who do not have money can find a place to castrate themselves with a knife. Those who have neither money nor courage should find a tree and hang themselves so that they can be reincarnated as a real man" (S. Bao 2008). "We should castrate these people first and then insert a 40-mm steel club into their rectum, and then transport these perverts to Tibet to build railroads" (M. Yi 2008). Health-related websites also published articles labeling homosexuality as a crime against humanity and calling homosexuals "disgusting, shameless, filthy perverts" (S. Bao 2008; Shi Bo 2012; Si Bo 2012; M. Da 2008; D. Qiao 2005; Tang 2007).

Not surprisingly, such depictions of homosexuals sparked discrimination. A news story told of a mother who brought her twenty-year-old homosexual son to see Professor Zhang, who was identified as a national expert on homosexuality. The mother said to Zhang, "Had I known that (he would grow up to be a homosexual), I would have strangled him to death upon his birth" (Chai 2005). Media reports also related stories of doctors refusing to provide medical care to HIV-positive homosexuals (Chai 2005).[6]

These negative depictions also aligned with the opinions of many Chinese psychiatrists in spite of the official recognition of homosexuality (H. Wu 2011). In the 1997 and 1998 debate about whether homosexuality should be removed from psychiatry as a perversion, Shanghai psychiatrist Jia Yicheng published a number of articles arguing that a population of less than 5 percent should be considered abnormal from a statistical point of view and that homosexuality could lead to "spiritual pollution, moral degradation, promiscuity, crime, destruction of family happiness, and suffering of family members, as well as transmission of HIV and STDs" (Jia 1997). In 2001, after the removal of homosexuality from the category of mental illness, a reporter interviewed the vice president of the Psychiatry Council, Chen Yanfang, who was responsible for stipulating the diagnosis criteria and categories of mental illness (Honggu Li 2001). When the reporter asked if homosexuals were normal because homosexuality was no longer considered a mental illness, Chen responded, "No, you cannot use this logic. A negative statement is not equivalent with a positive statement. To say that they are normal has to be proven. People with mental illness are insane, but homosexuals are not insane" (*fengzi*) (Honggu Li 2001). Chen continued, "These people suffer a sexual impediment and require medical help because their sexual orientation is unique. Under this circumstance, we cannot assume that they are normal people. For us who are normal, is there any need to diagnose impediments?"

This viewpoint seemed to be representative of experts' points of view as portrayed in media articles. For instance, a woman sought advice from a psychiatrist about her homosexual husband (D. He 2012). The psychiatrist responded that homosexuality should never be supported as normal because it negatively affected psychological and physical health. According to the psychiatrist, no matter how progressive a society was, homosexuality would never be considered normal because it was against evolution. Although the Chinese Psychiatric Council declared that homosexuality is not a pathology, psychiatrists continued to see it as a moral deviation and an impediment to a healthy society.

A critical question for society is whether or not the individual has made a moral choice to be homosexual or is genetically predisposed to homosexuality. The Chinese Psychiatric Council simply ignored this question, which is, after all, central to the moral issues it has raised. To hold a person morally accountable, we must assume he is making a free choice. If he is born with a homosexual proclivity, he cannot be held responsible because he clearly is not making a free choice.

Homosexuality was labeled a "disease of sexual perversion" to be cured or corrected, as suggested by this article title, "What to Do If a Child Gets Homosexuality" (W. You 2012; see also Jian 2009). In general, homosexuals were called "patients" in the media (Wei 2009). According to many counselors, sexual orientation was a choice; to deem homosexuality genetic and for an individual to claim that he was unable to change was to avoid his personal responsibilities (G. Huang 2006; Z. Zhong 2006). Using terms such as "mistaken love" *(cuowei de ai)* or "impediment in sexual orientation," it was reported that the passive role in male homosexuality and the active role in female homosexuality were the real signs of perversion, caused by parents' misguidance, because the concept of yin and yang in Chinese culture insists that the yang (male) should be aggressive and the yin (female) should be passive (Pin 2004; Ru 2001; M. Yi 2009; W. You 2012). Doctors and psychiatrists claimed it difficult to correct and cure this kind of patient (Pin 2004; Ru 2001), yet these patients were urged to seek psychiatric help and undergo corrective treatments such as repulsion therapy and "early prevention in childhood" (Bai 2001; Xinyue Li 2009; Liu and Lu 2005; Ony 2007; H. Wu 2011; M. Yi 2009).[7]

At times, marriage was recommended as the "the best curing method," with doctors stating that "after you have a normal heterosexual life, your problems will disappear naturally" (Qi 2001, 2). For instance, a college student sent a letter to the Chinese Health Magazine requesting help (Qi 2001). He wrote that he was brought up by his sister because his parents were too busy working. His behaviors and mannerisms were affected by his sister, and he took on women's characteristics and became weak and effeminate. When he was eleven years old, he was sexually assaulted by a twenty-year-old man and later realized that had an interest in men's bodies. He wanted to stop having those desires. In the response letter, the counselor/psychiatrist stated that this story recorded the development of his psychological perversion. The counselor advised the student that, to have manly behaviors and take on a man's role, the most important thing for him to do was to marry a woman: "If you don't marry, you cannot experience your manly spirit. Once you experience it, you will have a man's courage. You can use this experience to be transformed into a normal person. Marriage is the best cure. After you have a normal heterosexual life, your problems will disappear naturally. Behaviors and psychology are learned and you need to start solving your marriage issue first" (Qi 2001, 5).

In contrast, the active role in male homosexuality and the passive role in female homosexuality were deemed "easy to cure" or "heal without treatment" through education or marriage because these homosexual activities stemmed from temporarily unfulfilled sexual desires (Bai 2001; D. Liu 2005; Pin 2004; W. You 2012).

Counselors and psychiatrists were cited throughout the media proposing methods to correct homosexuality. An article titled "How to Correct Youth Homosexuality" defined youth as a messy period and the process of correcting mistaken sexual orientation as going "from disorder to order" (S. Xi 2012). It recommended four steps: overcoming inferiority complexes, interacting with the opposite sex, learning about gender differences, and understanding that homosexuality could be corrected if there was a will on the part of the subject to overcome it (S. Xi 2012; see also D. Nan 2011). Boys were encouraged to overcome fear and hesitation and "feel a man's pride and prowess" (S. Xi 2012). One sign of success was a boy's active interaction with girls. In addition, the article put forward the following questions for the youth to consider: What is the difference between a man and a woman? What are the social demands and requests of gender behaviors? How do you happily accept your own gender? The youth were encouraged to observe people, discuss the topic with friends and classmates, consult with adults, or find answers in literary works (S. Xi 2012).

The media put forth the reassuring message to youth that the "homosexual proclivity" could be corrected easily (S. Xi 2012). As noted by the psychiatrists, the reason why boys loved muscular men was because boys lacked masculinity and suffered "an impediment toward gender recognition" by believing that it was better to be a female. This impediment was explained as an expression of psychological immaturity. Boys were advised to exert efforts to improve the self and become mature, a stage when homosexuality would be corrected (Ony 2007; S. Xi 2012). A counselor in Jilin noted that setbacks in love made college students unable to form correct gender recognition, suffer distorted mentality, and exhibit unhealthy homosexual tendencies (Ony 2007). According to counselor Li Min, college students were not mature enough to tell right from wrong, and hence it was imperative to offer them education and treatment. Students with "abnormal sexual orientation" were encouraged to recognize their problem and get treatment from college counselors and psychiatrists in the community (Ony 2007).

Hospital websites also published articles that appealed to homosexual people "to bravely treat their disease to safeguard the happiness of their family" (Ning 2010). For instance, the Ningbo hospital publicized an article that called on homosexuals to use a wide array of imported cutting-edge technology to "cure their disease."[8]

These depictions of homosexuals had two interesting implications. First, the assertion that homosexuals create chaos and disorder in a society that emphasizes harmony and order suggests the role that the Chinese cultural inclination for harmony plays in determining the way homosexuality is conceived. Second, even though the psychologists and doctors were trained as scientists, they did nothing more than make simple conjectures about the causation and the harmful effects of homosexuality that fit the cultural pattern in China without any kind of empirical follow-up to test their validity. As a result, these conjectures are clearly little more than a reflection of common prejudices in the society. This is particularly insidious because for ordinary people these speculations both had the power of scientific validity and reflect the lowest common denominator in the society.

CRIMINALS

Homosexuals were castigated and reviled as borderline criminals associated with a plethora of crimes, including prostitution, murder, rape, child molestation, deliberate transmission of sexually transmitted diseases, abetting others to be homosexuals, and engaging in homosexual activity in public (Lai 2006; Yuan 2007). Following the disorder theme, some social scientists argued that homosexuals tend to feel hatred toward society and employ extreme measures to gain revenge against society for the ostracism they have received (Ony 2007). In a media report, two experts from the Chinese Medicine and Science Council and the Chinese Xiehe Medical University advised homosexuals to control themselves and avoid any defiant behaviors against the law (Bai 2001).

Even female homosexuals were considered a threat to society and were often portrayed as sexy, murderous psychopaths in popular murder mysteries (see Y. Zhong 2007). For instance, a media article reported a murder mystery involving a homosexual couple who turned into enemies (Zhuan 2004). In the story, Qian, who was a very attractive woman, broke up with her long-term lesbian partner Lan in search of a man to marry. Furious that Lan deliberately destroyed her relationships with men, Qian invited Lan out one night, clubbed her, and pushed her into a river. This story suggested a connection between murder and homosexuality (Zhuan 2004).

The predator theme in the media associated homosexuality with the rape and molestation of teenage boys. In a news story, Zhi was described as "different from normal people" because he was interested in members of the same sex. He watched homosexual porn at home and afterward looked for opportunities to release his sexual desires and "satisfy his abnormal habit." He used money to lure two teenage boys to a cave where he raped both of them. Later he invited his homosexual friend to reenact the crime, raping two boys multiple times. Zhi was sentenced to three and a half years in prison and his friend to two and a half years (L. Xuan 2006).

Many media articles associated homosexuality with blackmail. For instance, in one news story, a homosexual man, abandoned by his lover, not only stole his lover's computer and printer but also blackmailed his lover with a threat to publicly reveal his homosexuality (S. Lan 2006).[9] In another article, a homosexual man sued his ex in court for blackmail, asking for compensation for financial losses and spiritual damage (N. Jiang 2003). In a third news story, when a year's relationship ended with Yong's breakup with Zeng, Zeng took out a DVD of their love making, which he planned to share online to blackmail Yong for 200,000 yuan (Liao Wang 2009). Yong first decided to commit suicide but eventually reported it to the police and had Zeng arrested (Liao Wang 2009).

As mentioned earlier, the media feature many news stories concerning prostitution and homosexuality. In reports about homosexual prostitution the settings varied from personal residences to homosexual bars, bathhouses, clubs, and websites (Cui and Xiao 2012; W. He 2009; X. Lan 2006; M. Liu 2005; Tian 2009; X. Yan 2009; N. Zheng 2003).[10] The following three examples help illustrate the nature of the news reports. In the first story (Tian 2009), two homosexual men rented a place and recruited young men to engage in prostitution. Both were arrested and sentenced to five years in prison with a fine of 5,000 yuan for disturbing the social order and destroying social morality (Tian 2009). In a second story (Cui and Xiao 2012), it was reported that the police destroyed an "organized male prostitution gang" at a Nanjing homosexual bar. The boss was a homosexual man who kept a male mistress. He and his wife recruited a large number of young, handsome men to offer sexual services to homosexual customers. The organizers were arrested and sentenced to eight years in prison and a fine of 60,000 yuan (Cui and Xiao 2012). In a third story, it was reported that Hangzhou police stopped group sexual activity involving forty men in a homosexual bathhouse and subsequently closed down this "homosexual prostitution place," which housed eight good-looking young male prostitutes (Hu 2008). As reported, this homosexuals' "free heaven" visited by homosexuals twenty-four hours a day was the first and biggest orgy site closed by the police (Hu 2008).

In these crime stories, with the police's intervention, a healthy, social order was protected from a homosexual threat. Homosexuals were depicted as undesirable, distasteful, and repellent murderers, rapists, prostitutes, predators, recruiters, and sex maniacs—only interested in satisfying their own perverted lust. *straight ppl murder too! molest assault*

EFFEMINATE IMAGES

In my interview with a local man in his forties, he said, "I can spot a homosexual immediately because they look effeminate with an inadequate yang energy force *(yang gang qi bu zu, niang niang qiang)* and they talk like women." In Taoist ideology, yang represents the masculine principle, which is defined as being positive, bright, active, dry, and hot. According to Taoist ideology, it is natural for men to be dominated by the yang principle, and it is natural for women to be dominated by the yin principle. In this interview, my respondent perceived homosexuality as violating the natural order of things. He used the term "yang energy force" to refer to masculinity, and the Chinese derogatory category *niangniang qiang* (literally, "women's voice") to refer to effeminate, sissy men (see also Sears 2005a, 2005b). His perception was a representative one in my interviews. Indeed, images of homosexual men are almost always couched in effeminate representations. The popular media are filled with effeminate homosexual men who look more feminine and alluring than real women; they are defined as "fake women" *(weiniang)*.[11] Fake women originally appeared in Japanese animation and comic games, where male actors displayed feminine beauty and, after the extensive use of makeup, possibly equaled or at times exceeded the beauty of real women (J. Xia 2010).[12]

This phenomenon of fake women has sparked competing media discourses. On the one hand, commercial interests have appropriated the phenomenon to sell commercial products, thereby driving and reinforcing the trend. On the other hand, indignant discourses abound in the media chastising this phenomenon as an epitome of the loss of Chinese manhood and a threat to the nation-state. Experts, counselors, and educators have called for "saving boys" through revamping the education system and emphasizing gender-difference education in schools and families.

In the 2010 *Happy Men's Singing* contest, a TV show similar to *American Idol*, Liu Zhu, a teenage boy dressed as a woman, participated in the event. Wearing a rainbow blouse and blue skinny jeans, Liu appeared as a beautiful woman. Due to his strikingly feminine voice and his own stylish long hair, Liu's performance was interrupted three times by the judges who questioned his gender and even threatened him with a strip search. In spite of the setbacks, Liu's performance of the song he wrote won over the audience and made him famous overnight. Pictures of him as a woman abound in the online media.

Special interest groups immediately took advantage of Liu's fame and his portrayal as a fake woman to sell their products. Accessories that helped men look like women proliferated in online and brick-and-mortar stores; these products included male bras, male perfume, male skin care products, male makeup, and male wigs. Displaying photos of Liu and of other fake women, advertisements read, "Do you believe that they are men? You can also be this sexy and alluring!" "This is the tribe of Fake Women. We are a supermarket to mold Fake Women!" (P. Liu 2012; J. Xia 2010).

Commercial interests in fake women heightened society's worries about the loss of manhood and the growth of the homosexual orientation. Through the prism of the burgeoning homosexual bar scene, newspaper reporters went undercover to explore the "secret" homosexual population. In the stories, they portrayed them as fake women wearing outlandish, ostentatious clothes (Ai 2007; Ju 2009; Ony 2007; D. Qiao 2005; Ying 2009).

News reports rendered the stereotypical image of a homosexual man as effeminate, a comic spectacle for the heterosexual audience. For instance, in a visit to a Dalian homosexual bar, a reporter categorized the clients as ecstatic when they were called "sisters" (Ying 2009). The report called them "female customers" and depicted them as slender "fake women," wearing makeup and women's clothes, speaking in a feminine voice, having undergone cosmetic surgeries, addressing each other as "sisters," and extolling each other as "beautiful" (Ying 2009). Similarly, another newspaper reporter paid a visit to a "homosexual bar" in Taiyuan city and wrote a piece on Taiyuan homosexual men. The report also described these men as effeminate fake women who either underwent or pursued breast augmentation surgery and "looked more beautiful than ordinary women" (Ai 2007). The report stated that these men appeared as men during the daytime but as women at night: "Meng Meng who had had breast augmentation surgery wore a low-cut dress to show off her cleavage. Xiao Yu was tall, slender, white-skinned, with long and beautiful hair. I would have never believed that he was a man" (Ai 2007, 2). These two reports were representative of a host of others that focused on how these homosexual men used thick facial powder and makeup to make them look like women (D. Qiao 2005).

Media reports not only stereotyped homosexual men's effeminate appearances but also underscored their feminine personalities. Recalling our earlier analysis of yin and yang, it was reported that homosexual men's energy level was lower than "ordinary men" and that they rarely liked outdoor activities or bodybuilding, probably because "they tried to protect their skin" (Y. Lan 2008, 3). It was said that they only relished singing songs and playing musical instruments and that they were more emotional than "ordinary men," yet rarely displayed their true emotions (Y. Lan 2008, 4).[13] Like women, they also enjoyed eating snacks. One account was written by a female college student who was dismayed that male students in her college liked to eat snacks. One summer when she was riding the train home, two male students sat across from her, carrying two huge paper bags. They took out a huge amount of snacks from the bags and were eating them for one hour straight without rest. She wrote, "How womanly these male students have become! Men nowadays—why are you all turning into women?" (Sheng 2009). Because of their "feminine traits and personalities," media reports stated that it was not surprising that their typical work was as hair stylists and makeup specialists (Ju 2009; J. Xia 2010), although many were not able to land a job because of their effeminate personas (Zhuang 2008).[14]

Demeaning and mocking commentaries about effeminate homosexual men proliferated in the media (S. Bao 2008; M. Da 2008; Y. Lan 2008; D. Qiao 2005). Juxtaposed to "normal men," homosexual men were described as "despicable fake women," "whining," and "swinging hips while walking *(yiniu yiniu)*" (S. Bao 2008). A reporter wrote that he was so petrified that his hair stood up when he saw an effeminate homosexual man dressed up like a woman, raising his pinky finger, and calling another man "husband" with a coquettish voice (M. Da 2008).

EFFEMINATE HOMOSEXUALS, MANHOOD, AND THE NATION-STATE

The anti-feminized men discourse suggested a serious crisis of manhood and a crisis of the nation-state. "A China with too many "fake women" is dangerous," the media bellowed (Yue 2012). Deviation from the heterosexual norm and feminization of men were castigated as symptoms of social degeneration, ultimately becoming a trope denoting a nation-state put in danger by a dysfunctional Chinese manhood. Experts, educators, and counselors argued that the feminization of males in the past had led to the colonial domination of China. "The future of our nation is worrisome with the disappearance of manly heroism and masculine spirit," as the discourse lamented (Yue 2012). Authors contended that a harmonious nation should have men who behave like men and women who behave like women; otherwise the nation would cease to be harmonious (Limei Zhang 2012). To save the nation, men's gender-appropriate code of conduct needed to be emphasized and reasserted.

The ideal attributes for men were defined as fearless, heroic, and militaristic—a vital component of the national spirit. In 2010 Yuan Luo, general of the Chinese Military Council, published an article that was posted, cited, and disseminated throughout the Internet (Y. Luo 2010). For China to become the strongest nation in the world, he contended, men's militaristic, fearless, heroic spirit was imperative. Luo traced the problem back to China's humiliating past when military backwardness caused China to descend into a semi-colonized nation after losing the opium war and being forced to pay war debts to colonial nations. Military power, according to Luo, reflected national integration and economic power. Now that China's dream to become a strong nation was finally realized, it had to be supported by a strong military.

The "bad phenomenon" of effeminate men and fake women, according to Luo, was an imminent disaster to the nation-state *(guonan lintou)*, especially when China was still not unified and separatists constituted a threat (Y. Luo 2010).[15] He lamented that this phenomenon of "yin waxing and yang waning" (ascending female role and descending male role) would destroy national integration and vitality. "A nation that does not valorize heroes will have no heroes" (Y. Luo 2010).

Luo's indignant diatribe about the phenomenon of feminized men echoed the feelings of many commentators, pundits, politicians, scientists, and military men (Chong 2010). They articulated men's proper code of conduct: "A man should be like a man. A man needs to be strong and re-silient. Men are born to protect and care for women" (S. Bao 2008; Sheng 2009). "The true meaning of masculinity lies in the spirit of exploring nature, challenging physical limits, and having an unyielding will, rather than sissy clothing and outlook" (Yue 2012). Many people formed "anti-fake-women" groups. A C-block (sissy-block) group appeared at the *Happy Men's Singing* contest, waving a flag that read "Protect pure men. Eliminate fake-women folks" (Chong 2010). An online Anti-Fake-Women League under the banner of "Real Chinese Men" was also formed (Chong 2010).[16]

Invoking the self-strengthening movement at the turn of the twenti-eth century, the creator of the Anti-Fake-Women League castigated fake women for damaging the image of Chinese men in an article titled "Protect Our Testosterone!" Chong, a young professional, asked, "How do youth without testosterone make the country dominate the earth? When the youth are strong, the country is strong. When the youth domi-nate the earth, the country dominates the earth" (Chong 2010).

Many people joined him in the league, agreeing with this declaration: "At this juncture of the dearth of pure, real men, a man should live like a man" (Chong 2010). Fake women, according to the league's members, suffered from psychological perversion and biological regression. Self-defined as "pure men" *(chun yemen)* and "real men," members claimed that they loved sports and outdoor activities, did Wushu *(kungfu)*, performed sword play, revered real men such as Arnold Schwarzenegger and Alain Delon, and worshipped brotherhood and army troops (Chong 2010). Chong himself spent 10,000 yuan on a heavy Tang Dynasty sword, wav-ing it every night and imagining himself as a hero rescuing the good and combating evil. An ex-soldier member went through survival training in the woods with little sustenance for seven days during which time he drank spring water and ate snakes, rats, and birds. Members convened online every night to discuss strategies to fight the phenomenon of fake women (Chong 2010).

EFFEMINATE MEN, GENDER CONFUSION, AND GENDER MISRECOGNITION

Criticisms of a profit-making consumer society and of an education system that was believed to perpetuate the phenomenon of effeminate men abounded in the media. Articles proclaimed that companies should stop using fake women in advertising and instead should guide youth toward the "correct gender recognition"; schools and families should also underscore gender differences and enhance boys' gender-specific education (J. Xia 2010; Limei Zhang 2012).

The consumer society was partially blamed for the loss of manly traits in society as commercial interests appropriated fake women to sell products and increase sales (P. Wang 2012; J. Xia 2010; Limei Zhang 2012).[17] For instance, companies hired members of the Wuhan Fake-Women's League to perform at sales events at the price of 500 yuan for each performer. These fake women provided entertainment and were treated as a comic spectacle, as audiences received pleasure through deriding and taunting them (Limei Zhang 2012).

Yet companies were called upon to exercise their social responsibility for the betterment of youth and to stop the negative influence on them by terminating their use of fake women performers to advertise their products (Limei Zhang 2012). These performances were criticized as misleading youth and affecting boys' sexual orientation, leading to "gender misrecognition," which "was not beneficial for their healthy growth" (Lu 2012; see also Limei Zhang 2012). Articles pointed out that the advertisements inverted gender by employing "beautiful boys" to sell products. For instance, the famous female impersonator and Peking opera singer Li Yugang impressed the audience with his effeminate performances and both female-voice and male-voice singing. He was made a star overnight in the CCTV Spring Festival gala show, thereby creating a vogue and example for boys to follow. Commentators pointed out that this kind of entertainment, in which boys were no longer like boys and girls were no longer like girls, affected boys' values and sexual orientation (Lu 2012). One news editorial asked, "Under the influence of special commercial interests, when real men have disappeared as fake-women, who will assume the roles of father and brother for our kids?" (J. Xia 2010).

Although media portrayals were criticized for their harmful effects, family and schools were identified as the source of gender misrecognition.

The current education and exam systems, as well as parents' guidance, were conducive to the phenomenon of effeminate men (Y. Luo 2010; Yue 2012). Sun Yunxiao, editor-in-chief of Youth Studies and board director of the Chinese Family Education Council, published a book entitled *Saving Boys* (Y. Sun 2009). Sun believed that the education system that focused on college entrance exams was the most violent killer of manhood. He stated that boys' testosterone level was fifteen times higher than girls, which determined the difference between boys and girls on birth and led to boys' sports-oriented, adventurous, and competitive traits. He argued that because schools planned no outside activities, provided no sports equipment, and prohibited students from running between classrooms, boys, whose biology required extracurricular activities, believed that schools were set up against them. Schools did not recognize boys' natural advantages in sports and visual and spatial competence. Girls, he stated, could sit still, but boys tended to jump around, which was incompatible with the school system and led to boys' lower grades than girls. The educational model that lacked recess and enslaved students with books repressed boys, and the lack of positive feedback in schools also damaged boys severely.[18]

Sun's criticism of the education system reverberated throughout the media. Many agreed that the stringent education system rewarded obedience and docility as the only criteria for a good student, thus robbing children of ingenuity and creativity, extinguishing their personalities, and turning them into domesticated cats (Lu 2012; Yifei Mu 2012; Yue 2012). Authors also affirmed Sun's argument that a lack of outdoor activities and the enclosed school-home environment hindered the development of masculinity (Lu 2012; Yifei Mu 2012).

The education system was berated for generating a "yin waxing and yang waning" phenomenon. Because girls were more meticulous than boys and had better self-control and better memorizing skills, their grades tended to be higher than boys and allowed them to enter better schools, putting boys at a disadvantage (Lu 2012). In one junior high school, only three of the twenty-six leaders were male (Yifei Mu 2012). Women also eclipsed men in professional performance and exam grades for government work (Yifei Mu 2012). Science majors in universities used to be dominated by males but were now equally divided between males and females; equal admission of women into medical schools also ended the era of male domination (Yifei Mu 2012).

Others such as Shao Yiming, committee member of the Chinese Political Association, also pointed out that the ratio of male to female teachers resembled an inverted pyramid. Almost no male teachers could be found in nursery schools, and very few taught in elementary schools (D. Gu 2012). Shao concluded that the lack of contact with male models led to the lack of "manhood education." Having almost exclusively female teachers bred delicate boys who lacked manhood (D. Gu 2012; Lu 2012; Yifei Mu 2012).[19]

The family was identified as the other source of mistaken gender (Lu 2012; D. Xu 2005).[20] Parents were blamed for their many failings. They were castigated for making too much demands on boys to study and for fostering an "excessive timid and weak" personality in boys (Yue 2012). They were also chastised for doting on only children and for prohibiting boys from climbing trees, climbing mountains, or playing in water, thereby preventing boys from being independent, adventurous, and taking challenges, and robbing them of strong wills and sharp edges (D. Gu 2012; Yifei Mu 2012).[21] Boys were described as "little emperors," enjoying the love and care of both parents and four grandparents (Lu 2012). They were also depicted as seedlings in a greenhouse that could not withstand any wind or sunshine: In an enclosed environment, it was natural for boys to "degrade" into fake women (Lu 2012; Yifei Mu 2012).

Fathers were specifically blamed for failing in their role (Y. Sun 2009). In his book *Saving Boys*, Sun identified the father as the key to nurturing manhood in his son. When fathers were busy advancing their careers, they deprived the boys of an opportunity to learn to be a man.[22] Hence Sun argued that the lack of the father's role led to the lack of manhood in boys.

In turn, mothers were criticized for being domineering in families. Authors pointed out that in too many families, mothers were dominant and fathers were submissive like lambs (Lu 2012; S. Xi 2012). Domineering mothers affected sons in a negative way (Lu 2012). Sun's book intimated that mothers should safeguard fathers' images in front of boys, which would stimulate boys' yearning to assume a man's role (Y. Sun 2009). One media story described Luo Ming, who grew up in a family where the father was weak and the mother was strong and dominant; he later discovered that he was a homosexual and exerted all efforts to change it (Z. Zhong 2006). In another media story, a man was brought up by a timid father and a fierce and violent mother who often beat him, and he later became a homosexual because he did not like his mother or any other women

(D. He 2012).[23] A psychologist provided commentary to this story that underscored the overwhelming role parents play in inducing children's "mistaken sexual orientation" toward homosexuality. According to the psychologist, in normal situations, daughters are closer to their fathers and sons to their mothers. A disruption of this normal situation by a bullying mother and a weak father and child abuse by the opposite-sex parent could cause boys to feel fearful of women and be embarrassed by their father's humiliation and, consequently, develop a "mistaken sexual orientation" (D. He 2012).[24]

Many online websites on homosexuality cited sociologist Li Yinhe's analysis of the relationship between gender misrecognition and child rearing. In her book on Chinese homosexuality (Li and Wang 1992), Li argues that her research demonstrated that the lack of their fathers' love and participation in child rearing is the underlying cause of homosexuality. Li also notes that boys who look effeminate are likely to be homosexuals. The causation process is as follows. First, the missing father leads to the son's attachment to the mother and distance from the father. As a result, the son self-recognizes as a female rather than a male, exhibiting timid and submissive sensibilities and displaying female postures, female mannerisms, and a female disposition. In addition, his mother worship either causes an inability to feel attracted to any woman, who is seen as far inferior to his mother or makes him revere all women as holy, inaccessible mothers.[25] Second, parents who raise their boys as girls, requiring them to wear girls' clothes and teaching them female-specific work such as knitting and embroidery, are also an issue. Third, effeminate looks and a weak physique make some boys want to play with girls and miss their male-role education. Because of their lack of courage and decisiveness, these boys seek protection from strong men and attachment to strong lovers.[26] Fourth, abuse by women in childhood leads to their disgust toward women (Li and Wang 1992).

In consonance with Li's theory, "abnormal gender misrecognition" as a result of poor parenting was repeatedly reported as the predominant reason for homosexuality throughout the media (Lun 2005; Pin 2004; H. You 2005; Z. Zhong 2006).[27] Gender misrecognition was also recognized to be a two-way street. In a media story, a college sophomore in physical education stated that she had been raised as a boy by her parents (Wo 2006). At the age of six, she learned to play basketball and spent her time playing with boys. In college, she had a girlfriend. A psychiatrist in

Changchun Sunshine Psychiatric Center offered commentary on this story, attributing the student's failure to recognize her own gender and her homosexuality to her parents (Wo 2006).[28]

There seem to be considerable inconsistencies in the examples given by media stories. Although the prevailing narrative seems to be that dominant mothers create homosexual boys, it is also possible to find stories in which the opposite is the case. For example, in another media story, a homosexual man, Lu Tu, came out to a news agency and asked that his story be reported. In the published news report, a section on causation had the headline, "These environments easily brew homosexuality," under which were listed parents' divorce, boys living with the father or girls living with the mother, and so on (Qi 2001; M. Yi 2001; Zhuang 2008).[29] Parents were urged to visit a counselor's website and consult with the counselor (Zhuang 2008). Dr. Kong Fanyu, a counselor for the Nanguan Counselor's Center, was cited as an expert who stated that gender-role education provided by the parents from the age of two to six was imperative. He noted that the problem of homosexuality was difficult to resolve, but that through counseling, he had discovered that many homosexuals became so because of their parents (Zhuang 2008).[30]

Allowing homosexuals to become parents was deemed extremely detrimental to children's growth and therefore was to be rejected (Shen 2007); these homosexual parents' distorted value system would be the root cause of their children's crimes and social chaos. The children of homosexuals would suffer serious damage both physically and psychologically and would themselves become homosexuals (Shen 2007).[31] Because homosexuality was not normal from the perspective of human reproduction and social development, Shen's article recommended that the marriage law should stipulate the prevention of homosexuality and that homosexuals who are willing to seek treatment should receive a discounted price from the Hygienic Development (the Chinese equivalent of the U.S. National Institutes of Health). Schools, army, and other social institutions were also advised to establish approaches to prevent homosexuality (Shen 2007). In the news report described earlier about Lu Tu who came out to a newspaper agency, Lu expressed his trepidation that his child would also be a homosexual (Zhuang 2008).[32]

Psychiatrists in counseling centers advised parents to prevent homosexuality beginning in early childhood (Si Bo 2012). The most crucial time for intervention was between the ages of one and three, and certainly before the age of twelve. Parents were urged to look for preliminary "symptoms" to "diagnose" whether their children had developed a "gender recognition impediment." These "symptoms" in children were deemed discernible between the ages of two and four. They included the child wishing to become the other gender, wanting to wear the opposite gender's clothes, imagining the self as a different gender, aspiring to participate in the opposite sex's entertainment or games, and yearning to become playing partners with the opposite sex. It was noted that boys' feminine behaviors led to homosexuality when they grew up. On discovery of these issues, parents were advised to work together to solve the problems or seek guidance from counseling centers (Si Bo 2012).

Parents' prohibition of opposite-sex interactions was also blamed for resulting in effeminate boys and homosexual relationships. Media reports were filled with panicking parents who feared their kids' homosexual inclinations (H. Pan 2009; X. Zi 2010; Zuo 2006). According to counselors and health educators, the prohibition of heterosexual contact at an early age made kids fear the opposite sex. Parents' rejection of early heterosexual relationships caused children to seek intimacy and emotional needs through homosexual relationships (X. Du 2007; Lin 2012; H. Pan 2009; X. Zi 2010; Zuo 2006).[33] Early heterosexual dating was believed to encourage independence and adaptability to social situations (X. Zi 2010). This led parents to encourage kids to become involved with the opposite sex at an early age (X. Du 2007; Lin 2012).

In one rare instance, when a mother actually supported her son's homosexuality in public, online posts responded quickly with condemnation (M. Yi 2008). The case of this mother was unusual in that she had displayed a nude portrait of herself, hanging on the wall of her bedroom, which the TV report emphasized; online posts immediately latched onto the hanging of that portrait as the cause of the child's homosexuality. The bizarre nature of this situation made the mother an easy target; she was labeled as "disgusting, perverted trash" (M. Yi 2008). Although the intense criticism of this mother does not have the analytical quality of the previous criticisms mentioned, what ties it to the theme is the failure of the mother to accept social norms and thereby once again introducing social chaos and disorder. Disorder is not only a result of homosexuality but, apparently according to this criticism, also a cause of homosexuality.

SOLUTION: REVAMPING THE EDUCATION SYSTEM AND REINFORCING GENDER-DIFFERENCE EDUCATION

Educators around the country criticized the phenomenon of feminized men and declared that China was facing "a crisis of manhood" and that China was losing a generation of men (D. Gu 2012; Y. Sun 2009). In the 2012 National People's Congress and the Chinese People's Political Consultative Congress, Ronghua Wang, the head of the National People's Representatives and board director of the Shanghai Education Development Council (the equivalent of a U.S. state school board), called on the nation to pay attention to the "crisis of manhood" and recommended gender-difference education *(yinxing shijiao)* (D. Gu 2012; Y. Sun 2009).

As educators and the media discourse argued, the education system had to change (Yue 2012). Ronghua Wang contended that the crisis of manhood was inextricably linked to problems in the education system: The exam system and evaluation standards failed to build on boys' advantages and led to their setbacks in study. He argued that gender-difference education should be carried out nationally and men's junior high schools should be established to provide boys with multidimensional educational choices (L. Zheng 2012). The lack of coherence in the strategies to fight the feminization of boys is made clear in the recommendation to create men's junior high schools in which boys would be separated from girls during the critical period of their development. As we saw earlier, encouraging heterosexual dating was seen as one solution to stopping the growth of male homosexuality in China.

The new men's junior high schools would reverse what was perceived as a trend toward the feminization of Chinese men. First, national educators and leaders, following the lead of General Yuan at the Chinese Military Council, argued that a militaristic, patriotic, heroic, and fearless spirit training should be incorporated in the national education system (Lu 2012; Y. Luo 2010; Yue 2012).[34]

Second, gender-difference education was underscored as urgent and pressing (Y. Sun 2009). In his book *Saving Boys*, Sun argued that it could combat the phenomenon of feminized boys and gender ambiguity, thereby creating a new generation of real men.

In addition, boys and girls should be placed in segregated classes, and the education system should apply different evaluation standards to each

gender. Evaluation of boys should emphasize their sporting and adventurous nature, whereas evaluation of girls should be based on their
superior memory and language skills. Because playing sports was in boys'
nature, Sun argued, a sports-oriented education would sharpen boys' will
and increase their ability to withstand setbacks.

Third, parents, especially fathers, were called on to assume the promi-
nent role in educating boys (Y. Sun 2009). They should encourage boys to
accept challenges in life, provide boys with personality training, and in-
culcate in boys the meaning of manhood (D. Gu 2012; P. Wang 2012;
L. Zheng 2012).[35]

Following national educators' call to battle the phenomenon of feminized men, some schools have already started to change. For instance,
in Zhengzhou City, the Eighteenth Junior High School has stipulated
twenty-eight evaluation standards for boys and twenty evaluation standards for girls, requiring boys to be masculine and girls to be demure
(D. Gu 2012).[36]

In Shanghai, East China Normal University signed a contract with
Huangpu District Government to turn Shanghai's Eighth Junior High
School into a men's junior high school (Yifei Mu 2012; L. Zheng 2012). The
headmaster Lu Qisheng stated that the primary purpose of establishing
the men's junior high school is to combat "the crisis of manhood" and
solve the problem of "yin waxing and yang waning" (Yifei Mu 2012; see
D. Gu 2012). It will instill in boys a sense of manhood and terminate the
phenomenon of feminized men.

In this men's junior high school, as reported, boys' needs would no
longer be ignored, nor would their advantages be undercut as in coed
schools (L. Zheng 2012). As noted by the headmaster, this school would
tap into experts' resources and employ a model of boy's education to
mold boys' personalities and advance their latent talents. This personality education was designed to take advantage of boys' perceived logical
superiority and to target their disadvantages of weak will and poor planning. The "masculine" curriculum would include boxing, Chinese chess,
and male music bands. The faculty, as noted by the headmaster, would
continuously adjust and perfect its teaching techniques to increase boys'
self-confidence and make up for their disadvantages (L. Zheng 2012). On
March 30, 2012, the Shanghai Education Development Council autho-
rized Shanghai's Eighth Junior High School to establish trial classes of a
men's junior high school (C. Ji 2012).

Although the Shanghai Huangpu government, the Education Bureau, and East China Normal University supported the establishment of this school and believed that this environment would benefit boys and ensure their growth as real men, some expressed worries that a few qualified, real men trained by the men's junior high schools would not be enough to change the entire society's problem of feminized men (Yifei Mu 2012; L. Zheng 2012). To completely eliminate the problem of gender misrecognition, authors argued that both schools and parents, especially the fathers, should indoctrinate boys with male gender roles and girls with female gender roles (Limei Zhang 2012).

CONCLUSION

Media discourse about homosexuality in postsocialist China is responsive to the broad cultural changes produced by market reforms—reflecting the anxieties about gender, social security, and the nation-state. In this chapter, I argue that underpinning the discursive depiction of homosexuals as deviant, effeminate, criminal, gender confused, and HIV positive is the need to ensure the heterosexual matrix, safeguard the immutability of gender roles, build the prestige of medical professionals, and strengthen the nation-state.

Indeed, as we have seen, homosexuality has become a scapegoat on which anxiety over current social problems such as dissolved marriages and the AIDS epidemic is displaced. Although a dissolved family is pinpointed as one of the key factors that can lead to a child's homosexuality (X. Zi 2010), the media portray homosexuality not only as a public menace and a threat to the family but also as a metaphor for passive masculinity and national crisis. Homosexuality is considered a peril to the security of the nation because it reflects powerlessness, inferiority, feminized passivity, and social deterioration, reminiscent of the colonial past when China was defeated by the colonizing West and plagued by its image as the Sick Man of East Asia. Reviving and strengthening the nation require building a strong manhood and sharpening proper male gender roles.

Distinctive gender roles, considered crucial in safeguarding the security of the nation, are supported and controlled through media discourse. Indeed, sexuality is appropriated to control gender in the same way that gender is used to control sexuality. Although homosexuality is pathologized, the central concern of media discourse is gender behavior, rather

sexuality conflated w/ gender

than sexual behavior. As illustrated, media articles focus on homosexuals' deviant or mistaken gender behaviors and lack of understanding of gender distinction. The characteristics ascribed to homosexual men—being effeminate, passive, and weak—are considered deviant. Their mistaken gender identities and misrecognition of gender are depicted not only as creating a crisis of manhood in the nation but also as an indicator of poor parenting and a problematic education system. As shown in this chapter, educators, psychiatrists, and psychologists have proscribed myriad preventive strategies involving parenting and the education system to strengthen socialization and education of proper gender roles and combat "the crisis of manhood." As such, gender deviance is governed and controlled to prevent and control sexual deviance.

In exploring the root cause of homosexuality and methods to avoid homosexuality, the scientific expertise of doctors is sought. Media articles tend to end with a doctor's comments and appraisals, thereby emphasizing the authority of doctors. The kind of power and authority that media bestow on doctors' "scientific" narratives exerts far-reaching impact in the social milieu. This resonates with Foucault's (1978) theorization of governance operated through professional discourse by experts and scientists.

The attitudes of medical professionals, as this chapter illustrates, reflect the social mores of postsocialist China. The rising middle-class medical professionals in contemporary China subscribe to the mainstream sexual morality and advocate cures and prevention of homosexuality. In an effort to advance their profession and procure influence, medical professionals have a vested interest in producing narratives that do not counter cultural norms. Producing such narratives will not only ensure their prestige and influence but will also draw more income to their profession, as parents and homosexuals continuously pay fees to seek their professional advice.

It is the application of the scientific method that is the basis of medical professionalism, and yet ironically that is exactly what is missing in their analysis. Rather than making a hypothesis and empirically testing it, the medical professionals simply have made a hypothesis based on common cultural biases. In fact, the conclusion they draw seems very much at odds with Western studies about homosexuality that are empirically based. Although not absolutely conclusive, evidence at this point seems to suggest that homosexuality is not caused through socialization, but is something with which people are born.

The question arises as to why this masculine narrative is so popular in China. To understand why, we have to look again at Chinese history. In traditional China, a self-contained culture that paid little attention to outside opinion, there was a masculine ideal that gave prestige to those who were not particularly physically robust. The mandarins who represented the highest social ideal in China were people who worked with their minds rather than their bodies. The symbols showing that they worked with their minds were their long robes, which today we would consider feminine clothing, and their practice of allowing their fingernails to grow into extraordinary lengths of six inches or more, making their hands unfit for physical labor. These were powerful status symbols that rejected physical activity as a defining factor of masculinity. When China finally succumbed in the twentieth century to Western aggression after stubbornly clinging to this traditional culture, it rejected its traditional culture in favor of what was called a New Culture Movement. This movement accepted Western culture and, with it, Western definitions of masculinity as sexually potent and aggressive. Implied in this acceptance were great shame about China's past and a belief that the traditional male's feminine nature was the cause of China's troubles in the twentieth century. In spite of Mao's rejection of the Four Olds—his attack on traditional Chinese culture—in many ways, Mao represented a return to traditional China. Mao represented himself as an all-knowing emperor whose wisdom brooked no challenge and required complete conformity with his values. Mao's emasculation of men certainly did not follow the traditional lines, but nevertheless was very effective, even while ironically using the Western ideology of Marxism. The rejection of Marxism in 1978 and the affirmation of the need for a new culture and a new economy led, once again, to a rejection of the traditional view of masculinity as emasculated and feminized and an affirmation of a macho, Western-style masculinity in its place. The powerful driving force in the post-Mao reaffirmation of a Western-style masculinity was a new capitalist economy that emphasized a masculine entrepreneurial spirit (T. Zheng 2009a).

CHAPTER 3

The 1s and the 0s

Defining, Socializing, and Disciplining Gender Roles in the Tongzhi Community

Before entering the tongzhi community, same-sex-attracted men are not aware of the gender division between 1 and 0. On their entry into the community, they find themselves overwhelmed by the question of whether they are 1s or 0s. 1, symbolizing the penis, is identified within the community as the male role, whereas 0, symbolizing the vagina, is associated with the female role. Conversations in Internet chat rooms and at the tongzhi cruising areas often start with tongzhi introducing themselves as either 1s or 0s. Even registration forms on online friend-making websites for same-sex-attracted men require self-identification as 1s or 0s. New members in the community, who have no clue whether they are 1s or 0s, find themselves slowly socialized into these two categories. Some choose their own role, whereas others are assigned a role by assuming a sexual position in their first sexual experience with someone who has already self-identified as a 0 or a 1. Once their gender role is determined, tongzhi are disciplined by the community to fit into it. This discipline is imposed and maintained through derision, gossip, and admonishment. For instance, my informant Wan, a self-identified 1, told me that he quit wearing his big bag on his shoulder because he was mocked and derided by tongzhi in the community for acting like a 0, not a 1. He learned from the community that wearing a big shoulder bag was associated with the female gender, whereas having a small bag at the waist was associated with the male gender. He adapted by buying a small bag and carrying it around his waist. When Wan tried to share his relationship problems with other tongzhi in the community, once again he was laughed at, disparaged, and even berated for being emotional and committed like a 0. He had to adapt again by readjusting his behaviors toward his 0 and fulfilling the expectations of being unfaithful and promiscuous like a 1. Thus, through relationships and experiences, over time, tongzhi in my research are formed into the

75

identities of 1 or 0 according to the tacit rules and expectations shared in the community.

In anthropological studies of same-sex identities, Parker and Gagnon (1995, 15) assert that local systems of meaning are crucial to understanding sexual identities: "[We need to] move from the isolated sexual individual to sexuality as existing not only within but between individuals. The attempt to understand sexuality through an understanding of the social networks in which people live sexual and non-sexual lives is a way to concretize this movement." By placing same-sex-attracted men in their local cultural context, in this chapter I explore the gender dynamics implicit in the roles of 1 and 0 and answer the following questions: What are the cultural meanings of 1 and 0? How do their identities as 1s and 0s shape the romantic experiences of same-sex-attracted men? How are gendered identities of 1 and 0 played out in romantic relationships? How are hegemonic gender norms reflected and challenged in the lived experiences of 1 and 0? I argue that 1 and 0 frame their different gendered identities, rather than common sexual identities, according to normative expectations of women and men. Their appropriation, negotiation, and transgression of cultural norms denote a gulf between upheld ideologies and lived realities, which often results in upheavals and volatility in romantic relationships.

SAME-SEX-ATTRACTED MEN IN LOCAL CONTEXTS

Dennis Altman (1996a) points to a "global queering" process in the shift from gender-based identities to Western sexual identities that are not hinged on gender identities. This trend, according to Altman, is triggered by Western influences disseminated via media, entertainment, consumer culture, and tourism.

Numerous researchers (Boellstorff 1999, 2005; Elliston 1995, 1999; Godelier 1986; Herdt 1994; Parker 1999; Sinnott 2004) have countered Altman's prediction of a globalized, Western style of sexual identity with detailed, contextualized accounts of local same-sex identities. These local same-sex acts and identities differ from the Western concept of sexuality and have a distinct embedded history. As shown in Melanesia and New Guinea, boy's ingestion of adult men's semen as a rite of passage into adulthood denotes a cultural, rather than erotic or sexual, exchange of substances to form social identities[1] (Elliston 1995; Herdt 1994). As such, same-sex acts do not warrant or imply a homosexual identity and hence can only be understood within their local contexts.

It is imperative to analyze local practices by placing them in their local contexts (Parker 1999).[2] The identities of same-sex-attracted men in Indonesia, for instance, cannot be understood until they are studied in their local system (Boellstorff 1999, 2005). On the one hand, the Indonesian national culture is the driving force for same-sex-attracted men to marry heterosexually. On the other hand, local cultural patterns inform and structure their emotional and sexual attachment. Hence the identities of same-sex-attracted men in Indonesia are constructed by forces that include both local culture and state policies (Boellstorff 1999, 2005).

In my research, the formation of 1 and 0 identities is a result of a multi-faceted confluence of the local cultural system and economic and social transformations in the postsocialist era. Whereas social class was often the determining factor for same-sex relationships in classical China, in the postsocialist era, it is gender dynamics that plays a salient part in shaping the identities of 1 and 0, as I show later.

In this 1/0 system, it would be problematic to use the Western lens of sexual orientation, which obscures gender and accentuates sexuality. As I show, the categories 1 and 0 are entrenched in the local gender paradigm that denotes masculine and feminine categories. Rather than sharing a sexual identity based on a common sexual orientation, 1s and 0s differ from each other as two different gendered identities. As such, gender difference is more pivotal to their identities than sexual identities. This gender-denoted same-sex relationship is found elsewhere, such as in Thailand and Latin America (Adam 1986; H. Bao 1993; Carrier 1985; Epps 1995; D. Goldstein 2003; Green 1999; Kulick 1998; Parker 1999; Prieur 1998; Sinnott 2004[3]).

The gender difference between 1s and 0s not only debunks Altman's argument but also refutes Murray's assertion of a universal homosexual identity based on same-sex acts (S. Murray 1992). In contrast to Altman's contention, the identities of 1 and 0 are gendered entities produced by comprehensive forces, rather than sexualized identities produced by Western influences. Although two same-sex-attracted men in my research did cite Western models to question the 1/0 system, the presence of such few voices has been unable to destabilize the 1/0 system, which remains intact and hegemonic in the community.

GENDER IDEOLOGY IN THE 1/0 SYSTEM

The 1/0 system is relatively pervasive among same-sex-attracted men, although it does not encompass all same-sex-attracted men's identities. In my research, only two men identified themselves as 0.5, somewhere between 0 and 1. According to them, their increasing age and a loving relationship necessitated a change of roles, resulting in a flexible role as 0.5.

Same-sex-attracted men in my research construct their 1 and 0 identities in compliance with the implicit norms in their community, just as American butches and femmes structure their butch and femme identities in accordance with the strict rules in their community (Kennedy and Davis 1993). Before entering the community, same-sex-attracted men are not usually aware of the division between 1 and 0. They are either ushered into the gender role of 1 and 0 through their first sexual experiences or assign themselves the gender role of 1 or 0. Although their first sexual experience can at times, influence their future roles as 1 or 0, ultimately, it is the gender roles—the cultural categorization of traits and characteristics as either masculine or feminine—that decide their roles as 1 or 0.

The gender division of 1 and 0, according to the men in my research, "naturally imitates" and "emulates" the hegemonic gender roles in heterosexual relationships. 1 takes on the role of the aggressive inserter and is considered "not physically damaged" *(bu po sun)*; 0 assumes the role of the inserted receiver and is considered "physically damaged" *(po sun)*. Same-sex-attracted men usually call each other "husband" *(laogong)* and "wife" *(laopo)* in alignment with their gender roles. The complementary roles of 1 and 0 in a relationship are believed to be more harmonious than having two 1s or two 0s in a relationship, a situation that is often expressed as "stuck" *(ka huo)*.

1s and 0s in my research render themselves differently from each other, invoking the Chinese philosophical theory of yin and yang. As they contend, the two fundamentally different principles of yin and yang are helpful in understanding the meanings of 1 and 0. Yin, or 0, conveys the meaning of being negative, dark, passive, cold, wet, and feminine. Yang, or 1, carries the meaning of being positive, bright, active, dry, hot, and masculine. According to the same-sex-attracted men in my research, it is natural to have a union of 1 and 0 in a relationship, just as it is natural to have a union of yin and yang in the universe. 1 is believed to be able to marry and have a heterosexual relationship with a woman, whereas 0 is believed to be incapable of doing so.

Although sex positions vary in a relationship, it is gender roles that invariably determine who is a 1 and who is a 0. Even if a man has experienced the inserted position of 0 for the one he loves, he may still self-identify as a 1 because of his individual traits. Conversely, although a man may feel pleasure in the inserting position of 1 rather than the inserted position of 0, he may still choose to be the latter as he self-identifies as a 0 because of his individual traits. As a result, most 1s are believed to be able to choose the inserter's position to satisfy their physical needs, whereas most 0s are believed to endure the pain in their initial sexual experiences to satisfy their psychological needs. In other words, gender roles usually lead to sex positions.

In my research, many same-sex-attracted men choose to be 0s because they perceive themselves as passive, submissive, obedient, and dependent, not because they are unable to be the inserter. According to them, few people are willing to be 0s because, to use Xiao Ming's words, "There is no pleasure in being inserted, but for the person you love, you are willing to accept the pain." Those 0s in my research discussed with me at length the horrible physical pain they had to go through for a long time before they finally became accustomed to and even enjoyed the feeling. For instance, Xiao Lu said to me, "The pain was excruciating. I was biting my teeth the entire time. When he asked if I enjoyed it [sex], I lied to him and said yes. In fact, I was in pieces because of the pain. I love him, so I want *him* to feel the pleasure." 0s such as Xiao Lu disregard their own physical pain and feel gratified for giving physical pleasure to their 1s. Love makes them "sacrifice" and "dedicate" (*fengxian*) their bodies to their 1s. Love makes them derive pleasure from their 1s' pleasure. Here I am not making a universal claim that all penetrated men in China feel that assuming that role is a sacrifice. Rather, I am simply reporting that both 1s and 0s in my research agreed on the physical pain of being 0s and that it usually took a while for 0s to finally get to the stage of physical pleasure.

As I was told by tongzhi in my research, the assignment of 1 and 0 is determined by the traits and personalities that are associated with idealized categories of masculine and feminine qualities. Tongzhi told me that 1s have a controlling tendency, a desire to protect others, a strong sense of security, a callous mind, and an interest in violence. In contrast, 0s accept control, require protection, lack a sense of security, submit to domination, rely on intuition, and have an interest in music, art, and aesthetics. More specifically, 1s like eagles, wolves, and dogs, whereas 0s like cute things such as dolls, squirrels, and cats.

Indeed, it is the tongzhi community that defines proper male and female behaviors and roles and uses the rules to structure the identities of 1 and 0. Whereas 0 is expected to be faithful, dedicated, and understanding of 1's promiscuity, 1 is expected to be promiscuous and controlling; he is believed to assume the superior position because he considers himself the "master" and 0 the "sex object." Whereas 0 gives 1 his body and soul in a loving relationship, 1 gives 0 a wandering heart as in a "migratory bird," coming and leaving freely. 0 is often warned that 1 will get tired of him quickly and leave, leaving 0 grief-stricken for the lost love. I often heard complaints from 0s that, although they longed for a loving relationship, many 1s only wanted a one-night stand. A 0, Xiao Feng, for instance, met several 1s online who requested either a threesome or a one-night stand right after they initiated the chat. Another 0, Xiao Liu, lamented that the 1s he went to bed with told him they loved him before sex, but left him right after sex. These distressful experiences led to a conclusion that "1 only thinks with the lower part of his body and values sex more than emotions." 0s usually warned each other that if they were interested in a 1, they should put off sex, because they believed that 1 would not fall in love with a 0 with whom they had a one-night stand.

According to the men in my research, the lopsided ratio between the large number of 0s and the much smaller numbers of 1s further contributes to the superior status of 1s and inferior position of 0s. During my research in the cruising areas, many 0s complained to me that there were too few 1s and too many 0s. Whenever a 1 came to join the group, several 0s would yell out, "A 'big man' *(da yemen)* finally came! Sisters, come over and watch!" They joked that they were competing with each other to serve the 1. Like the cruising place in the park, online chat rooms were also filled with more 0s than 1s. Indeed, the community was likened to a "Kingdom of Women" *(nv er guo)* where a magnitude of 0s fought against each other for the attention of a limited number of 1s.

Tongzhi generally describe 1s as *hua xin*. The translation of this term is "having a florid heart," which means a playboy or unfaithful heart. Their unfaithful heart tends to lead 1s into promiscuous behaviors with multiple sexual partners, whereas 0s tend to be more loyal and dedicated. During my research, it was commonplace to hear 1s brag about their voluminous and high-quality sexual conquests. They often told me that it was "natural" for them to have the desire to conquer as many 0s as possible and that, no matter what they did, their 0s were always patient and obedient. Xiao Tan said to me, "After being with a 0 for a while, I usually run out of passion and need to seek new stimulations from one-night stands. I long for the feeling of fast heartbeats." Some 1s expressed to me that they loved the "animal-like sex"; others ticked off a long list of women and men with whom they had slept. Xiao Zhang bragged to me that he had sexual relationships with fourteen sexual partners per week, including many male waiters at the bathhouses and every single hostess in the sauna bar that was adjacent to his house. In his grandiose account of his sexual conquests, he did not fail to mention that he was so strong in his penetrating role that his male partners usually begged him to be less harsh.

In consonance with the rules and expectations in the tongzhi community, some 1s told me that it was sufficient to satisfy their biological needs without getting entangled in the complexity of emotions. Xiao Ming, a 1, for instance, got to know a 0 through an online chat room. The 0 sent Xiao Ming his picture and told Xiao Ming that chatting with him online made him very interested. The 0 went on to say that he wanted a long-term relationship and suggested that both meet each other's parents. Xiao Ming responded that a long-term relationship was impossible because he was going to marry a woman and "have a normal life." Xiao Ming also emphasized that his parents knew nothing about his sexual behaviors, so it would be inappropriate to bring a man home to see his parents. According to Xiao Ming and many other 1s I talked to, 0s are more interested in long-term commitment, whereas 1s are more interested in short-term physical pleasure without emotional attachment.

Here are some more comments that 1s shared with me about their 0s: "In the bones (*guzi li*) of 0, they desire to be conquered, loved, and cared for." "0 needs someone to care for and someone strong to lean on. They like the feeling of being possessed." A 1 told me that his 0 drove his car very slowly "like a woman," at only sixty miles an hour and never dared to exceed 70 miles an hour. Another remarked that his 0 was "like a woman" because he was indecisive, spoke slowly and not concisely, handled things slowly, and tended to procrastinate. These comments evince patriarchal, discriminatory views of women that are part of the dominant gender ideology in society.[4]

The tongzhi community applies heterosexual cultural expectations of women and men to the gender relationships between 1s and 0s. Tongzhi are socialized into their gender expectations and gender roles in the relationships. As I was told by tongzhi in my research, 0 is expected to accept 1's control. A 0, Xiao Zhao, described to me his 1's control over him: "My boyfriend watches me very closely *(kande kejin)*. He doesn't allow me to send or receive any text messages or phone calls. Whenever a text message or a phone call comes in, he interrogates me the whole night about my relationship with that person. So when we are together, I keep my phone off the entire time. It's been really tiring." Another 0, Xiao Feng, said that his previous 1s forbade him from looking at their cell phones. Later he managed to find out that both 1s had sexual partners in addition to him.

In the tongzhi community, the hegemonic gender rules and expectations indicate that being male and female is more pivotal to 1 and 0 identities than being "homosexual." 1s often told me stories about their dominance and 0s' obedience. A 1, Han, told me that his 0 listened to him in every matter. Whenever a decision had to be made such as where they should meet, his 0 always deferred to Han. His 0 hand-washed Han's underwear, socks, and clothes every day and begged him not to let others wash his clothes for him. When Han asked what he was going to do if he tested HIV positive, his 0 answered that he would be with him forever; if Han tested negative, his 0 responded that he would be with him for 1,500 years. Thus his 0 used every opportunity to express his loyalty to Han in the relationship.

The hegemonic gender rules and expectations in the tongzhi community also stipulate different obligations to 1s and 0s. Whereas 1s take on the husband's role as rational, aggressive, protective, and financially supportive, 0s take on the wife's role as emotional, passive, delicate, and financially dependent: 1s are expected to protect 0s and take care of them financially. A 1, Xiao Zhao, said to me, "When I love a 0, I will protect and care for him. When he is hungry, I will buy him his favorite food. When he is thirsty and there is no water nearby, I will run to a far-away place to buy him bottled mineral water and soft drinks such as Red Bull that he likes. In return, my 0 obeys me and listens to me in everything." This account crystallizes the different responsibilities of 1s and 0s: the husband's breadwinner duties and the wife's submissive duties.

Anthropologists who have conducted research in Polynesia, Mexico, Peru, Brazil, and other parts of Latin America have written about this pattern of same-sex relationships based on gender differences and of men assuming the female gender role (Adam 1986; D. Bao 1993; Besnier 1993, 2002; Caceres and Rosasco 1999; Carillo 1999; Carrier 1985; Ellison 1995; Epps 1995; D. Goldstein 2003; Green 1999; Klein 1999; Kulick 1998; Parker 1999; Prieur 1998; Sinott 2004).[5] Besnier (1993, 2002), for instance, analyzes men who are identified in "gender-liminal" categories as *fa'afafine* in Samoa and *fakaleiti* in Tonga. These men's female gender role is determined by their social role rather than sexual behaviors. More specifically, these men engage in work traditionally associated with women, such as domestic chores.[6] In Latin America, studies show that males who are dominated take on the female role and males who dominate take on the male role, despite myriad variations in their sexual behaviors. The local cultural pattern of gender binaries between femininity and masculinity shapes the gender divisions in same-sex relationships. The masculine primacy of the male-gendered men in same-sex relationships cannot be captured by Western terms of "homosexual" or "heterosexual." Nor can it be encapsulated by the term "bisexual," because it accentuates the sexes of their sexual partners, not the masculine primacy that constitutes their social identities.

The gender rules and expectations that tongzhi implicitly and explicitly articulate and follow in the tongzhi community seem to derive from heterosexual patterns in the dominant cultural system; they are entrenched in dynamics of power and social sanctions and dependent on the fulfillment of gender roles and social obligations. As illustrated, the hegemonic gender rules and expectations constructed in the community enforce strict and, at times, repressive gender roles for both 0 and 1, with 1 functioning as the economic and financial provider. Both 0's experience of a subordinate position and 1's experience as a financial supporter can be oppressive.

0's identity as a biological man and a social woman engenders an unstable and contentious gender identity, as I describe next. Despite men's socialization into 1 and 0 identities in the community, the gender rules and expectations are under constant and creative manipulation and contestation by men to advance their own interests. More specifically, as I show, 0s not only appropriate the female privilege to be financially supported but also assert their male prerogative to be sexually free.

0S' APPROPRIATION OF FEMININITY

0s in my research often appropriate femininity to receive emotional care and financial support from 1s. Their manipulation of femininity is similar to the urban Brazilian *travestis* who usurp femininity to attract male lovers (Kulick 1998). Male *travestis* in urban Brazil appear feminine in feminine outfits and feminine makeup so that their male lovers can envision them as true women and imagine their relationships as heterosexual rather than homosexual. Like urban Brazilian male *travestis*, 0s often deploy femininity as a strategy in the same-sex relationship.

Like women in heterosexual relationships, 0s in my research tend to use their body shape, skin texture, fashion, and feminine behaviors, such as a coquettish voice, feminine mannerisms, and a buttock-swinging walk style to attract 1s' attentions and earn their love and appreciation. I was told that 1s usually display a muscular look with a rough style, whereas 0s usually exhibit a feminine look with a trendy style. Unlike 0s, very few 1s wear casual, tight, or pullover clothes; instead, they wear dress shirts, dress pants, leather shoes, and small bags along their waists—in contrast to 0s, who carry big bags over their shoulders. A 1, Xiao Wen, said to me, "My 'wife' behaves like a woman. He calls me 'husband' in a coquettish voice, turns up his lips, and asks me to embrace him or carry him on my back. He also moans loudly like a woman, which we men love." Another 1, Xiao Lin, commented that his "wife" knew how to dress up, looked "anew" *(huanran yixin)* to him every day, wore tight clothes and tight jeans to show off his body shape, and coordinated the colors of his clothes aesthetically. His "wife" even took contraceptive pills to soften his skin texture and develop his chest.

0s in my research often expect 1s to have a good career, be able to support them, and aspire to a goal to achieve success, which 0s define as the accumulation of wealth and consumption power. To most 0s, it is 1's responsibility to satisfy both their material and emotional needs.

The intersection between romance and material concerns, as research has shown, characterizes postsocialist romantic relationships. Research on youth in China (P. Sun 2012; Zhang and Sun 2013; T. Zheng 2009a) has documented the commodification of romance in postsocialist China, where cars, apartments, income, and consumption of luxury goods are important concerns in romance, love, and marriage. Farrer (1998), for instance, in his research with youth in Shanghai, discusses the ways in which material and romantic motives permeate sexual relationships in the market society where "getting rich" has become the ultimate motive. For Shanghai women, choosing partners necessitates a balance between material conditions and romantic feelings, between pragmatism and romance. Farrer (1998, 15) points out that in the market society where masculinity is tied to economic prowess and a perception of sexual potency, women generally desire to "marry up," choosing husbands who will provide the best economic conditions for them and whom they also love. Jankowiak (2013), in his research with youth in Hohhot, also states that men on dates discuss their future prospects to attract women by describing the money they will make, the kinds of cars they will purchase, and the sizes of the apartments they will have. His findings illustrate that young people, much like their parents, continue to marry to gain material resources and fulfill social expectations. In another study of matchmaking of youth in Shanghai, Zhang and Sun (2013) argue that economic factors are a priority for urban youth, who believe in the importance of self-centered pragmatism. Social class and economic hierarchy are central concerns at the matchmaking corner where most young people require future spouses to have a certain social rank, prestigious educational background, wealth, and networking resources.

My research showed that 0s often valorized 1s' money and care in a relationship, and many expressed their wish to find a wealthy and considerate 1. The following four vignettes from my research were representative of 0s' pervasive expectation for financial support and meticulous care from 1s.

In the first story, Xiao Peng's 1 deposited 100,000 yuan in his savings account as a proof of his love. When Xiao Peng was hungry in the morning, his 1 would immediately rise from the bed and cook for him in his underwear, wasting no time putting on his clothes.

In the second story, Xiao Tao's 1, a physician, paid for his rent, took him out to high-end restaurants for every meal, and bought him nutritious food, snacks, and other daily necessities so that Xiao Tao did not need to work.

In the third story Xiao Sun's 1, a university professor, took him on several trips to exotic, foreign countries and bought him foreign brand-name clothing and luxurious fitness and massage machines. When he took Xiao Sun to restaurants, he always put food on Xiao Sun's plate, poured wine for him, and ordered his favorite dishes.[7]

In the fourth story, Xiao Luo's 1 either cooked for him or bought him meals every morning and every evening despite his busy work schedule. His 1 also carried a basin of warm water for him and helped wash his feet and his face every day. When Xiao Luo asked for a dog that cost 800 yuan, his 1 immediately promised to buy him one on receipt of his salary that month.[8]

0s' stories prompt us to wonder what 1s think about the sacrifices they have to make to satisfy their 0s' material needs. It is quite ironic that although 1s enjoy sexual agency and gender dominance in the power dynamics, 1s suffer from this prestige and power. Indeed, they are often exploited by having to serve the role of financial provider. The following story offers another example of the kind of pressure and anguish embedded in this obligation.

A 1, Xiao Fang, to keep up with his financial support of his 0, sold his blood and worked in a sweatshop, unbeknownst to his 0. Xiao Fang moved to the city a few years ago and entered the tongzhi community. Ever since he established a relationship with his 0, he found himself forced to keep up with his 0's material needs to make him happy. His 0 always depleted his own salary and demanded he pay for eating out, taxies, trendy clothes, and high-end consumption places. He also paid for his 0's phone services, apartment rent, food, and other necessities. Xiao Fang expressed to me his concern that he was not fit to be with his 0 because of the gap between what he could give and what his 0 wanted: "I feel that we are a mismatch *(men bu dang, hu bu dui)*. He is a skilled make-up artist, and I am a common laborer."

To close the gap, Xiao Fang exhausted all possible means of earning money, including doing direct sales, working at sweatshops, selling blood, and working at a local AIDS NGO. He said, "I eat bitterness; I sell blood, but I can't let him know. I don't want him to feel my financial burden, because he would despise me for not having money. He doesn't know the pressure on me. He always thinks I have a lot of money, and he will get upset if I don't buy him what he wants."

Xiao Fang said that he gave his 0 money to prove his love. Extremely thrifty when spending on himself, Xiao Fang saved almost all the money he earned to support his 0. He said, "I never spend money on myself but save every cent for him. I want to show him how much I care about him. I want to show him that I can help him out when he is in need. I don't believe other people will ever give him as much money as I do." When his

0 borrowed money from him, he loaned him all the money in his bank account and left himself practically nothing. Not surprisingly, the money Xiao Fang loaned to his 0 was never returned. When Xiao Fang made one attempt to mention the loan, his 0 called him a "cheapskate." After that, he never mentioned the loan any more.

Was his 0 grateful for his selfless sacrifice? In my conversation with his 0, he expressed that Xiao Fang did not have any aspirations in life. I asked, "What do you mean by aspirations?" He replied, "You know, goals in life. My goal is to own a car and a house. These are the signs of success. Having a car is much more convenient, you know. However, his [Xiao Fang] response to my need was: the city has such a convenient bus transportation system, what do you need a car for?" He paused here, shook his head, and sighed at what he believed to be Xiao Fang's fatal shortcoming.

Of course I did not tell Xiao Fang what his 0 told me. To understand Xiao Fang better, I asked him why he was willing to suffer for his 0. Xiao Fang said, "It's 1's responsibility to spend money on his 0 and support his 0. 0 feels happy when 1 buys things for him. No matter whether 1 is rich or not, 1 has to continuously give (*fu chu*) and keep buying things for his 0." However, Xiao Fang did criticize 0s' pursuit of material life as "crazy and feverish" (*feng kuang*). "Without money, it is difficult to keep a relationship," Xiao Fang said, "When I am unable to satisfy my 0's needs, my heart will tell me that I should back off as I am unfit for my 0. If I have the money, I will definitely give it. If I don't have it, he will be eating bitterness with me since I can't give him what he wants. Then I feel unworthy of him" (*duibuqi ta*).

Once Xiao Fang's bank account was completely wiped out by his 0, Xiao Fang started keeping a distance from him. He said, "I am unable to hang on much longer." Nonetheless, he was determined to explore new ways of making money. In the end Xiao Fang concluded, "To be a man is difficult, but to be a 1 is even more difficult." hm,

Many other 1s in my research shared Xiao Fang's distress and plight caused by the repressive system. They complained that the 1/0 system endowed 0s with such an easy life that 0s usually lacked a sense of responsibility, often overspent, were too materialistic and too much doted on. Many also resented the fact that they were expected to act like "men" and make apologies to resolve disagreements. As a result of such visceral agony, some 1s in my research resisted the role of financial provider and called for shared responsibilities.

In my research 0s interpreted some 1s' rebellion against and recasting of the hegemonic rules as their evasion of their rightful responsibilities. They insisted that 1s fulfill their financial obligations as prescribed by the normative codes in the community. They chastised those 1s who failed to do so as irresponsible and derelict in their duties.

0S' REJECTION OF FEMININITY

Anthropologists have written at length about the rift between ideology and reality in the gender system (Ortner 1990). Although many researchers have insisted on a universal male dominance in all human societies, other anthropologists have urged us to pay heed to the discrepancy between the ideology of male supremacy and the reality of female power (Ogasawara 1998; Ortner 1990).[9] As Ortner contends, just as female power can be found in male-dominated societies, male power can be located in egalitarian societies. Hence neither the ideology nor the behavior patterns are "total" (Ortner 1990, 78).

This gap necessitates a scrutiny not only of the hegemonic gender rules in the tongzhi community but also of grounded experiences in lived relationships. Whereas the last section depicted conformity to the gender rules and expectations in the tongzhi community, this section describes a more nuanced relationship in which 0s often highlight their male identity. An analysis of this gap between ideology and reality indicates that it is erroneous to assume that all 1s and 0s conform to the gender rules and expectations in the tongzhi community. Rather, as I show in this section, challenges and contestations in everyday lives often complicate the hegemonic ideology and create contradictions between ideology and practice.

Although in theory, gender rules in the tongzhi community hold 0s to be submissive and faithful and 1s controlling and promiscuous, in practice, this norm is subject to constant contestations that often produce complex and contradictory relationships. Like the urban Brazilian *travestis* who render their male bodies as superior to women (Kulick 1998), 0s in my research often simultaneously appropriate and reject femininity as the object of control and reassert masculine prerogatives that society bestows on men.[10] As I demonstrate next, many 0s are unwilling to relinquish their masculine privileges. Although the feminine status endows them with the benefit of being financially cared for, 0s often renounce the subordinate social role accorded to women by society.

The prestige and respect associated with the male role cause some 0s to present themselves as 1s in the community. In the cruising areas, I encountered quite a number of men who proclaimed to everyone that they were a 1, not a 0, and that they had always been a 1 and never a 0. These men bragged about sexual conquests they had made to prove their sexual potency. Later their partners told me that they were 0s. The same scenario repeated itself on online friend-making websites and chat rooms. Xiao Han said to me, "When I first met my boyfriend, he pretended that he was a 1. It was not until we entered an intimate relationship that I knew that he was a 0." Many 1s in my research were aware of such false claims often made by 0s.

The social stigma and inferiority linked to the female role was conducive to some 0s' efforts to efface feminine traces in their "body habitus" (Bourdieu 1977). Bourdieu discusses how one's body habitus—bodily appearance, mannerisms, speech style, consumption habits, life styles, and habitual behaviors acquired through socialization—gives away a person's social class. The classed body, according to Bourdieu, is "the most indisputable materialization of class taste, which it manifests in several ways" (1977, 195). The class distinction is revealed through the uses of the body in work and leisure. In short, people embody their class in the way they act, talk, stand, gesture, and move—all unconsciously. Stigma attaches to those whose body habitus indicates their lower social class.

This concept can be applied to gender: Some forms of gender body habitus invite stigma. Xiao Gao, a self-identified 0, attributed his "C" (sissy) behaviors to his socialization by his doting parents and female playmates during his childhood. He said that in school, his feminine body habitus earned him the pejorative nickname of "second-class" *(er deng)*. To counteract the stigma, he said he underwent a long, painstaking journey to shed his feminine *(nuxing hua)* attributes and cultivate masculine traits. He first terminated what he considered feminine behaviors such as reading fairy tales and comic books, loving dolls and teddy bears, enjoying snacks, and relishing quietness. He then increased his interactions with male friends and scrupulously corrected what he thought were lapses in his behaviors. Despite his distaste for sports, he forced himself to watch soccer games with his male friends. He also recorded his own speech to identify what he believed were feminine tones *(niangniang qiang)* and endeavored to obliterate them. Xiao Gao said, "It's depressing to be a 0, despised by society. The community is filled with 0s, who are getting younger and younger. I can't compete with them. I want to be a 1 and satisfy my own desires."

0s such as Xiao Gao resist what they and the community perceive as the inferior female role with its vulnerable character and submissive mind; they embrace what they and the community perceive as a superior male role with its resilient character and rational mind. They openly express a disdain for "C" (sissy) behaviors and endeavor to alter their own body habitus. In work and leisure, these 0s dress up as 1s and profess to others that they are 1s, not 0s.

To maintain what they called "man's nature" *(nanren de bense)*, 0s in my research reminded each other not to restrain themselves by complying with restrictive cultural codes of female conduct. Indeed, they often openly expressed their love and unabashedly pursued desirable men. Many engaged in relationships with multiple sexual partners, yet at the same time convinced their 1s that they were faithful. A 0, Xiao Ning, told me that being in a relationship did not preclude him from looking for hookups, as long as his search was kept secret from his boyfriend. Another 0, Xiao Hong, was in two relationships simultaneously, without the knowledge of his two 1s, who resided in two different cities. These kinds of behaviors would be considered culturally inappropriate or degrading for women in society.

Although 0s are expected to tolerate 1s' promiscuity, the reality is often more complex and nuanced. Some 0s in my research, on discovery of their 1s' unfaithful behaviors, terminated the relationships. A 0, Xiao Ye, for instance, never had a chance to access his 1's phone record until one day when his 1's phone ran out of a charge. When his 1 borrowed his phone, Xiao Ye charged his 1's phone where he found pictures of him with another man, as well as with a woman and a child. It turned out that his 1 not only had two boyfriends at the same time but was also married with a wife and a child. The discovery of the deceit led Xiao Ye to end the relationship.

Lived experiences reveal that the hegemonic gender rules and expectations in the tongzhi community are under constant challenge and contestation by both 1s and 0s. Just as some 1s complain about their masculine role as the financial provider, some 0s eschew the feminine role as the object of control. These 0s strategically alter their body habitus, repudiate the expectation that they endure their 1s' promiscuity, and enjoy free sexual expressions with hookups and multiple sexual partners. In the cultural context where men's sexual desires are deemed biological and hence difficult to be quenched (T. Zheng 2009b),[11] these 0s reclaim their socially ascribed masculine prerogatives. In so doing, they rework the normative gender rules in the tongzhi community by imbuing new meanings to femininity and masculinity.

THE STORY OF WANG AND TAN

In this section, I tell a story to detail the ways in which reconfigured gender roles are played out between two lovers. Both in their early thirties, Wang, a 1, and Tan, a 0, had been together for more than six years. Tan was married with a child, and Wang had a girlfriend. Their long-term relationship was heralded as an exemplary model of a harmonious relationship in the community. However, below the surface, as I show in this section, it was tumultuous and turbulent. Wang's assertion of masculine control and Tan's simultaneous appropriation of, and rebellion against, the feminine role often resulted in a volatile, tenuous relationship filled with tensions and conflicts.

In this long-term, committed relationship, although Wang surreptitiously engaged in one-night stands with 0s whom he met online, he demanded absolute loyalty from Tan, using a variety of strategies including the following. When apart, Wang would call Tan and ask where he was. Afterward he would travel to that place to confirm Tan's story. At night, Wang always saw Tan home and waited outside his door for an hour and a half to make sure that Tan did not leave the house. Wang often posed as a stranger and used a new chat-room number to ask Tan out to test him. Wang also used Tan's account numbers and passwords to log onto Tan's accounts where he deleted Tan's group account and all the friends whom Wang deemed suspicious. Wang took on Tan's identity to chat with friends and test the nature of their relationships. In addition, Wang demanded access to Tan's phone records, text messages, and online chat record. Wang contended that everything he did was a proof of his love for Tan. *omg, complete invasion of privacy/independence*

One day Wang called Tan, telling him that he would be gone for a whole night on business and would not be back until the next day. Tan responded that he would stay at home and watch TV. Wang immediately traveled to Tan's house to monitor his activities. Seeing Tan walk out of his house, Wang followed him. Tan went to a nearby Internet café, where he met his previous boyfriend. They played online games for several hours and left together. Wang followed both of them into a hotel and stopped them as they were walking up the stairs to their room. Both were stunned at the sight of Wang. Tan explained that it was too late for them to go home. Wang asked Tan to go with him if he loved him. Tan eventually followed Wang out of the hotel, leaving his previous boyfriend behind.

In this scenario, Tan subverted Wang's control and engaged in multiple sexual relationships. Indeed, Tan was not compliant with Wang's assertion of power. On the contrary, as I show next, Wang's dominant behaviors were invariably met with Tan's ferocious resistance and free sexual pursuits outside the relationship. For instance, when Tan caught Wang reading his online chat record, Tan unplugged the Internet and terminated the process. When Wang interrogated Tan about his whereabouts, Tan told Wang to stop controlling him. When Wang ordered Tan to stop contacting other men, Tan told Wang that he should do the same. At times, Tan's resistance even took the form of intense physical brawls that ended in injuries to both of them. To Tan's vehement protests, Wang contended that, as a husband, he had every right to monitor and regulate Tan's behavior and that, once Tan chose love, he could no longer have freedom. Confronting Wang's demands, Tan declared that he wanted love, but at the same time, he wanted freedom.

Although Wang pretended in front of other tongzhi in the community that he was the cat in the relationship, he said to me that he felt like a mouse. He felt distraught and confused by Tan's unyielding contestation. He said he wished to be like a man and end the relationship, but he was simply unable to do so. Although he was easily fed up with other 0s he slept with who were submissive, he was never tired of Tan. Nonetheless, Wang felt he was losing control when faced with Tan's incessant protests. Frustrated as he was, Wang said he was unable to share his concerns with other tongzhi in the community because he would then become a laughingstock. He said that one time when he could not help venting a bit of his anguish to other tongzhi in the community, he was greeted by laughter and ridicule for his loss of control and his emotional commitment. Other tongzhi also questioned his claim to the 1 role, repeating to him the rules and expectations for 1s. Comments from the tongzhi in the community and the adversities in the relationship also caused Wang to question his 1 identity. He told me that he did not think he was "man enough" because he was, in his words, "too emotionally committed and sensitive like a woman."

This was a story of a couple that evoked envy and admiration in the community for having achieved the ideal of a long-term relationship. My proximity to them over the years revealed a different story.[12] As shown in this section, although Wang carried out his controlling role to ensure Tan's loyalty, he found himself humiliated by Tan's persistent rebellions and claim of sexual freedom. As a result, their love journey was a contentious and negotiated process in which both of them felt deeply hurt and exhausted.

CONCLUSION

This chapter has demonstrated that 1 and 0 identities are constructed, socialized, and shaped in the local cultural context of the tongzhi community; they are informed by heterosexual gender norms, rather than just sex positions. This gender norm endorses masculine promiscuity and control and support of females, as well as feminine dependence and loyalty. As illustrated, tongzhi learn to develop disparate identities to fit the gender roles of 1 and 0 through established rules, expectations, and romantic experiences in the community.

Indeed, the paradox of conformity to and subversion of the heterosexual norm encapsulates the nature of the gender dynamics of 1 and 0. Although 1s and 0s are embedded in the hegemonic gender matrix, the enactment of their identities inscribes, reinforces, and at the same time resists and reconfigures heterosexual hegemony for their own advantage. As we have seen in this chapter, whereas 1s usurp the prestige prescribed to them, 0s simultaneously appropriate the heterosexual norm that heralds support of females and refute the heterosexual norm that denies female sexual agency. The lived realities of 1 and 0 are imbued with constant negotiations, challenges, and subversion of the gender system that is both repressive and liberating.

Gender norms in Chinese society strictly regulate and control women's sexuality and bodies. As I have argued elsewhere (2009b), social norms instruct men that sex is instinctive and biological, and they tell women that sex is an emotional commitment. Indeed, in China, girls are indoctrinated with the moral value of abstinence until marriage to protect their virginity and the social order as a whole (Hershatter and Honig 1988). The state instructs young women to manage and control men's sexual advances before marriage, to satisfy their husbands' sexual needs during marriage, and stay clear of extramarital affairs after marriage. In their study of advice literature, Hershatter and Honig note that it invariably rests on the shoulders of young women to "channel and control the sexual desires of young men as well as their own and to defer acting on those desires until they [have] reach[ed] the socially appropriate age for courtship and marriage" (Hershatter and Honig 1988, 53).

The hegemonic code of femininity is articulated, negotiated, and challenged by 0s in a revamped model of femininity. 0s appropriate femininity and enforce norms of masculinity on 1s as financial sponsors. At the same time, 0s rescind the negation of female sexual agency and resist social control over their sexuality. 0s assert the masculine prestige of sexual freedom and openly express and assert sexual desire. In so doing, 0s embody a recalibrated model of femininity that claims dominant power without the burden of financial obligation, grants women sexual license, and contests socially circumvented and stymied female sexuality.

As such, an alternative structure emerges through negotiations and contestations against the hegemonic gender codes. As seen in this chapter, the alternative structure arises when some 1s refuse to conform to the hegemonic code of proper masculinity and assume the role of financial supporter and some 0s renounce the female role as the object of control. 0s also appropriate femininity that they simultaneously subvert for their own benefits. Rather than imitating the hegemonic rules, 1s and 0s rework and reconfigure the norms in creative and challenging ways.[13]

Judith Butler (1990, 1993) argues that resistance against the dominant system does not originate from outside the system, but rather stems from social activities within the system. She contends that drag queens engage in political defiance against gender ideals and heteronormativity with their performance of a hyperbolic image of a woman on the stage. Their hyperbolic version of the ideal womanhood exposes the cultural imperative and reveals the parody of the gender norm. The drag queen's performance, which Butler (1990, 1993) calls "theatrical agency," demonstrates the malleability of gender ideals and gender norms, calling into question heteronormativity and the essentialist and naturalist view of gender.[14]

Like the drag queens in Butler's research, the way 1s and 0s inscribe, yet transgress, the cultural norms indicates that their challenges to the system arise from the system itself, rather than outside. Unlike the drag queens in Butler's research who openly defy heteronormativity, 1s and 0s in my research mask their same-sex behaviors from their families, parents, and friends. As I illustrate in the next two chapters, in public work and leisure, they frame their gender identities according to cultural norms of masculinity. Indeed, 1s and 0s usually pursue a nonconfrontational expression of their gender identities and do not usually describe themselves as openly defying the heterosexual gender norms.

CHAPTER 4

The Normal Postsocialist Subject

Class, Wealth, and Money Boys

Xiao Huang was a self-identified heterosexual migrant worker from a rural area in a distant province. He came to the city to realize his dream of opening his own business and becoming a wealthy entrepreneur. He worked at a heating factory in the city, where the urban manager favored him so much that he sent him to skill training for several months free of charge, during which time he continued to receive his full salary. Xiao Huang felt indebted to his manager, but as a migrant worker from the countryside, he did not have any way to reciprocate except by inviting him to meals, which the manager declined. One evening Xiao Huang's manager asked for his help arranging furniture. Xiao Huang felt ecstatic that the opportunity had finally arrived to express his gratitude. After work the next day, Xiao Huang's manager took him to the market to buy food to cook at home. That night after dinner, Xiao Huang's manager played X-rated videos and initiated sexual contact with him.

That evening inaugurated a five-year "contracted relationship" (T. Zheng 2009a, 216) between the urban manager and the rural migrant worker Xiao Huang. After five years, the manager gave Xiao Huang 500,000 yuan to open a laundromat in the city. I met Xiao Huang at the cruising spot where he told me his story. Xiao Huang said to me, "I always thought, what's the difference between me and xiaojie (female sex workers)? We're the same! Xiaojie sell their bodies. Aren't I doing the same? But I couldn't resist because I needed the money. Now I am a successful business owner in the city and have finally realized my dream. I've made it, and it's not important how I got here. What matters is that I'm here and I'm successful."

This story highlights the relationships between sexuality, class, and political ideology in increasingly stratified postsocialist China. As I show later in this chapter, a rural migrant worker is relegated to second-class citizenship as a result of cultural discrimination, institutional constraints, and economic deprivation. In this vignette, the urban manager capitalizes on his prestigious urban status and economic power to lure Xiao Huang into a hierarchical renting relationship. Xiao Huang's agreement to this transactional relationship is informed by the dominant neoliberal ideology that prizes economic profits, individual responsibilities, and free choice.

Xiao Huang's rationale that the ends justify the means is rooted in the dominant state ideology—expressed pithily in political leader Deng Xiaoping's famous aphorism related to China's pursuit of a market economy: "No matter whether it's a white cat or a black cat, as long as it can catch mice, it's a good cat." This theory prioritizes economic gains, arguing that economic development takes precedence over everything else. In other words, it does not matter whether anything is capitalist or socialist; what matters is whether it helps with economic development and achieves economic gains. This new neoliberal ideology steered the country away from class struggle to economic profits as the fundamental principle and put blame on individuals for their failure to achieve economic wealth. As we see in this story, Xiao Huang contends that the route to economic gains does not matter; what matters is economic success. Xiao Huang follows this ideology by defining success in purely economic terms and justifying the commodification of his body by the end result of his ownership of a business.

This chapter unravels tongzhi's negotiations and interactions with the neoliberal discourse that defines a "normal" postsocialist subject as heterosexual, wealthy, and consumerist; it also examines the impact this discourse has on class structure, career choice, and romantic relationships among tongzhi. As I show, class structure among Chinese tongzhi is largely shaped by wealth, with these classes in descending order: the red and gold collar (red collar refers to government and Party employees, and gold collar refers to people with an annual income from 400,000 yuan to millions of yuan); the white, blue, and gray collar (white collar refers to well-educated, mental labor workers, blue collar refers to manual labor workers, and gray collar refers to college students); and the money boys, who are male sex workers. I first discuss the neoliberal ideology of a normal postsocialist subject in the rapid transformation of China. I then explore the diverse sexual practices that are facilitated by the social hierarchy and, at the same time, enact social class in the process of the tongzhi's embrace of neoliberal ideology in a society with increasing social inequalities. I illustrate the ways in which economic wealth, social class, and political ideology impinge on sexual practices, intimacies, and career choices (as sex workers). In the final section, I conclude with insights and findings.

The goal of this chapter is twofold. It demystifies the universal model of Chinese tongzhi and highlights the politics of difference based on social hierarchies and economic inequalities. This chapter also argues that the embrace of the neoliberal ideology reproduces the link between success and consumerism and legitimizes state power that is contingent on economic growth and consumerism.

A "NORMAL" POSTSOCIALIST SUBJECT: HETEROSEXUAL, WEALTHY, AND CONSUMERIST

In postsocialist China, decollectivization, privatization, and marketization of institutions including education, health care, and housing have both provided opportunities for individuals and enforced individual responsibilities. The economic reform has created new spaces for sexual expressions and personal desires, but only as long as they are circumscribed and self-disciplined within the purview of the state.

The simultaneously authoritarian and neoliberal governance in postsocialist China has created a new "enterprising and desiring" heterosexual subject by imposing new responsibilities on the individual to compete in the market economy and pursue wealth, happiness, and self-expression (Kleinman et al. 2011; Rofel 2007; Zhang and Ong 2008). Neoliberalism, instead of an economic theory or political philosophy, has been conceptualized as a form of governance, or "governmentality" in Foucault's term, to produce responsible and governable citizens (Brown 2005; Rose 1996; Weiss and Greyser 2012). In China, economic development and the concomitant making of the normal postsocialist subject have been key state strategies to legitimize the state's political power (see also Hua 2012).

The state capitalizes on the role of the market to cultivate a consumption-oriented individual whose predominant goal is to maximize economic gains and profits (Kleinman et al. 2011; Kong 2012; Zhang and Ong 2008). Unlike the traditional Chinese person, whose identity hinged on collectivity and self-sacrifice, the new market individual seeks to maximize his or her self-interest and fulfill material and sexual desires (Y. Yan 2011). Unlike the traditional Chinese person, whose identity was predicated on class consciousness, the new market individual is a "desiring subject" who acts on the basis of material and sexual self-interest and who learns limitations through the characterization of proper and improper desires and aspirations expressed in diverse forms of public culture (e.g., soap operas, museums, cosmopolitan fantasies of consumption, magazines, the Internet; Rofel 2007).

This ideal or normal postsocialist subject is economically entrepreneurial and enterprising, sexually normative (heterosexual), self-managing, and politically docile (Kleinman et al. 2011; Kong 2012; Zhang and Ong 2008). This individual is not just "obliged to exercise diligence, cunning, talents, and social skills to navigate ever-shifting networks of goods, relationships, knowledge, and institutions in the competition for wealth and personal advantage" (Zhang and Ong 2008, 8) but is also nationalistic and patriotic in his or her loyalty to the Party and the state (Anagnost 2004; Hoffman 2008; Kleinman et al. 2011; Kong 2012; Zhang and Ong 2008).

This chapter shows how tongzhi, who do not fit into the normal heterosexual ideal, still deploy this dominant discourse and fashion themselves as normal postsocialist subjects who are wealthy, consumerist, and economically enterprising.

SOCIAL CLASS AMONG TONGZHI

Gold- and Red-Collar Tongzhi

The Chinese Communist Party first proposed the term "red collar" to refer to all Party officials; later its usage expanded to denote all employees working in government institutions, Communist Party agencies, and administrative authorities whose superior welfare and high-end salary were secured by the government. The color "red" was selected to commemorate the history of the Party, echoing the red star on the hat worn by Chinese Communist Party members and the People's Liberation Army, as well as the red national flag. Red-collar employees have to pass a competitive nationwide examination—China's First Examination—which has an acceptance rate of only one in sixty-nine test-takers. They are believed to harbor a unified value system of serving the people, as opposed to the so-called fragmented and weak value system of white-collar employees who work in diverse profit-making enterprises and organizations.

"Gold collar" refers to people with an annual income from 400,000 yuan to millions of yuan, who hold higher education degrees and who occupy high-level managerial positions such as CEO, CFO, or COO of joint venture companies and Chinese companies or who serve as Chinese representatives of foreign companies in China. This new class emerged with the market economy. People of this class are said to enrich their lives with brand-name merchandise, purchase fashion in Paris, eat Italian and French cuisine, live in aesthetically furnished villas, fly business class, own more than two luxury cars, frequent high-end bars and night clubs, own exorbitant club memberships, travel to exotic places for recreation, and stay in five-star hotels.

To my knowledge, nothing has yet been written in either English or Chinese about the sexual practices of the gold- and red-collar tongzhi. The only suggestion in both academic and popular media is that high-class tongzhi focus on emotional attachments and have romantic relationships, whereas low-class tongzhi focus on physical pleasures and merely have sexual encounters (Y. Li 2009; L. Xin 2009). The dichotomy between body and emotion is pinpointed as the fundamental difference between high- and low-class same-sex behaviors. By associating the body with the crude, corrupt, and lower realm and the mind with the refined and higher realm, popular belief associates high-class tongzhi with the mind and low-class tongzhi with the body. This is reminiscent of the values of classical China that made a distinction between lower-class people who worked with their body and upper-class people who worked with their mind.

In contrast with this popular conception, my research shows that gold- and red-collar tongzhi usually purchase sexual services or rent money boys to satisfy their sexual desires free of any emotional entanglements. This purely physical gratification runs counter to the presumed romantic endeavors among them depicted in the academic and popular media.

The invisibility of this group of tongzhi is conducive to their erroneous portrayal in the popular media. Gold- and red-collar tongzhi rarely venture out to visit areas where tongzhi congregate or expose their identity at public places such as tongzhi bars, tongzhi bathhouses, parks, or Internet chat rooms. This is because their reputation, family, and status are at stake if their same-sex behaviors are disclosed or if their same-sex contacts blackmail them. As my interviewees related to me, what they feared the most were slander, defamation, social sanctions, and a loss of their status, career, and family. Because the economic and political privilege they enjoy imposes constraints and limits on overt same-sex sexual practices, they practice secrecy and concealment, engaging in covert same-sex practices.[1]

To evade the punitive costs of overt practices, gold- and red-collar tongzhi execute a wide array of tactics to mask all traces of their sexual activities. These covert strategies include segregation from the tongzhi circle, purchase of sexual services, rental of money boys, and anonymous transactional relationships.

Xiao Wang, for instance, made the decision to extricate himself from the tongzhi circle after he was promoted to a high-level government law office. I had gotten to know Xiao Wang during my initial fieldwork in 2005 when he was a low-ranking office employee. After passing the nationwide China's First Examination, he was selected for a high-level position. Xiao Wang told me, "Ever since I was promoted, I have been terrified that others may know my sexual orientation." As a government law officer, Xiao Wang said he got to know many people in the public security office, the court, and other government agencies. With so many contacts in the government agencies, Xiao Wang deemed it perilous to visit tongzhi public places and risk being recognized. Indeed, he maintained that government agencies would not tolerate tongzhi and that the disclosure of his sexual identity would render him instantly powerless, strip him of his position, and cause him public disgrace. Xiao Wang said, "If any of them knew my sexual orientation, it would be unimaginable. People in my circle always deride and taunt homosexuality. I always follow them and do the same, but nobody knows how distressed and agonized I feel when I laugh with them!"

Before he was promoted, Xiao Wang was blackmailed once by an Internet friend he met through an online chat room. He said he was fortunate that this man had only made one monetary demand and had never returned for more. After his promotion, Xiao Wang changed his contact information, left his online tongzhi groups, and married a woman. Xiao Wang said to me, "It's been two years. During this time I've never dared to chat online, meet Internet friends, or have anything to do with my [tongzhi] circle. I've cut myself off completely." His success in keeping clear of the tongzhi community and maintaining his high-level position, however, was not enough to make him happy. Xiao Wang said, "I don't know how to overcome my loneliness and get rid of my sexual frustration. With this kind of job, I should be worry-free and happy, but I am not."[2]

Other men in my research also maintained that, before being promoted to a higher position or becoming wealthy, they had frequented tongzhi cruising areas. After their social and economic status was transformed, the number of their social contacts increased greatly. So did the fear of exposure of their sexual identity—hence the cessation of previous activities and withdrawal from the tongzhi circle. This same phenomenon was found in 1980s Germany where research found that the higher one climbed in the social hierarchy, the fewer one's sexual contacts (Pollak 1986).

Despite his repressed sexual desire, Xiao Wang, along with other men in my research, decided against getting involved in long-term romantic relationships. As they recounted, having a long-term relationship with a boyfriend would be a precarious move, because he would know their true identities. They emphasized that it would be a nightmare if, after squabbles or other emotional problems in their relationships, the boyfriend disclosed everything to the public. The most scrupulous way to shield their behaviors and remain anonymous was to engage in transactional sex in variegated forms: purchasing sexual services, renting money boys, and forming anonymous transactional relationships with monetary gifts. With these strategies, they were able to satisfy their sexual desires while stabilizing their social position.

The strategy that gold- and red-collar tongzhi use most frequently is to engage in transactional sex with money boys, free of emotional entanglements. My research with madams and money boys has revealed that, to hide their identities, gold- and red-collar men usually contact reliable madams of brothels to request sexual services. They often request a new money boy each time to prevent becoming involved with a particular sex worker and thereby jeopardizing identity disclosure. For the most prudent ones, these encounters usually take place when they travel to cities other than their own. My research suggests that they prefer five-star hotels, such as the Swiss Hotel, which costs more than 2,000 yuan per night, to complete the transactional sex, because these kinds of hotels are presumably safe from police surveillance. Police, as I was told, often patrol low-star hotels where managers are required to submit ID numbers of all guests to the police. During their business trips when the gold- and red-collar tongzhi stay at such hotels for a few days, they reserve two rooms—one for themselves and one for the sexual encounter—to make it impossible to locate them on the second day.

Indeed, brothels, under the cover name of "Man's Clubs" *(hui suo)*, target people of this class through advertisements. For instance, one advertisement reads,

> Our Man's Club is the biggest, safest, most private, most professional, and superior recreational club. With the fast speed of modern life and concomitant physical and psychological pressure, repressed deep desires have exploded. For many years our club has been providing intimate, recreational services to gold-collar and white-collar high-income people, to rejuvenate and reenergize their exhausted bodies. We have plenty of muscular and strong men with professional skills and all-round services, first rated service, providing service to male, female customers and couples. (Heze Yangguang Xing Nan Huiguan 2013)

As noted earlier, my research revealed that many gold- and red-collar men request sexual services from madams to ensure anonymity. On some occasions, money boys were driven to the client's home at night to ensure that they would not remember the route in the dark. Money boy Xiao Feng, for instance, told me that he was once picked up by a man and taken to a client's home. Xiao Feng's madam insinuated that the client was a high-ranking official at a police station. It was dark at night and the car made so many turns that Xiao Feng had no clue about the location of his client's home. Once there, he saw heaps of name-brand cigarette boxes filling five huge drawers, each box worth more than 1,000 yuan. Xiao Feng said he became frightened, worried about being criminally implicated should the corrupt police official be caught and arrested.

Although the most prevalent form of transactional sex is to employ intermediary instruments such as madams to purchase sexual services, other strategies are to rent money boys directly and to forge anonymous transactional relationships with economic benefits for younger men. For instance, one of my key informants, Xiao Liu, formed an anonymous, romantic relationship with a gold-collar man for monetary gifts and economic benefits. Xiao Liu, in his early twenties, was pursued by the government-appointed director of the tongzhi organization he worked in. This man told Xiao Liu that he was also a university professor. According to Xiao Liu, the man belonged to the gold-collar class because his monthly salary exceeded 25,000 yuan and he owned two villas.

Xiao Liu said to me, "The leader told me that he is an old cow wanting to eat tender grass. He pursued me. Personally, I don't have any interest in him—he's too old!"[3] Despite his lack of interest, Xiao Liu took into consideration the economic and social benefits associated with the relationship and agreed to it. Xiao Liu later enumerated to me the many material gains he reaped from the relationship, including traveling and sightseeing at exotic places, dining at high-end restaurants, consuming brand-name clothes, enjoying exorbitant gifts, and receiving an increased monthly salary.

Throughout the duration of this intimate relationship, Xiao Liu was never given the director's name, his work or home address, or the name of the university in which he worked. Despite the monetary and social advantages he gained from this anonymous relationship, Xiao Liu discovered that he had to pay the price of physical pain during sexual intercourse. Indeed, Xiao Liu, who had always been the inserter, found no alternative but to assume the penetrated role in this relationship. Xiao Liu said, "Sometimes when he touches me, I can get hard. But because I don't have any feelings for him, it [the penis] cannot remain hard. At the beginning I acted as 1 [the inserter], but it [the penis] lost erection very quickly. So I had to assume the inserted position in our sexual relationship."

The fact that Xiao Liu had to assume the penetrated position was less a signifier of status and social stratification, which it had traditionally been in Chinese same-sex acts, as presented in chapter 1. Rather, it was a physical necessity because Xiao Liu was unable to perform the inserter role due to his lack of interest. In this reciprocal relationship, Xiao Liu gleaned only material benefits because the liaison was purely transactional to him, whereas the director was able to satisfy both his sexual and psychological needs with a much younger man whom he favored, without jeopardizing his social position.

Through engaging in covert practices, gold- and red-collar tongzhi are able to project the image of being normal postsocialist subjects—wealthy, heterosexual family men. This is similar to upper-class lesbians in Jakarta who follow Indonesia's state ideal of the heterosexual nuclear family and maintain a heterosexual appearance while secretly engaging in lesbian relationships abroad (A. Murray 2001). Like the upper-class Jakarta lesbians, Chinese gold- and red-collar tongzhi hold onto the dominant state discourse and engage in covert activities to retain their power and status. In so doing, they are complicit in state power and heterosexual marriage.

In contrast to the upper-class Jakarta lesbians, Chinese gold- and red-collar tongzhi orchestrate clandestine activities at home, not abroad, but in such a muted form that there can be no disclosure of their true identities. As shown in this section, this usually involves an isolation of the sexual practice in time and place to minimize social risks and maximize sexual satisfaction.[4] Though most often they detach sexual acts from affection by purchasing or renting money boys, some do form controlled, anonymous relationships to meet both sexual and psychological needs.

White-, Blue-, and Gray-Collar Tongzhi

"White collar" refers to well-educated, mental labor workers, and "blue collar" refers to manual labor workers. "Gray collar" refers to college students who occupy a gray area between white collar and blue collar, being capable of both mental and manual labor and characterized by unstable income and random jobs.

Tongzhi in this group visit public tongzhi cruising areas such as public parks, online chat rooms, tongzhi bars, tongzhi bathhouses, and public toilets. Currently Dalian has three cruising spots in three parks, four tongzhi bars, and six tongzhi bathhouses. Although young people usually find no problem securing sexual encounters through visiting online video chat rooms, parks, and tongzhi bars, I was told that older and less attractive people found themselves exploring other possibilities. Xiao Li, a young man in his early twenties, said to me, "When you chat online, you actually view the person's face and body before you meet him for a one-night stand. At bathhouses, however, those old men's ten thousand eyes were riveted on you. They stared at you first and then they came to touch you. When I was there, they used force to drag me to the dark room—it was too much [to bear]. Only those who aren't desirable go to the dark room to have random sex." Like Xiao Li, other young men in my research described to me in detail how they were taken to the dark room by force and how they resorted to screaming for help while scratching their attackers' arms.

Online chat rooms, parks, and tongzhi bars expose a person to public scrutiny, and men who are unable to attract potential sexual partners in these venues usually either purchase sexual services or visit bathhouses where dark rooms mask their bodies and faces. When these bathhouses were shut down, these men's purchase of sexual services from money boys through online chat rooms, tongzhi bars, massage parlors, Man's Clubs, and parks increased.

Perils of Cruising

Online chat rooms, tongzhi bars, massage parlors, Man's Clubs, and parks are perilous places because they are the targets of regular police patrols and police surveillance. Indeed, the police had shut down several tongzhi bars and tongzhi bathhouses. A waiter at a bathhouse told me that two local bathhouses had been closed and never reopened. One bathhouse was told to submit 300,000 yuan to the police station as a condition to reopen, but the owner chose not to do so and instead closed the business. Another bathhouse was told to hand over 100,000 yuan to reopen, and the owner chose to do so. Yet another bathhouse owner, whose business had not yet been shut down, told me that he was ordered by the local police station to attend weekly meetings, register customers' ID numbers as the condition of their admission, and dismantle private rooms in the bathhouse. Because of his connection with the government officials, he was often informed of police raids ahead of time. I was told that when the other bathhouses were shut down by the police, he closed his bathhouse for renovations for one month and so evaded the police shutdown. The eight waiters who worked for him left the city during that month and stayed at their rural home-towns until the bathhouse reopened. However, in our conversation, the owner lamented that, despite his ongoing bribery of government officials and the police, the police had recently raided his bathhouse and arrested customers on the charge of public display of promiscuity *(gonggong chang-suo yinluan)*, which scared visitors away and affected his business.

During my fieldwork, I was told that the police raided several local bathhouses, arrested all the guests, beat them up, and detained them for twenty-four hours. This was part of the crackdown campaign to "purge" entertainment places, which I have discussed in detail elsewhere (T. Zheng 2009a). These crackdown raids usually occurred just before festivals, conventions, and other national events such as the Olympics. During my fieldwork, police raids of bathhouses took place prior to two major events: "Two Conferences"—the National People's Congress and the Chinese Political Consultative Conference—and the Annual World Economic Forum. Although bathhouse managers maintained close contact with the local police station by offering them regular bribes, it was the district police bureau—the subsidiary of the city police bureau—that executed the raids. As I have illustrated elsewhere, police raids constituted an efficient way for the police to collect exorbitant fines (T. Zheng 2009a). I was told that the police charged a fine of 5,000 yuan per person, but some owners were able to negotiate it down to 3,000 yuan.

Although the tongzhi spots in parks, where I conducted most of my research, are open to everyone regardless of sexual orientation, tongzhi bars and tongzhi bathhouses are selective and prudent, screening every visitor, mainly to ward off civilian-clothed police. Every time I attempted to enter a tongzhi bar or bathhouse, I was stopped by the gate guard, who told me that this was a special place for a special population that was off-limits to others. Each time, my tongzhi companions had to assure them that I was a friend of tongzhi and was not associated with the police. Access for me always involved a negotiation process, which was indicative of the constant, high alert against undercover police at such places.

The unguarded public places have their own dangers. I was told that it was common to run into not only friends and colleagues there but also robbers and thieves. Several key informants of mine, for instance, were robbed at cruising spots in the park: Xiao Fang had his wallet stolen by a man to whom he had gotten close at the park. Penniless and ID-less, Xiao Fang had to borrow money from friends in the park to take public transportation home. Another informant said he was seduced by a man in the park, who took him to a hotel. The next morning, when he was in the shower, the man took his wallet and left. During my fieldwork at the park, several men came to the cruising area at 1:00 a.m. and attacked people with knives. The next day I learned that two of my key informants had been knifed and hospitalized. Although the motive for the attack was not clear, it certainly added to the sense of danger constantly confronted by a tongzhi in China. The police also came to the cruising area to record information from witnesses. Although crimes were commonplace in the park, they were not enough to hold the men back from visiting.

Benefits of Cruising

Perilous as the public places are, they help form a tongzhi community where men in my research said they not only feel free, relaxed, and unleashed but also are able to keep abreast of the latest news about tongzhi. In the park, for instance, they feel safe and free to express their sexual desires and entertain each other without concerns and worries. They touch each other's sexual parts, fake love-making movements with loud moaning sounds, and play around with each other. The park also provides a forum wherein men are able to discuss every conceivable topic, especially same-sex issues. It was in this forum where men in my research learned about police patrols of certain tongzhi bars, police closure of certain tongzhi bathhouses and bars, and police arrests of certain people, information on which they adapted their activities accordingly.

A support group was also formed in the park that provided its members not only with news but also with brotherly friendship and support, and sometimes even job opportunities. I was told that face-to-face communication in the park trumps Internet communication because the latter is unable to provide direct contact. Every day and every night scores of people come to the park to socialize with one another and find friends, boyfriends, and sexual partners. Xiao Ming said to me, "In this circle, it only takes a few hours to turn strangers into friends, but in non-tongzhi circles, it can take months or years." I was told that tongzhi's same-sex activities are the main impediment in maintaining friendship with non-tongzhi. When one party discusses his private life, as my research subjects asserted, it would be unfair for the other party not to reciprocate and talk about his. When in need, many approach tongzhi friends rather than non-tongzhi friends for help. For instance, Xiao Tan secured a bank loan from a bank clerk Xiao Min whom he had met in the park. In the park, men in my research shared their emotional travails and received invaluable advice from each other about relationships, sex, romance, and family.

Internal Economic Hierarchies and Social Class

The price of entrance into these cruising areas—bathhouses, bars, Man's Clubs, and the parks—further divide tongzhi into different social strata. The highest-priced places are tongzhi bars, affordable only to the top strata in this middle-tier category of tongzhi. Tongzhi bars generally charge an entrance fee of 60 yuan and high prices for drinks and snacks. One of the tongzhi bars that I visited was in a two-story building adorned with beautiful Chinese calligraphy and Chinese paintings with traditional motifs of bamboo, horses, and peony flowers. About one hundred people were present each night, engaging in different activities such as sitting around, chatting, drinking, dancing, and singing karaoke. Some bars provide a romantic ambience with aesthetic decorations and a large platform for dancing and karaoke-singing activities, whereas a few others that I visited stage entertainment shows such as drag performances.

Some exclusive online groups also mark class differences by admitting only white-collar tongzhi. For instance, one online tongzhi group restricts access and participation to white-collar "elite" who were born after 1980 ("Zhengzhou 80hou Bailing Jingying" 2013); the website defines these clients as office workers or company employees. As I show in chapter 3, romantic relationships are often shaped by material concerns. For instance, Xiao Fan commented that he was a salesman and financially stable and was looking for a boyfriend with the same kind of financial soundness. The bottom line was, in his words, "Our class background has to match" (*yao mendang hudui*). Tongzhi such as Xiao Fan consider financial background and social class to be important criteria in their choice of partners.

Although the top echelon of this class can often be found in tongzhi bars that charge the highest fees and prices, a mix of white-, blue-, and gray-collar people are found in many public places that are either free or require a low fee, such as the bathhouses. People in this middle-tier category usually visit a wide array of places rather than just one place. For instance, in the winter, when it is too cold to gather in the park, they go online or visit bars and bathhouses. When bars and bathhouses are closed down, they visit the park or go online.

As shown, leisure spots and recreational resorts are stratified by social and economic status. Precarious as these areas are, medium-tier tongzhi continue to visit them to overcome social isolation and indulge in sexual encounters within the tongzhi circle. At the same time, however, the prestige attributed to certain spots, the exclusion of rural migrant tongzhi and money boys, the discrimination against certain self-presentations, and the selection of appropriate partners all reinscribe and solidify class differences and the social hierarchy. Nothing is farther from the truth than to characterize this community as harmonious and homogeneous. Instead, medium-tier tongzhi deploy the neoliberal discourse to justify and reproduce economic hierarchies and social distinctions that cut across the community, causing profound dissension and exclusion.

MONEY BOYS

Class differences among tongzhi are epitomized by the cultural and moral values associated with rural versus urban origin, type of work, and cultural traits. Red-, white-, blue-, and gray-collar tongzhi express moral repugnance and social discrimination toward the "low-class" category of tongzhi of rural origins who have a migrant status, engage in sex work, and are too flamboyantly and overtly feminine in self-presentation. In creating these boundaries, tongzhi demonstrate that, just like non-tongzhi, they are interested in drawing class distinctions to their advantage.

Men in my research construed money boys as low-class rural migrants who bring disgrace to and pollute the tongzhi community. The marginalization of money boys within the tongzhi community has been attributed to the "quality discourse" *(suzhi)* that marks money boys as uncivilized, uncouth, and immoral (Ho 2009; Jeffreys 2007; Kong 2011a, 2011b; Rofel 2007, 2010). In my research, tongzhi's charges against money boys ranged from their conduct, such as engaging in blackmail and robbery, to their low education levels, dishonesty, laziness, and immorality. Discriminating comments against money boys were harsh and extreme throughout my fieldwork. For instance, Xiao Gao commented, "We should alienate and trample on money boys like garbage. They are poorly educated and immoral. They detest work and favor laziness *(haoyi elao)*. They disgust me. They should be punished by law." Other men in my research likened money boys to "a group of wolves," socialized to be immoral and shameless robbers, thieves, and criminals.

In addition to the outright discrimination against money boys, flagrant insults against rural migrant tongzhi were ubiquitous. Pejorative adjectives used to describe them included but were not limited to the following; dark, dirty, ugly, crude, and repellent. In one instance, Xiao Wen recounted to me a story about a bathhouse: "I ran into two rural migrant guys at the bathhouse yesterday. They looked very dark and very dirty—none of that dirt could be washed off no matter how hard they washed themselves. While they were doing each other, we all laughed loudly and commented that they needed to rinse their mouths and purge their intestines first."

Denigrating comments against rural migrants focused not only on their alleged dirtiness and dark skin color but also on their clothes, speech, and behavior. As noted by many men in my research, clothes and manners could betray a person's low education and low social status. They despised rural migrants who "had no clue how to wear clothes, how to pair shoes with clothes, or how to carry themselves." Xiao Ming, for instance, commented, "Rural migrants always wear ugly clothes and look ugly. They are abhorrent. Once I was on a bus, a rural migrant got on the bus and sat next to me. I immediately stood up and left. There's no way

I'll allow such a rural migrant wearing dirty clothes and worn-out shoes to sit next to me!"

In the tongzhi community, a too glaringly feminine disposition is also denigrated and stigmatized as underclass. Tongzhi use derogatory term "too C" (sissy) to describe men who act, dress, and talk in an egregiously feminine manner. For instance, some tongzhi assume feminine postures, stick out their pinky fingers, waggle their buttocks, speak and laugh in a feminine voice, and dress up in tight, feminine clothes. This is similar to the 1950s and 1970s gay community in North America that stigmatized gay men who were too extremely overt in self-presentation (Leznoff and Westley 1956; Newton 1979).

Internal Hierarchy among Money Boys

My research showed a hierarchy among money boys—rural migrant men around seventeen to twenty-six years old who provide same-sex sexual services. High-tier money boys usually work in high-class brothels *(huisuo)* under the pretext of providing massages and similar services to "cultivate men's body and health." Money boys are advertised as "advanced-level technicians" *(gaoji jishi)* and could earn about 7,000–10,000 yuan per night, after submitting one-third of the fee to the management. The high-class brothels offer both protection to money boys and clients and a stable supply of reputable and wealthy clients. Madams and managers continuously replenish their pool with new money boys to keep their clients intrigued. Applicants to these brothels are required to report their ages, heights, weights, sex skills, and the size of their penis, and only attractive money boys are accepted. Some brothels only have an online presence; their websites display numerous photos of half-naked young men, with an employee number assigned to each picture. Customers then call the establishment's phone number or the twenty-four-hour online customer service and provide the number of the money boy they want. As discussed earlier, red- and gold-collar tongzhi engage in the covert practice of contacting madams rather than visiting public places to request the services of money boys; often they then engage in transactional sex at five-star hotels.

Medium-tier money boys work in medium-level brothels, hotels, online chat rooms, bars, and bathhouses. They charge 300–400 yuan per sexual service or 500–2,000 yuan for the evening; like the high-tier money boys they pay one-third of the earnings to the management. On this basis they could earn more than 3,000–5,000 yuan per month.

Freelance money boys send out information about their ages, heights, and weights to all public chat rooms and wait for users to request a private chat. It is in these private chats where they disclose their identity as money boys and negotiate prices, with the video enabling clients to check out their appearance. Clients have to pay for hotels and taxi costs, and money boys meet them at the designated places. Online solicitation can be perilous and erratic, because clients could leave without paying the money boys for their service or the clients could be civilian-clothed police.

Low-tier money boys solicit customers in the park or on the street next to entertainment places. Whereas the high- and middle-tier money boys are secretive and clandestine, low-class money boys work out in the open. Charges range from food and shelter for a night to 50–100 yuan for oral sex and 100–300 yuan for penetrative sex. Negotiations are not limited to the price but also involve the place and the type of service provided (oral, 1, 0, or versatile). Some money boys I met in the park agreed on sexual services in exchange for a night's stay at a nice hotel. They preferred hotels not just for their comfort but also for their safety. Money boys expressed a fear of the unpredictable when they were asked to go to the client's place, but felt more in control at hotels. The complaint I heard the most was that, after their service, clients left without paying them.

Some money boys are kept in an apartment and receive a negotiated monthly payment. These rented money boys do not self-identify as money boys because the exchange of sex for money is not as straightforward as in the other forms. The ambiguous category makes it difficult to define the parameters of sex work (see also Mitchell 2011).

Rural Origin and Historical Baggage

More than 70 percent of the money boys in my research self-identified as heterosexual and less than 30 percent as bisexual; in their words, "half and half." This ratio is similar to the one published on online tongzhi websites (T. Xin 2009); it echoes that found among 1960s young male sex workers in the United States who served adult gay men sexually, but did not self-identify as gay (Reiss 1961). In that context, sexual services were, in principle, restricted to oral sex, with the young male sex workers serving as penetrators and the clients as penetrated. Although these young men did engage in oral sex with adult gay clients, they construed clients as sexual deviators and did not perceive themselves as such. They drew a boundary between "homosexual behaviors/acts" and "homosexual identities" (Reiss 1961, 225).

Money boys in my research came from the countryside. According to them, their lack of marketable skills doomed them to low-wage jobs in factories with hard physical labor. Sex work, in contrast, provided them with a free, enterprising lifestyle that offered the most profits with the least investment.

Money boys carry heavy historical baggage because of their rural origins. In postsocialist China, 260 million rural people have crossed the urban-rural border, fleeing intolerable poverty created by decades of government policies biased against rural people. The house registration system *(hu kou)* has divided the population into permanent urban "citizens" who have urban residence permits and rural/migrant people who do not.[5] Without urban residence permits, rural migrants are denied subsidized housing, health care, employment, children's education, and other benefits that are associated with urban residence permits (Goodkind and West 2002; Li et al. 2007).

Although the household registration system has been reformed since the late 1990s, it continues to lead to rural-urban disparities (K. W. Chan 2010; Chan and Buckingham 2008; Kong 2012; Li and Piachaud 2006; Fei-ling Wang 2010; Zhu 2007). It is deemed as "the most serious form of institutional exclusion against mainly rural residents" that produces "rural-urban apartheid" in China (Chan and Buckingham 2008, 583–87). In Dalian, for instance, the most recent policy, laid out in 2009, dictates that rural migrants who meet the specified requirements can apply for urban residence (Dalian Metropolitan City Government 2009). These requirements include being under forty-five years old; having a legitimate, state-recognized university BA degree; and having a legitimate stable job in the center of the city or a five-year contract with a company located in the new zone or the satellite zone (the city is divided into the center zone, new zone, and satellite zone). Those rural migrants who are not able to meet these designated requirements need to purchase either an apartment worth at least 800,000 yuan or a commercial building worth at least 1 million yuan in the center zone to be able to apply for urban residence. In addition, there are restrictions on bank loans to rural migrants, and only those who have a stable job and are able to provide evidence of having paid at least one year of taxes and social insurance are allowed to purchase an apartment. The policy restricts the number of apartments—only one apartment per household—that rural migrants are allowed to purchase. A person who marries someone who holds city residence still needs to purchase an apartment in the city and wait eight years before being allowed to apply for urban residence (Dalian Metropolitan City Government 2009).

In 1958, the Maoist state institutionalized the household registration system: Every household was required to register all of its members with the local public security station. It constructed a bifurcated—urban versus rural—hierarchical state structure that classified citizens according to their differential entitlement to political, economic, social, and legal resources (Christiansen 1990; Dutton 1998; Gui and Xian 1992; R. M. Li 1989; Solinger 1995a, 1995b, 1999; Siu 2007). Rural second-class citizens were ruthlessly excluded from the urbanites' privileged access to state-subsidized goods (e.g., grains), services (e.g., health care) and opportunities (e.g., jobs, mobility).

For almost three decades, rural people's mobility was severely prohibited, and the countryside was completed isolated as a discrete unit. Peasants were condemned as the reservoir of backward feudalism and feudal superstition—a major obstacle to national development and salvation (Brownell 1995; M. Cohen 1993).

Rural-to-urban migration was permitted beginning in the 1980s in China, but the urban-rural gap is still the dominant contributor to overall inequality (Khan and Riskin 1998). Government policies have intensified rural-urban inequality by promoting a skewed distribution of housing assets and by instituting a regressive rural fiscal policy that has worsened rural poverty, creating greater income polarization and inequality (Khan and Riskin 1998; Khan et al. 1992).[6]

In the cities, despite migrants' great contribution to the national and local economy, they still encounter severe institutional constraints *(hukou)* and social denigration (Kipnis 1998; Pun 2003, 2005; Pun and Chan 2008; H. Yan 2008; Li Zhang 2002). Urbanites deem the city "modern" and consider the countryside "backward" and "barbarian" (Kipnis 1998). Categorized as "outsiders" *(wai di ren, wai lai gong),*[7] migrants are not only isolated and excluded by the state and urbanites but also mistreated and blamed for all kinds of social problems. For instance, in 2003, a college graduate, Sun Zhigang, was detained by the police because of his failure to show a temporary resident card and was subsequently beaten to death at the repatriation center (Luo 2003). In addition to police harassment, wage withholding, reductions of wage payments, and physical abuse toward rural migrants drove many to commit suicide (Xu 2003; see also Chan 1993, 1996, 1998, 2001; Chan and Senser 1997).

Entry into Sex Work

Social discrimination and government policies biased against migrants have forced the vast majority of rural migrant men onto the lowest rung of the labor market, where they often work as construction workers, garbage collectors, and factory workers. Some have decided to replace low-wage jobs and exhausting physical labor with sex work. Some were introduced into sex work via friends, whereas others solicited their own clients or applied to brothels. As they told me, living in cities with rampant consumerism, a monthly income of 1,000 yuan is simply not attractive. Indeed, it is estimated that, in the city of Beijing alone, four to ten thousand male rural migrants offer same-sex sexual services (Jeffreys 2007).

I next present the life stories of two money boys: a low-tier money boy who solicits clients in the park and a high-tier money boy who works for a high-class brothel. These stories illuminate two central themes. First, both rural migrant men chose sex work as the path to realizing their dream of success, which they defined by wealth, consumption, and a cosmopolitan lifestyle. Second, the class difference within sex work shapes these money boys' experiences, structures their lives, and influences their chances to fulfill their dreams. The money boy in the park is exposed to the public, open to ridicule, and forced to cope with clients who leave without paying for his sexual services. The money boy at the high-tier brothel, however, is hidden, protected, and always remunerated for his sexual service. Of the two money boys, the money boy at the high-tier brothel has a much better shot of fulfilling his dreams.

Xiao Dan: A Money Boy in the Park

I first met Xiao Dan in the park when he was soliciting clients. Xiao Dan, a twenty-year-old good-looking fellow from a rural area outside the city, self-identified as a heterosexual.

The tongzhi in the park called Xiao Dan "little stammer-er" because he stammered while talking, presumably as a result of several episodes of epilepsy between the time he was ten months old and his tenth birthday. His father died in an accident when he was ten. He always loved reading and could read for an entire day. He was also so intrigued by everything around him that sometimes he could easily get distracted. When he was in high school, his mother could no longer afford his school education. Although he enjoyed school, he had to quit school to work in a paper factory at a nearby town.

In the paper factory, although he worked very hard and was exhausted every day, the monthly wage of 800 yuan was always either withheld or delayed. Sometimes he was given only a one-month wage for six months of work. Life was hard, and he found himself in constant deprivation.

When he was seventeen, he quit the job and left for Dalian to pursue a better living and realize his dream of becoming a successful businessman. He stayed at a dirty, crowded hostel that cost only 5 yuan per night and looked for work every day at the city's central labor market, but to no avail. One day, a fifty-year-old guy approached him at the labor market, offering him 2 yuan per night and free meals in his hostel. The older man took him to a nearby restaurant and bought him some food to feed his empty stomach.

Thereafter Xiao Dan became that man's rented boy for six months. After he turned eighteen, he learned about the career of money boys and left the man.

Xiao Dan lied to his mother and embarked on a career as a sex worker. In the park, Xiao Dan charged 50 yuan for hand jobs and oral sex, and 300 yuan for penetrative sex. In the winter when the park was cold, Xiao Dan shifted his work site from the park to the bathhouse to solicit clients. Xiao Dan ran into many clients in the park and at the bathhouse who left without paying for his service, for which he had no recourse. The work was not easy: It was psychologically tiring for him to repeat the same acts over and over. Nothing could excite him anymore, which caused problems with ejaculation. One time it took him five hours to ejaculate, not because of the pleasure but because of the long sexual repression.

Xiao Dan's dark skin color, rural background, and money boy status invited pejorative and disdainful remarks and comments from tongzhi in the park. Indeed, he was the object of constant ridicule. During my fieldwork in the park, tongzhi denigrated Xiao Dan in front of me, making fun of his clothes and shoes and calling him "a dirty, lazy, and immoral rural migrant." Xiao Dan, however, responded that it was the urban clients who were immoral and uncivilized because they did not pay for the services they received.

Despite the low fees and occasional nonpayment for his sex work, Xiao Dan loved the free and mobile lifestyle and quick remuneration that other kinds of work were not able to provide. Xiao Dan was determined to realize his dream to open his own business and become a successful entrepreneur in the city. Distant as the dream may seem, he was convinced that he could, down the road, encounter enough wealthy clients to help him achieve it. Indeed, prior to engaging in sex work, he had not been able to have any friends in the city because of his rural migrant status. Sex work changed that situation and provided Xiao Dan with a network of urban friends who were important resources for him. Xiao Dan valued these friends very much and was intent on using them to realize his dream one day.

Xiao Kun: A Money Boy at a Brothel

I met Xiao Kun at a restaurant next to the hotel where he had just completed a session of sexual service. Xiao Kun, a handsome man in his early twenties, came to Dalian from a faraway rural area and had been working in the brothel for two years. He enjoyed the free and mobile lifestyle provided by sex work, as well as the financial gains.

Self-identified as half and half (bisexual), Xiao Kun was very proud of the progress he had made in the city—from a monthly wage of 400 yuan to one of 7,000 yuan. His first job in the city was as a worker in a bread factory. He quit the job to work in a restaurant with a monthly wage of 700 yuan and then in a sauna bar with a monthly wage of 3,000 yuan. Working as a money boy topped all the previous jobs with its monthly wage of 6,000–7,000 yuan. The more than doubled monthly salary, to Xiao Kun, was a testament to his success, of which he was very proud.

His brothel did not have a physical location; appointments were made through phone calls to his boss, who, in turn, would call him. A total of fifteen money boys worked in the brothel. Clients varied in age and occupation. One client in his fifties had assets of 3 billion yuan. He paid Xiao Kun 10,000 yuan for his one-time service.

It was not easy to be chosen to work in the brothel: "You have to have everything—a handsome face, an appealing appearance, a good body type, and skillful sexual technique." His work was so good that he was guaranteed clients every single day. His boss heard so much wonderful feedback about his work that he always recommended him to new clients. In fact, his boss was so confident in his work that he would promise return of a client's money if he were not satisfied.

Xiao Kun was very proud of his raised living standard, seeing it as a token of his success. When he first migrated to the city, he shared a tiny, crowded room with many others, paying a monthly rent of 400 yuan. After working as a money boy, he was able to afford a two-bedroom apartment with a rent of 1,500 yuan per month. In two years he was able to send home 50,000 yuan.

Xiao Kun was en route to realizing his dream of opening his own business as a boss. In a couple of months he would have saved enough money to launch his own massage parlor (euphemism for a brothel). He decided to set up his business in another city, so that he could exchange money boys with his previous boss to ensure a fresh supply. His boss had already signed a contract with him to this effect. Xiao Kun was thrilled that he had climbed the social ladder and become a successful businessman with wealth, a high-consumption rate, and a cosmopolitan lifestyle.

Money Boys' Rationale for Engaging in Sex Work

Money boys in my research told me that they wished to "gain a footing (*lizu*) in the city," with wealth and an urban status. With wealth, they could establish their own business and settle in the city as legitimate residents. They could also consume brand-name fashions, cultivate their bodies, and appear "modern." A modern persona would help prove their cultural sophistication and heighten their social status. Having a successful business would help them attain a house, a car, and a high standard of living.

As shown in the two stories, money boys harness an entrepreneurial spirit by engaging in sex work as an effective option to reach their goals and achieve success in the city. Ironically, by moving away from "normal" kinds of jobs, money boys achieve status as "normal" citizens (see also Kong 2012; Rofel 2010). In a rural-urban apartheid society, sex work provides them with ample opportunities to accumulate economic capital and proclaim themselves as self-managing, self-reliant, and self-enterprising normal postsocialist subjects.

Money boys like the free and laissez-faire lifestyle in sex work, which cannot be afforded by lower-paying jobs. As I was told, no one controlled them in their work, enabling them to quit and resume the work any time they wish. They are transient and travel from site to site, from cities to cities, to work as money boys. They are avid consumers of the gym, high-quality cosmetics, and fashionable clothes. The remuneration of sex work allows them to live a cosmopolitan lifestyle.

In my research, quite a few money boys, such as Xiao Kun in the early story, were able to reap the benefits and became business owners and housing owners in the city. Some rented boys had their urban clients buy them apartments in the city as well as provide cash payments. For instance, an urban man offered Xiao Sun 6,000 yuan per month for renting him, in addition to purchasing him an apartment under his name. At the end of the renting relationship, Xiao Sun entered sex work. He said, "When I was a factory worker, I was exhausted every night, earning only several hundred yuan a month. Now I deposit at least 4,000 yuan every month."

Like Xiao Sun, money boys in my research commented that one client per day could earn them more money than a full month of white-collar work. The rationale for sex work was, in their words, "People mock poverty but not prostitution" (*xiaopin bu xiaochang*). Indeed, the theme that money mattered, no matter how it was attained, ran through the interviews with money boys in my research. Money boy Xiao Ben, for instance, said, "I want to continue working to strengthen my economic power, to control what I have, and to solve all of my problems. Then I can go to a city I like and live my life as if nothing has happened."

Embracing the neoliberal ideology to become normal postsocialist subjects, money boys engage in sex work to enjoy a cosmopolitan lifestyle, and some do achieve upward mobility, despite the risks involved in sex work. As I have discussed elsewhere (T. Zheng 2009a), sex workers are the main target of police raids in China's crackdown campaigns; if caught they are fined, detained, jailed, or deported to the countryside or to rehabilitation centers. Faced with biased state policies and cultural prejudices against rural migrants and sex work, money boys find it imperative to negotiate the risks and perils associated with sex work through a wide array of strategies. They conceal their work from family and friends, segregate their work from their life, move from one place to another, shift from one type of sex work to another,[8] and endure discriminating insults. Some are able to refashion themselves by transforming from low-status rural migrants to postsocialist successful and wealthy entrepreneurs. As shown, some earned enough money through sex work to own a business in the city. Sex work becomes a new niche in the market economy that provides them an expedient route to becoming normal citizens with wealth and mobility.

CONCLUSION

This chapter debunks the monolithic, unified model of Chinese tongzhi by engaging in a political economic analysis of sexuality that links sexuality with class, socioeconomics, and politics in postsocialist China. Through scrutinizing the internal differences in the tongzhi population, this chapter illuminates the diverse sexual practices and identities shaped by hierarchies of social class, economic stratification, and political orientation. The embrace of the neoliberal ideology not only legitimizes and consolidates state power contingent on consumerism but also normalizes and perpetuates the dominant state ideology that good subjects are heterosexuals motivated by economic interests.

In this chapter, I have shown how different sexual practices are produced by and enact hierarchies of social class, reflecting the effectiveness of the dominant neoliberal ideology. Differently situated individuals negotiate with the dominant framework by engaging in a variety of sexual practices as the "technique of the self" (Foucault 1984). As defined by Foucault (1984, 27), the technique of the self is the "arts of existence"—the work "one performs on oneself, not only in order to bring one's conduct into compliance with a given rule, but to attempt to transform oneself into the ethical subject of one's behavior." With the postsocialist state providing rules and ideologies for normal citizenship, tongzhi in my research deploy a multitude of skills and strategies as the "techniques of the self" to refashion themselves as normal postsocialist subjects.

My research on the gold- and red-collar tongzhi fills a gap in the literature. Elaine Jeffreys (2007, 164) writes, "To date, the available literature does not address the question of who precisely demands the services of male sex sellers in present-day China." Ho (2009, 97) also notes, "The question of who consumes the body of money boys is still under-investigated and requires dynamic research attention."

The gold- and red-collar tongzhi, as demonstrated in this chapter, have a stake in the status quo, as they engage in covert practices to maintain their power and prestige and evade social ostracism, political damage, and economic costs. They capitalize on a hidden network to satisfy their sexual desires through purchasing and renting money boys. By not making their sexual practices legible, they are complicit in perpetuating heterosexual practices as normal. It is possible that in the future when the punitive costs of overt practices diminish, there will be less muted forms of expressing sexual desires among this group, but this is not the case today.

Despite the risks and perils involved in frequenting public places, white-, blue-, and gray-collar tongzhi visit public cruising areas and create their own subcultures. As shown, recreational spots and cruising areas are stratified by economic cost and differentiated by social status, with some places off-limits to tongzhi from lower socioeconomic status. Precarious as these public places are, white-, blue-, and gray-collar tongzhi congregate there to enjoy a sense of community and a support group. Visits to these places help them overcome social isolation and indulge in sexual encounters in the tongzhi circle. Nonetheless, this community is anything but harmonious and homogeneous. As illustrated in this section, social discrimination and economic hierarchies cut across the community, creating profound dissension and exclusion.

Money boys, carrying heavy historic baggage due to their rural migrant status, contest social inequality and cultural stigma by valorizing state ideology and claiming themselves as normal postsocialist subjects. Money boys in my research reject urbanites' discrimination against them, castigating urban clients as low-quality, immoral, and uncivilized for not paying them after using their sexual services. Sex work, for money boys, is an expedient and effective route to becoming normal citizens, who they define as wealthy and successful consumers. Through engaging in nonnormative sex work and sexual practices, money boys are able to participate in urban consumption and a cosmopolitan lifestyle and prove to the urbanites that they, too, can be wealthy consumers. Their success in becoming normal postsocialist subjects helps challenge cultural prejudices against migrants.

Although sexual practices of tongzhi in high- and middle-tier categories reproduce their social class, money boys' negotiated economic power allows them to climb the social ladder and achieve social mobility. At the same time, paradoxically, their strategic self-fashioning runs the risk of further stigmatizing and excluding rural migrants by validating the correlation between cultural identities and economic purchasing power, consumerism, and market potential. In so doing, money boys divert attention from unequal state policy to individual responsibility. Obscuring the cultural and political root causes of rural poverty, they contribute to the neoliberal discourse that justifies social inequality by blaming it on migrants' immutable, authentic worthlessness or "low cultural level" (see T. Zheng 2009a, 197–98).

The tension of class differences, as I have highlighted, constitutes a dividing factor among Chinese tongzhi. The gulf engendered by class creates mutual misunderstanding, stigma, and prejudice, which can be further exacerbated by physical segregation. The result is a community that is often fraught with conflict and dissent. As shown in this chapter, the gold- and red-collar tongzhi go to extra lengths to avoid associations with the tongzhi community, preferring instead their isolated connections with money boys through sex. Middle-class tongzhi relegate rural migrant tongzhi and money boys to an illegal and immoral status and disassociate themselves from them. Tongzhi in general distance themselves from those who appear "too C" (sissy).

These entrenched divisions among tongzhi prohibit them from uniting, and the embrace of the neoliberal ideology further reproduces the legitimacy of a heterosexual, self-disciplined, and self-enterprising consumer. One may imagine that challenges to the existing hierarchy, prejudices, and discrimination within the Chinese tongzhi population would be difficult, if not impossible, to overcome without candid and honest communications that cut cross class barriers.

CHAPTER 5

Organizing against HIV in China

On May 26, 2007, I participated in Dalian's fifth International Walk Convention as a member of a local AIDS organization, Ai Xin Work Group, where I served as a volunteer consultant. That morning more than 100,000 participants from over 800 local work units[1] began the walk. When I arrived at the starting spot, about twenty self-identified tongzhi were already standing there, holding a rainbow flag. As we talked and walked along the way, we ran into a number of bulletin boards set up outside a tourist spot, on which tourists could write about their impressions of the city. These bulletin boards were filled with walkers' graffiti, such as "I have toured here." As we were reading the graffiti, Xiao Lin, a volunteer from our organization, took out a pen and wrote on the bulletin board: "When one person becomes a gay, the whole family becomes glorious (*yiren dang gay, quanjia guangrong*).[2] Ai Xin Work Group—a partner of the Beijing Olympic Games."

This was the first time the word "gay" appeared throughout the whole event. I was told that the purpose of the walk was to "wish all the tongzhi in the world can live proudly under the sun"; its slogan was "Let us walk together under the sun!" I attended the event in spite of warnings from my heterosexual friends that walking in a "homosexual" group in such a public event could potentially generate violence against us. These concerns turned out to be unwarranted; throughout the event, the tongzhi identity of our organization was concealed. The group left no signs indicating that its members were tongzhi. Although all the other attendees in the event held flags that identified the names of their work units, the flag of our group was simply a rainbow, leaving our identity ambiguous as no one knows the meaning of the rainbow flag. No wonder there was no hassle, no fear, no violence, and no worries throughout the walk. With the walk participants' tongzhi identity hidden from the public, the slogan "Let us walk together under the sun" seemed meaningless.

In writing the phrase, "When one person becomes a gay, the whole family becomes glorious," Xiao Lin was creatively reconfiguring the government's prevailing slogan: "When one person becomes a soldier, the whole family becomes glorious." That slogan had been created to counter Confucianism's negative view of the military. As a famous Confucian saying held, "You don't make nails out of good steel; and you don't make soldiers out of a good man." In the twentieth century, if China was to survive colonialism and Mao and the communist insurgents were to be successful, this attitude toward soldiers needed to be changed. Hence, the new phrase proclaiming the value of the military. In the same way that it was necessary to change society's attitude toward soldiers, Xiao Lin created a parallel statement to help change the attitude toward tongzhi. In appropriating and reconfiguring the state-endorsed propaganda, Xiao Lin proclaimed that being a tongzhi is as glorious as being a soldier, thereby resignifying the derogatory and demeaning symbol of "gay" as the exalted and extolled symbol of "soldier."

By inscribing his statement, Xiao Lin seized control of the mainstream discourse that deems that soldiers glorify families. Tongzhi are excluded and rendered invisible in this discourse because they do not glorify families but blemish and taint them, causing them to feel shame. This is compounded by the traditional belief that being childless is the most unfilial thing a son can do, making it even more difficult for tongzhi to come out to their parents. Xiao Lin endowed this mainstream discourse with a new message about tongzhi, thus proclaiming glory in being "gay." In so doing, he attempted to implicate the system of domination and suppression of tongzhi, from which they create for themselves a sense of pride.

This identity-oriented action involved boundary crossing and label disruption. Tongzhi individuals such as Xiao Lin draw on their knowledge of the state-endorsed discourse and both appropriate and disrupt the state's vocabulary to resignify and rectify the tainted and tarnished label of homosexuality.[3] Furthermore, by claiming tongzhi's affiliation with the nation's 2008 Olympic Games in his graffiti, Xiao Lin is expressing their narrative of belonging. By placing tongzhi as a part and parcel of an organization in support of the nation, this claim embodies and bespeaks their desire for national belonging and their worthiness for social and political inclusion through their active engagement with the state-propagated cause.

In this chapter, I argue that tongzhi's manipulation and subversion of the mainstream discourse express their longing to be included in the mainstream. This paradox captures the nature of tongzhi's health and social activism in postsocialist China. I first discuss the background of emerging AIDS organizations in contemporary China and then present their goals and strategies for promoting health and social activism. I argue that these AIDS organizations' strategies actually mitigate and undercut the goals they aspire to reach, perpetuate social prejudice against homosexuality, and thwart the activism they purport to pursue. In the last section, I conclude with theoretical findings.

THE HIV/AIDS EPIDEMIC AND THE EMERGING AIDS ORGANIZATIONS IN POSTSOCIALIST CHINA

UNAIDS (2010) estimates that 0.1 percent of the total population of China is HIV positive, which is about 1.3 million people; the comparable statistic from the Chinese Center for Disease Control is 780,000 HIV carriers (An 2011). The Chinese government also reported that the number of new AIDS cases rose almost 13 percent in 2012 ("HIV/AIDS Cases Rising in China" 2012). Of the new cases reported in 2009, 42.2 percent were transmitted through heterosexual contact and 32.5 percent through homosexual contact (Ren and Xing 2010; UNAIDS 2010).[4] The proportion of new infections caused by homosexual contact had increased from 12.2 percent in 2007 to 32.5 percent from 2007 to 2009, making homosexual contact a growing source of HIV transmission (Ren and Xing 2010; UNAIDS 2010).

In response to the increasing number of people infected by HIV through homosexual contact, the central government proclaimed that the MSM group (men who have sex with men) was an important target for AIDS prevention (Fu 2009). Hundreds of nongovernmental organizations sprang up all over the country, carrying out AIDS prevention work in the MSM population.[5] Currently there are more than four hundred grassroots NGOs, government-organized NGOs (GONGOs), and online AIDS networks and forums working to combat HIV/AIDS in China (Micollier 2003, 2005, 2006). Leaders, participants, and volunteers in these grassroots organizations are almost exclusively tongzhi.[6]

"THE POWER OF EXISTENCE": HEALTH AND SOCIAL ACTIVISM AND COMMUNITY BUILDING

The Ai Xin (A Loving Heart) Work Group for which I volunteered was established in 1999. Its slogan is equality, happiness, care, and health, and it advocates monogamous sexual relationships. Its goals are to advance health education among tongzhi, eliminate prejudice against homosexuals, advocate care for HIV-positive people, and help them receive social support.

The organization runs several hotlines: a health hotline to discuss issues related to homosexuality and health, a love hotline to discuss relationship issues, and a tongzhi parent hotline presided over by the parent of a tongzhi for parents to discuss issues with their children with other parents. The head of the organization also runs a tongzhi bar where tongzhi can socialize with each other and enjoy spending time together. Organization members set up and man health booths in some designated places in the city to make the dissemination of condoms more convenient. The organization sponsors a variety of activities—discussion panels with college students who self-identify as tongzhi, singles events for tongzhi, and many summer trips to tourist spots in the surrounding areas where they dispense AIDS prevention materials and provide AIDS prevention information to all participants. It holds workshops about AIDS prevention and drug abuse and provides peer education about HIV and STDs to tongzhi college students, money boys, and migrant workers. The organization also provides HIV testing.

Every June at the beginning of summer the organization would attract around thirty to forty self-identified tongzhi to hike the twenty-seven-kilometer scenic seaside road that crosses the mountains—with their rainbow flag aloft. During the height of the summer, the organization would lead tongzhi in swimming activities while distributing AIDS information on the beach. The director of the organization also flew to Hong Kong to participate in the one-day Hong Kong anti-homophobia demonstration and pay a visit to local tongzhi organizations there.

Other grassroots tongzhi organizations throughout the country are run along similar principles; for example, "promoting human rights and enhancing the strength of tongzhi through collaboration with all walks of life and building a forum" (Beijing Tongzhi Center) and "supporting, advocating, and organizing the rights and benefits of Chinese LGBTQ groups to push forward public recognition of LGBT issues through public education and social advocacy activities, eliminating prejudice toward tongzhi, and fighting for equal rights for tongzhi" (Beijing Tongyu) (Zhao 2010). This latter group further advocated a dream of "a free country where there is no prejudice, hatred, crime, or war; a country that can tolerate red, orange, yellow, green, blue, and purple; a country that contains sex, love, power, hope, freedom, and art" (Zhao 2010).

The tongzhi population seems to be more politically active in large cities such as Beijing. On international anti-homophobia day the Beijing Tongzhi Center invited French foreign activists and American scholars to discuss a host of issues relating to community building and tongzhi relationships. Another of its offerings is a "one yuan activity," where each person contributes one yuan to support tongzhi activities such as film screenings. In Beijing, other activities have included a tongzhi literature forum in which authors and translators of books on tongzhi issues discussed tongzhi literature and increasing tongzhi voice in the current discourse; its goal was to expand tongzhi literature and the social influence of "the LGBT groups" (Kuer 2010; X. Wu 2009).

In the tongzhi pride month of June, Beijing Tongzhi Center staged an activity called "I am tongzhi, I am proud," setting out to collect photos of Chinese tongzhi worldwide (Zixuan Zhang 2010; Zhao 2010). Its members went to public places such as cafés, squares, shopping malls, bus stations, and subway stations to collect photos. The purpose of this activity was to bring more tongzhi out of the closet, to encourage them to recognize and acknowledge their sexual identity, to make more people understand tongzhi, and to decrease prejudice and misunderstanding. The style was peaceful and nonconfrontational. People who were asked for their photos were told the following: "There is no need to yell on the street; there is no need to clad yourself with a rainbow flag and run in groups on the street. You only need to paint a picture or write a couple of sentences, describing your wishes or exploring your imaginations. You can write 'I love peace, I am against prejudice,' or 'Sister, I only love women,' or 'Please respect every single life on earth.' ... Then write down your age, sexual orientation, province, city, and forward it to us at this email address" (Zhao 2010, 5). This public proclamation of sexual identity is unusual in China because, as shown in the next chapter, most Chinese tongzhi are eager to fit into a very tight communal society that has socialized them.

Across China, AIDS NGOs emphasize "the power of existence" rather than the power of resistance (Jun Wang 2010). They believe that by merely existing in society and by proclaiming that "I am present," they make a powerful public presence that will eventually change society. Tong Ge, a famous writer and sociologist, for instance, in 1997, proclaimed his tongzhi identity at the First AIDS Intervention International Symposium in front of government officials and members from international NGOs (G. Tong 1997). Tongzhi organizations claimed that his behavior was "the beginning of Chinese tongzhi declaring that 'I am present'" in public

(Jun Wang 2010). In 2010, seventy-four tongzhi, then registered members of the online Chinese Tongzhi Health Forum, affixed their names to a declaration that read, "I am a Chinese male tongzhi. I insist that my sexual orientation is a normal human behavior. I insist that everyone is equal upon birth and is not different from one another on account of gender, sex, or sexual orientation" (Jun Wang 2010). This declaration was seen by tongzhi activists as clarifying the goals of Chinese tongzhi social activism and increasing recognition, pride, and a sense of community.

The online Chinese Tongzhi Health Forum, which sponsored the declaration, has mobilized Chinese tongzhi from AIDS organizations around the country. This site disseminates international news concerning tongzhi and provides a space where AIDS organization members can interact. The significance of the Forum is captured in its mission statement:

> It [the Forum] is an independent social force that arises on the stage of history with confidence and pride. It marks the end of an era when Chinese tongzhi—one fifth of the world's tongzhi—had no impact on the international tongzhi movement. The Chinese tongzhi will play a significant role in ameliorating the world's tongzhi's role in AIDS prevention and improving their rights. Representing tens of thousands of tongzhi in China, at the advent of the sixth International Anti-homophobia day, here in China, we solemnly proclaim that we are tongzhi, we are present. We will change the status of tongzhi in this country. We will change this country. We will change this world. (Jun Wang 2010)

NONCONFRONTATIONAL STRATEGIES

In the two local grassroots AIDS organizations for which I volunteered, the leaders, employees, and volunteers were exclusively tongzhi. About twenty tongzhi (four employees and sixteen volunteers) worked for Ai Xin, and fewer than ten (one employee and eight volunteers) worked for Cheng Xin (Trust), the other local organization for which I volunteered. The secure environment that the organizations fostered enabled tongzhi to socialize with each other and to be incorporated into a tongzhi community.

The organizations operate largely by staging events and providing a space for tongzhi to come together and act on issues related to AIDS. By organizing events such as parties and trips to resort spots, they provide an opportunity and a space whereby tongzhi can share experiences, reaffirm their commonalities as members of a tongzhi community, obtain romantic fulfillment, and seek advice from each other without fear of social reprobation. In so doing, they facilitate the emergence of a tongzhi community in the city and help construct an embryonic collective identity.

When tongzhi interact with each other during these organized events, they engage in dialogues about their personal journeys toward realizing and accepting their tongzhi identity, their negotiations with society and family, their previous sexual experiences, their dynamics with their parents, and so on. Sharing these experiences allows strangers to identify as members and promotes a sense of closeness and bonding among the men. It satisfies the needs of many young tongzhi seeking a space for emotional and psychological support and interactions. For instance, Xiao Peng said to me, "This is the only place where we feel relaxed and at ease. We can talk about topics that we can never discuss in public. We talk about our parents, our experiences with other men, pressures to marry, and our relationship problems—all the issues that tongzhi face in their lives. Friends here will give us advice about our relationships. We feel safe here." Creating a community for the tongzhi is particularly important because these people are not able to communicate their problems to the outside world.

Tongzhi activist groups use nonconfrontational methods to negotiate with multiple sectors in society. In addition to manipulating and subverting the mainstream discourse as illustrated in the vignette at the beginning of the chapter, strategies include online postings, open letters, and self-criticisms. Few of these strategies have yielded any productive results.

In China, the media form the institutional mechanism through which normalization and domination of heteronormativity by the state are most effectively disseminated. Local grassroots organizations write letters and online postings to challenge reports that medicalize and pathologize homosexuality.

During my research in 2006, a major local newspaper published a one-page article on a psychology clinic that promised to "heal teenage homosexuality through psychological therapy and restore it to a normal state"; the article stated that "homosexuality is not healthy, not allowed by Chinese law, nor is it recognized in society" (Luan 2006, 38).

After the report was published, Da, the director of Cheng Xin, immediately posted on the online Chinese Tongzhi Health Forum a response of defiance against the newspaper and the clinic (L. Da 2006). The post launched three charges against the article. The first charge targeted its claim that homosexuality is not allowed by Chinese law, citing the fact that homosexuality was recognized as healthy in the United States in 1973, by the United Nations in 1992, and by Chinese psychiatry in 2001. The second charge contested the article's assertion that psychological therapy could restore homosexuals to a normal state. Instead, Da wrote that the psychology clinic harmed many tongzhi he knew, who spent hundreds of thousands of yuan on therapy, trusting the clinic's claim of a high cure rate of homosexuality.[7] According to Da, these tongzhi suffered not only financial loss but also insults, humiliation, and indignities at the clinic. One tongzhi in particular endured so much physical torment and psychological trauma at the clinic that he expressed a fantasy to bomb it. The third charge attacked the article's implication that adult homosexuality was pathological. After enumerating these charges, the post demanded that the newspaper explain its claim that "homosexuality is not healthy and not allowed by the law." The post accused the newspaper of "betraying its moral responsibility, promoting heresy, and harming healthy homosexuals" and demanded that the newspaper make an official apology to the tongzhi group (L. Da 2006).

After this article was posted on the Chinese Tongzhi Health Forum, it was copied and posted by a handful of tongzhi websites and blogs (Baidu 2006; Danlan 2006; Sina Blog 2006). Although one person commented that the newspaper article should not be taken seriously because the newspaper was just trying to sell copies, most people reasoned that ignorance *(wu zhi)* and lack of knowledge *(yu mei)* were responsible for its claims. However, responses stopped short of recommending any kind of action. One person posted, "Yes, we must protest when we should protest. However, it is a pity that we are never able to stage a sit-in demonstration *(jingzuo shiwei)* in front of the newspaper building. However, we should impose pressure on them. We cannot allow them to write such nonsense to vilify us."

It is worthy of note that even though some tongzhi were infuriated by the medicalized portrayal of homosexuality in the media, the subversive response they used was in the form of an online post, in the hope that it could exert power or pressure on the local newspaper. Although it did stir up some irate sentiments, cultivated a collective identity, and increased vigilance toward public media, the effect this post had on society as a whole and the media in particular was almost nil. The local newspaper never responded, and the organization never pursued the issue.

In addition to online posts, grassroots organizations also write open letters to challenge mainstream culture. Again and again these open letters invoke the following themes: There is no law against homosexuality, since 2001 homosexuality has no longer been classified as a mental illness, and tongzhi groups are an indispensable resource for the government in the state-run fight against AIDS.

For instance, in Tianjin City in northwest China, local grassroots organizations sent an open letter to the mayor, appealing for redress of several issues. The letter enumerated many AIDS patients' stories of doctors' cold and prejudiced attitudes toward AIDS patients, casual breaches of confidentiality of their identities, and lack of medical knowledge and competence in treating them, as well as the city's lack of financial subsidies for AIDS patients. Drawing on the vast gap between Tianjin and Beijing in the infrastructure of AIDS hospitals; doctors' attitudes, care, and competence; and financial subsidies for AIDS patients, the letter contended that Tianjin AIDS hospitals, doctors, and city policies were in violation of state policies that clearly stipulated care and financial support for AIDS patients; it appealed to the mayor to bring AIDS care into compliance with those state policies. In response, the mayor wrote that these issues were beyond the scope of his authority and that he had passed on the letter to the hygiene department (the equivalent of the U.S. National Institutes of Health). The local organizations immediately sent another letter to the mayor, clarifying that the letter was not addressed to the hygiene department and that he needed to abide by the state policy and offer an aid mechanism for AIDS patients. The second letter received no response. Nor were there any changes in the status quo.

A Fuyang local grassroots organization sent an email to the Chinese Tongzhi Health Forum reporting that the local Center for Disease Control (CDC) displayed a calendar on an office desk emblazoned with this slogan—"Stay Away from Drugs and Do Not Engage in Homosexual Behaviors"—as its AIDS prevention strategy (S. Su 2009). In response, the Health Forum decided to write an open letter to the national CDC, stating that the Fuyang local CDC's use of this slogan would lead to distrust from the tongzhi community and hence obstruct and thwart AIDS prevention work (Gay Men Health Forum 2009a). The letter used the protective umbrella of AIDS prevention work to accuse the local CDC of alienating the tongzhi community by publicizing prejudiced comments about homosexuality. To put an end to this kind of prejudiced behavior, the letter recommended a list of measures, including supervision of the local CDC by the national CDC and requirement of an antidiscriminatory training by employees in the local CDC and the other hygiene offices (Gay Men Health Forum 2009a).

The head of the national CDC finally responded to the open letter months later (Gay Men Health Forum 2009b; Z. Wu 2009), but his response made no mention of the specific issue of the Fuyang CDC's dissemination of prejudiced comments against homosexuality. Instead, the letter made general statements about the importance of the AIDS cause among "the MSM (men who have sex with men) community" and called for support from "the MSM community" in this cause.

Nor did the letter respond to the Health Forum's recommendations to address this problem at local CDC offices, particularly the proposed measures to educate local CDC employees. Rather, the letter deflected responsibility from the CDC to society as a whole: "We need the entire society's efforts to strengthen education and reduce prejudice." "To change reality, we need the entire society to work together." The letter also emphasized the increasing AIDS infection rate in the tongzhi community and the need for a combined effort of the CDC and tongzhi community:

> The AIDS infection rate in the MSM group has been increasing, putting us at a critical stage for AIDS prevention. We urgently need the entire society to act upon it. We especially need the hygiene department and MSM community to communicate, tolerate, and cooperate with each other to fight against this enemy of human kind and to prevent AIDS from spreading in the MSM community. I believe that the government's strong leadership and the MSM community's support can curb the spread of AIDS in the MSM group. Let us work together for this, hand in hand!

This letter from the national CDC was an official response designed to appease the tongzhi community not by addressing the issue, solving the problem, or setting up rules to regulate local government officials' prejudiced behaviors, but rather by acknowledging the tongzhi groups' important role in the fight against AIDS and by attempting to make AIDS, not the CDC, the enemy of humankind (Z. Wu 2009). It reflects the national

CDC's perspective that the tongzhi community serves as army troops to advance the state's interest and legitimize the state. Issues concerning tongzhi, in this perspective, are only relevant when they impede or enhance the focus of AIDS work. When there are clashes between the interests of tongzhi groups, which are primarily concerned with tongzhi rights, and the interest of state officials in AIDS prevention, the state representatives reconnect the two by stating that the state interest coalesces with, and actually represents, the interests of tongzhi groups regarding "preventing the AIDS virus from spreading in the MSM community" (Z. Wu 2009).[8] This official approach disarms the tongzhi groups, realigning the state and the tongzhi community as a cooperative team.

In the end, the tongzhi groups accepted this rationale and upheld the state interests. The online Health Forum celebrated the fact that the national CDC had responded, noting, "The National CDC welcomes the tongzhi community to propose similar issues and hopes to get more suggestions and opinions from the community. Health Forum welcomes the positive and open attitude of the national CDC, and hopes that this good relationship between us will continue" (Gay Men Health Forum 2009b).

From 2005 until 2011, tongzhi websites were blocked for months each year because they were considered "pornographic sites" (see X. Tong 2010). In 2007 during my fieldwork, many local tongzhi websites were blocked. I talked to a manager of a local tongzhi website, who contended that, although he was frustrated that his website was blocked, he had to support the state and he agreed with the state's surveillance because the websites posted solicitations for sex workers and 419s (the term for one-night stands). In fact, he was looking for volunteers to help with surveillance work for his website: "Chat rooms should be regulated and monitored. In Shenzhen for instance, you cannot write numbers such as 419 in the chat room. The country has rules and regulations, and they are for the good of the people. Money boys advertise themselves on the website, and they aren't acceptable to people. There is also the danger of blackmail, extortion, and other illegal crimes. So the websites need to be regulated." My research found that this manager's support of the state's surveillance of tongzhi websites represented many tongzhi's opinions.

A growing amount of research and scholarship has explored the issue of China's Internet censorship (Alford 2010; Casey 2013; Jason Ng 2013). The Chinese central government censors the Internet via software systems such as the Great Firewall and the Golden Shield. The Great Firewall targets foreign websites, whereas the Golden Shield targets domestic websites. Local and provincial governments are also equipped with their own surveillance systems. Since 2005, state-hired employees post government messages online and regulate online chatting by steering conversations away from sensitive topics. It is reported that 100,000 employees hired by the state and private companies spend every workday monitoring the Internet (Alford 2010; Casey 2013; Jason Ng 2013).

The surveillance system mainly censors organized activities that galvanize people to campaign for or support a political cause. For instance, as I mentioned in chapter 1, in 2004, before the opening ceremony of the Gay and Lesbian Film Festival at Beijing University, the government learned about the film festival by monitoring websites. The police broke in, ordered the students to leave, and then canceled the event. Although Internet censorship is intended to prevent people from using the Internet to organize political activities, all Internet access is blocked in some extreme cases (e.g., post-Xinjiang riots in northwest China in 2009). Researchers argue that because some minor social complaints are generally tolerated, people are given an illusion of participating in public debates where they feel free to voice their concerns (Alford 2010; Casey 2013; Jason Ng 2013).

During each crackdown in 2007, Ai Xin terminated all its activities, and its websites were shut down. Because any forms of congregating were deemed illegal by the police, it stopped organizing meetings and gatherings. During this time, the tongzhi bathhouse, then recently opened by the director of Ai Xin, was closed down by the police and visitors were arrested and fined severely. When Xiao Chen, an employee at Ai Xin, called the director and asked when they should start updating their website, the leader responded, "In view of the current situation, I don't want to manage it. We'd better just stay at home and do nothing."

From 2007 to 2011, the police arrested hundreds of tongzhi in major parks in Beijing and other cities in many incidents (see G. Li 2010). In Dalian and elsewhere, the police raided and closed down some tongzhi bars and tongzhi bathhouses, arrested tongzhi, made crude insults and humiliating comments, and even physically abused tongzhi in the process (Wan 2010; Long Wang 2010a). Only a few tongzhi responded with indignation.

On September 26, 2010, hundreds of armed police cracked down on the tongzhi cruising area in Mudan Park in Beijing and arrested hundreds of tongzhi (Long Wang 2010b). These tongzhi were forced to surrender their IDs and blood samples. They were also compelled to have their pictures taken and leave their fingerprints. The next day the police attacked this place once again. The police rationalized it as a necessary part of an annual security check before Chinese National Day, October 1[9] (G. Li 2010; Long Wang 2010a, 2010b).

After this raid was publicized on the AIDS networks and among tongzhi email groups, a local grassroots organization leader responded:

> Tongzhi visiting this kind of place should be arrested. It is these tongzhi who have brought stigma to the tongzhi community and created a bad image of the tongzhi community. Blackmail, robbing, and extortion often take place in this park. These people should be arrested and sentenced to jail. I need to speak the truth because I have been to the place and seen a very ugly scene. I myself am a tongzhi, but I know that as a tongzhi, we need to know decency. (Dou 2010)

The director of Cheng Xin, the local grassroots organization I also worked in, seconded this response:

> I agree with his response. His opinion should be a representative one in the tongzhi community. He is a person who dares to speak the truth. . . . Sex workers abound in places such as Mudan Park and Dongdan Park and their existence has created an adverse social effect on the MSM community and increased the spread of HIV/AIDS. The problem rooted in the MSM group itself is the ultimate reason for social prejudice. The MSM group has become the first high-risk group for HIV/AIDS transmission. Scientific data showed that many people in the tongzhi community are promiscuous, do not have any moral integrity, and are not conscious of safe sex practices, generating a serious HIV/AIDS epidemic in this group. These phenomena explain why society has prejudices and discriminates against the MSM group. I believe that the method the police utilize is not right, but tongzhi should look for reasons within themselves for the so-called "prejudiced" treatment of the police toward the MSM group. (L. Da 2010)

The NGO director's belief that problems rooted in the tongzhi community are conducive to social prejudice bespeaks the acceptance of the dominant moral order and the high level of self-censorship and self-criticism within the tongzhi community. He subscribed to the dominant moral order and used it as the moral benchmark to criticize the tongzhi community for being immoral, licentious, and loose. The scientific evidence of the tongzhi community as the first high-risk group for HIV/AIDS transmission was, to him, a strong proof of the deeply rooted problems within the tongzhi community on which discrimination and bigotry were grounded.

Such self-criticism was a common practice among tongzhi in my research. Although they sent open letters to the authorities, silence from the tongzhi community followed each physical assault. The rationale was that, when tongzhi bars and bathhouses were closed down, most reopened at a different time or in another, more secret place.

Despite the general silence, the main office of the Tongzhi Health Forum sent open letters to Internet companies, the Public Security Ministry, and the Information Ministry to challenge the blockage of tongzhi websites—but again to no avail (Long Wang 2009). Although the director of Ai Xin let its website go dark, a few other organizations chose to move their web servers outside of China, even though there was no web maintenance service and the Internet speed was extremely slow. Despite the intractable situation, distraught website leaders still expressed their support for the state's monitoring of tongzhi websites but appealed for a better method: "Please give our tongzhi websites a chance to breathe. All we want is a survival space—it is that simple. Please set up an isolated space for all the tongzhi websites so that we can be easily supervised and monitored."

Among all the tactics used to challenge discrimination and the mainstream culture, writing open letters has been the most frequently used strategy by tongzhi activists. Every open letter invokes the state-endorsed discourse on AIDS prevention to combat prejudiced behaviors, reflecting the desire of the grassroots organizations to work with the government as collaborators, rather than against the government as enemies, in efforts to educate government staff members, media staff members, and Internet company employees as a means to eradicate prejudice. Indeed, the letters evince their belief in the government and their aspirations to be included

in the nation. Such a national longing and belief in the state not only legitimize the state but also encourage self-censorship and self-criticism that
divert attention from challenging the system and making social change,
thereby maintaining the status quo social and political order.

CONCLUSION

Researchers who study social movements in China have paid special attention to the emergence of NGOs and their significance in ushering
in democracy in China (e.g., Brook and Frolic 1997; Chamberlain 1993;
P. Huang 1993; Q. Ma 2006; Madsen 1993; Rankin 1993; Saich 2000; Unger
1996; Unger and Chan 1995). Some researchers predicted that AIDS activism would lead to an unintended consequence of a flourishing homosexual
movement in big cities in China (see Micollier 2005). In contrast, this
chapter highlights the mutual constitution and dynamic interactions
between tongzhi, the state, and the dominant cultural order, which challenge the assumption that dichotomizes them as polarized entities.

In this so-called activism, Chinese tongzhi work in collaboration
with, rather than against, the state. Deploying and appropriating the state-
endorsed AIDS cause, they draw on the dominant moral order as a legitimate resource for engaging in tongzhi activism while still seeking
legitimacy in the mainstream culture. By declaring that the elimination
of homophobia is essential to curbing AIDS transmission, they use AIDS
activism to provide legitimacy for their tongzhi activism.

Chinese tongzhi's endeavors embody their paradoxical attempts at
conformity and subversion. On the one hand, their actions challenge the
dominant culture by resignifying the stigmatized label of tongzhi-ness.
On the other hand, they perpetuate the dominant culture by criticizing
tongzhi-ness and adopting the dominant moral ideal. These seemingly
contradictory behaviors both work together and conflict with each other.
They work together as they help tongzhi achieve legitimate integration and
membership in the dominant culture. They conflict with each other as
tongzhi accept the dominant moral order and reaffirm the negative and
stigmatized images of themselves, thus crippling the very goals of their
social activism.

AIDS grassroots organizations have a marginal status. Many are not
legally registered because state policy forbids the National Civil Affairs

Department from registering any NGOs; only a handful of organizations manage to get registered as companies (Long 2010). AIDS grassroots organizations are also prohibited from applying for global funds and other funding resources. Because their existence depends on financial resources from government organizations and GONGOs, this dependent and attached status requires that they have to cooperate with local government officials. They can only exist as volunteers for government organizations such as local CDCs and GONGOs such as the Red Cross. Although local officials take credit for the work of AIDS grassroots organizations in reports to their superiors, these officials deem the grassroots organizations to be illegitimate.

Such a relationship between grassroots organizations and the state has been theorized by Anthony Spires (2011) as a "contingent symbiosis," in which organizations can survive insofar as they refrain from democratic claims-making and are tolerated so long as certain state agents can claim credit for their work. This concept captures the mutual benefits and fragility that characterize the relationship between NGOs and the government, hence debunking the assumed linkage between grassroots organizations and democracy.

In my research, despite the fact that leaders, participants, and volunteers in these AIDS organizations are almost exclusively self-identified tongzhi, the tongzhi identity of the organization members is concealed from the public. None of these organizations' names refer to tongzhi. Some examples of names that conceal and hide the tongzhi makeup of the organizations are Consultation Agency of AIDS and A Loving Heart. In other words, they are only allowed to exist as AIDS prevention groups. The prominence of tongzhi in these AIDS-related organizations conveys the message that, because they bear the brunt of the AIDS epidemic, they have a vested interest in AIDS-related issues. Yet, for the tongzhi, engaging in state-endorsed AIDS prevention provides grassroots organizations with a sense of legitimacy in the eyes of the state.

Gramsci (1995) has stated that the capitalist state exerts and maintains control not only via violence and political and economic coercion but also, most importantly, via ideology. The bourgeoisie class creates and develops a hegemonic culture that propagates its own values, customs, and norms. The public soon adopts these values and norms as common sense. Rather than revolting against the dominant class or being forced into inferior positions, people of the ruled class voluntarily identify their values with the dominant ideology, thereby consenting to their own domination by the ruling class.

Having internalized the viewpoint/gaze from the hegemonic ideology, these tongzhi continuously reference this viewpoint/gaze to gauge their behaviors and activities and to engage in self-censorship and self-criticisms. This inward self-criticism and self-management bespeaks the power of the hegemonic narrative that diverts their attention from an outward collective social agency that would challenge the social order and propel social change.

By engaging in self-criticism and self-censorship, tongzhi in my research display a desire to change themselves. In envisioning the self as the ultimate opponent, tongzhi in my research engage in self-criticism and self-censorship rather than social criticism or a desire for social change. In so doing, agency is channeled inward toward the self to ensure self-transformation, rather than outward to ensure social change. Ultimately, the normalization process triumphs when tongzhi submit to fear and suppress their feelings.

This process reflects Foucault's conceptualization of the neoliberal technology of the self that makes each individual an entrepreneur of him- or herself, as the self is rendered both the object and subject of change (Foucault 1977, 170; 1988). In *Discipline and Punish,* Foucault (1977) traces a shift of technologies of control in the eighteenth and nineteenth centuries and the subsequent rise of surveillance techniques and the construction of the subject by scientific and expert discourse. In the neoliberal era, this technology of control involves a form of domination in which the delineation of normal and abnormal replaces violence as a technique of power, and power is maintained through a normalizing process in which "the whole indefinite domain of the non-conforming is punishable" (Foucault 1977, 178). Hence Foucault treats the pressure for conformity as a technique of power. Certain groups and behaviors are deemed abnormal through labeling and through systematically organized stigmatization. Unlike the previous era where the dominator was visible and oppression was institutionalized in the form of direct violence or force, in the neoliberal era, the dominator has become increasingly abstracted, disembodied, and invisible, and domination is exercised through the dominated themselves. Through the technique of the self, in the absence of a physical mechanism of control and punishment, individuals change themselves with an internalized disciplinary gaze to escape the peril of being excluded as abnormal.

This technique of power is both enabling and constraining. It is enabling in the sense that the deviant and derogatory label has become the basis on which these tongzhi forge a collective identity and organize collective activities, albeit in private and in a very limited scope. To resignify and disrupt the deviant nature of the label, they have to first build a community around the label (see also Gamson 1989). As the vignette at the beginning of this chapter shows, at times, they use the label to help remold and reorient its stigma as they challenge the normalization process through which domination is quite often effectively achieved. At the same time this technique of power is constraining in the sense that many of these tongzhi have internalized the disciplinary gaze and engaged in a technology of the self, resulting in a set of paradoxical and contradictory strategies of both resisting and embracing the norm to cope with domination.

In addition to the constraining effect of normalization, tongzhi activism is also severely undermined by the lack of independence of their organizations and by their tactics of deploying the state-legitimated HIV/AIDS cause. As we have seen, when adverse situations arise such as police arrests, police assaults, crackdowns of tongzhi websites, and prejudiced reports in the media, the tongzhi organizations avoid direct confrontations with local authorities, instead using passive means such as sending open letters or putting a halt to Internet activities and organized events. In their compliance with the state and active participation in the state-legitimized cause of HIV/AIDS, they hope to infuse a tongzhi activist agenda to bring about certain cultural outcomes, such as creating a cultural environment free of stigma attached to the tongzhi identity. However, because of the illegitimate social standing of these organizations that requires cooperation with a government institution, the kind of activism staged in their organizations must negotiate and move within particular institutional environments and is dependent on a variety of local authorities for institutional and financial support and legitimacy.

The fact that these AIDS NGOs rely on state-regulated funding systems and government organizations to exist legally shapes their tactics, forces them to mask their tongzhi identity in public, and impedes the extent to which they can infuse tongzhi activism in their AIDS cause. Their collaboration with the state mitigates their tongzhi activism, leaves the social norm unchallenged, and allows further stigmatization of their tongzhi identity. Consequentially, AIDS politics and tongzhi politics stand in tension, associated yet dissociated at the same time. Furthermore, AIDS politics, although serving as an important tool and opportunity for the tongzhi men to advance tongzhi politics, albeit in limited scope, paradoxically reinforces the association between tongzhi and AIDS and perpetuates the stigma that AIDS is a tongzhi problem (see also Gamson 1989).

CHAPTER 6

Embracing the Heterosexual Norm

The Double Lives of Tongzhi

I n a cruising area in a local central park, tongzhi gather and share their views on life. Tongzhi in my research define a "normal" life as being part of a heterosexual marriage and having children, and an "abnormal" life as a "crazy" transient time spent in the tongzhi group that is bound to end. Xiao Cheng said, "When a person is young, he can afford to be crazy in a place that cannot be exposed to the sunlight (*jianbudeguang*). However, when a person is older and wants to live like a normal person, he has to get married and do real and serious stuff. He cannot mess around anymore. He has to learn how to be normal." Other tongzhi nodded, and Xiao Ming said, "Yes, it's OK to play like this and seek stimulation and fun when you are young. When you reach your thirties, however, you need to embed yourself into society through heterosexual marriage because you want to be accepted as a normal person. Otherwise you'll be expelled and banished as an abnormal person and you will be living at the margin."

Responding to their statements, I shared my speculation that their attitudes toward a normal life and the tongzhi life would change if tongzhi marriage were legalized in China. The tongzhi around me immediately responded negatively to my suggestion. Xiao Yang stated, "Even if marriage were legalized among us, who would marry? Are you guys going to marry?" All the tongzhi around him shook their heads and said no. Xiao Yang went on:

Who wants to marry a tongzhi openly? Can you openly tell your colleagues that you are a tongzhi? Of course not! We don't want to do it because we don't even have this thought. When two people are together, it's just for play and no one thinks of marriage. If you marry, you'll become the focus of the world's attention and of course no one wants that—how shameful (*diu ren*) that would be! This kind

of thing cannot see sunlight, and there's no way we can openly be
tongzhi *(zhengda guangming)*.

This chapter examines the reasons why tongzhi do not unite or organize for formal protests against the status quo. I argue that the powerful postsocialist discourse about heterosexual masculinity and heterosexual marriage permeates tongzhi's everyday lives and aligns their
individual desires with the national desire of heteronormativity. The
failure of the tongzhi to stage collective action is an indication of the
ability of postsocialist heteronormativity to make a united form of
resistance seem hopeless.

As we have seen, young tongzhi in my research cope by imagining their
present situation as transient, only a youthful fling, and that they will lead
an ordinary life of conformity as they mature. Other times they are brought
back to reality and talk about how they will continue, behind the backs of
their wives, their same-sex practices after marriage. Whereas young tongzhi wrestle between imagination and reality, older, married tongzhi employ "everyday acts of resistance" in continuing to seek sex outside the
accepted framework of marriage, which suggests that the younger, unmarried tongzhi's projected imagination of their future is unlikely to be
fulfilled.

Anthropologists have contended that subalterns often engage in
"everyday acts of resistance" to resist domination, albeit with a lack of
class-based mobilization (Beemyn 2013; Montgomery and Stewart 2012;
Scott 1985; Thomson 2011). In his research among peasants in a Malaysian
village, James Scott (1985, 1990) maintains that peasants who face formidable repression engage in self-protecting compliance onstage and everyday resistance following a "hidden transcript" offstage. Similarly, in his
work in Rwanda, Thomson (2011) argues that on the surface, the rural poor
voice their support and compliance with the state policy of national
unity, but behind the scenes they use various strategies to avoid participation. Their every act of resistance, according to Thomson (2011), is driven
by their perception of the state policy as unjust and illegitimate, unlike
the tongzhi in my research who accept the state policy.

On the surface, tongzhi embrace heterosexual marriage and the heterosexual norm in society and fit themselves into the norm, while behind
the scenes they fulfill their personal desires and engage in same-sex practices. This act of everyday resistance—engaging in surreptitious same-sex

practices outside the socially acceptable realm—however, seeks not to overthrow state policies or to mitigate or minimize domination. Rather, it seeks to satisfy both social norms and individual desires. In so doing, it makes tongzhi complicit in reproducing and reinforcing heterosexual marriage and the heterosexual norm in society.

In their comments reported in the beginning of the chapter, Xiao Cheng, Xiao Ming, and Xiao Yang's disavowal and renunciation of same-sex marriage call into question anthropologists' celebration of everyday resistance, which has become an important terrain for researchers in locating marginalized people's agency. Tongzhi's renunciation complicates this resistance rhetoric. As we saw, young unmarried tongzhi protested that they would marry heterosexually and conform to the cultural norm. As young, unmarried tongzhi solicited sex and formed same-sex relationships behind the backs of their girlfriends, older, married tongzhi surreptitiously did the same outside their heterosexual marriages. Their discourse and behaviors place tongzhi not in a polarized relationship against the heterosexual norm in society, but rather in a dynamic relationship with it.

What made the tongzhi in my research want to change themselves rather than society, thereby relinquishing collective action? What made them reject their identity with their own group and lifestyle and feel self-negation?

Through an exploration of tongzhi's real-life existence, this chapter demonstrates the ways in which the power of the national discourse of heteronormativity is expressed in the tongzhi's double life, negative self-evaluation, and oscillation between identification and dis-identification with the tongzhi group—all of which undermine the group solidarity necessary to stage a formal, organized movement.

LIVING A DOUBLE LIFE

Tongzhi in my research straddle a cover-up and a true self-presentation while maintaining a discrepancy between a virtual identity and an actual identity. They describe this discrepancy as leading a double life. In their own words, they "live in the basement and [do] not see the daylight." They "live like a human being in the daytime but like a ghost at night," and they "have two faces: a yin face during the night and a yang face during the day." If discovered by society, this double life could discredit the tongzhi and turn the world against them.

Tongzhi identify many symbols or bits of information that could potentially convey their tongzhi-ness and so make concerted efforts to manage, conceal, and cover up these symbols so that they can "pass" as heterosexuals and avoid social stigma. Symbols, as Goffman maintains, possess social properties and convey social information based on which a social image of a person is formed. Hence they can establish a person's claim to prestige, honor, class, or stigma (see Goffman 1959, 43).

To manage the symbols of stigma and prevent slip-ups that might reveal their double lives (Goffman 1959; 1963, 45), tongzhi maintain a split self in public and in private—negotiating a constant tension of self-alienation, self-shame, and oscillation between identification and dis-identification with their own group. When they are in the tongzhi community, because they share the same stigma, their tongzhi identity is salient and collective. They can be expressive and relaxed and at the same time provide each other with moral support and the comfort of feeling at home and at ease. At the same time, however, they remain anonymous.

In public, tongzhi exert concerted efforts to pass as heterosexuals. It is through their focus on acceptance by the dominant world and their self-sanctioning strategies that the power of postsocialist heteronormativity is exercised. Indeed, it digresses, deviates, and undercuts their collective social agency.

ERASURE OF TONGZHI IDENTITY IN THE WORKPLACE

In their desire to be included in the majority straight world, tongzhi in my research scrub out their tongzhi identity in the workforce. The decision to hide their true tongzhi identity is reminiscent of the LGBT social movement organizations in Namibia and South Africa that wrestle with a similar strategic dilemma when they decide whether and how to become visible, modify their public profile, or forgo political opportunities (Currier 2012).

Xiao Liu, for instance, after being employed by the grassroots organization Ai Xin for two years, finally decided to leave it. He said, "I want to end my relationship with the tongzhi community. My career has nothing to do with tongzhi. I need to face society, not tongzhi. After all, tongzhi is non-mainstream" *(fei zhu liu).* Ever since Liu graduated from a local university, he had been working at Ai Xin. Like all the other employees and the director of the organization, Liu considered his work in Ai Xin peripheral and temporary and that a "mainstream" job is essential to a man's career. Through one of the social events organized by Ai Xin, he befriended a tongzhi who was a leader of a company. Desperate for a job, Xiao Liu sought his help and was hired to work under his leadership. Yet Xiao Liu was not satisfied; he said, "I don't want to work in a company with another tongzhi. Of course he will not disclose my tongzhi identity, nor will I disclose his. However, it creates an awkward situation. I want to use normal channels to deal with my leader. I don't like the fact that my leader is a tongzhi because I don't want to think about all this tongzhi business. Because I know he's a tongzhi, I have to consider so many things such as what tones I should use in talking to him. I need to be very careful." I asked him to elaborate on what he said, and he responded, "You know how you have to talk differently to men and women in face-to-face interactions because they are different. So of course when I know he is a tongzhi, I have to take that into consideration. I have to pay attention to my speaking tone and so on. I like to interact with other leaders because I am free from all this tongzhi business."

Knowing that his leader was a tongzhi created an uneasy burden for Xiao Liu, because of the gap between the tongzhi world and the mainstream world. To Xiao Liu, the tongzhi world and the mainstream world were antithetical entities. Anything related to the tongzhi world would jeopardize his efforts to be incorporated and integrated into the mainstream world. His aspiration to shed any associations with tongzhi-ness was thwarted by the fact that his leader was a tongzhi. Of course, it was ironic that it was his tongzhi friend who facilitated his integration into the mainstream world by hiring him. Xiao Liu said, "I want to be in the mainstream. Integration into the mainstream makes me more socially acceptable *(shehuixing)* and less marginal *(jubuxing)*. Tongzhi-ness is equivalent to marginality. To be socially acceptable is to erase the tongzhi-ness *(shuxing)*. I hope to be a normal social being. Otherwise there is no future for me career-wise."

Expunging any cultural traces of tongzhi-ness was a cynical strategy for Xiao Liu to use to deal with prejudice and marginality in his everyday life. Xiao Liu juxtaposed being mainstream against being tongzhi and asserted that there was no overlap between the two: To gain one meant to jettison the other. Indeed, many tongzhi conveyed to me the difficulty, if not impossibility, of reconciling the two realms. For instance, Xiao Cheng stated,

It's extremely difficult to keep ties with both tongzhi friends and straight friends. When my straight friends ask me to hang out with them on Friday or Saturday night, I have to lie to them and create a story. When they ask me what I have done over the weekend, I have to lie and create another story. When they call me and I happen to be at a tongzhi bar, I have to cover it up and make up another lie. It's too much nuisance, and in the end, I forget about previous lies, upset my friends, and damage the friendship.

As shown in this case, control of information about one's tongzhi identity negatively impinges on formed relationships in the straight world. On the one hand, relationships with straight people necessitate spending time together. The more time that friends spend together, the more chance that personal information will slip out and be acquired by the other. On the other hand, a certain level of trust and mutual commitment are expected from each relationship. Each person in a given relationship is obliged to reveal and exchange a suitable amount of intimate facts about him- or herself. As Xiao Cheng noted, the fact that he constantly had to conceal information made him deficient in shared information with his straight friends, hence compromising the relationships (see also Goffman 1963, 86).

Indeed, Xiao Cheng realized that to keep socializing in the tongzhi community, he had to decline or avoid friendships with straight people so that he could avoid the consequent obligation to divulge information. He had to maintain a distance from straight people because the more time he spent with them the more chance that unanticipated events could occur that would disclose his secret (see also Goffman 1959, 99).[2]

This incompatibility between the tongzhi and straight circles was also noted in a study of tongzhi in Shanghai: As gay men build social ties to other gay men, they often report an increasing degree of social separation from non-gay friends. Furthermore, among straight men a complete lack of self-disclosure about romantic and sexual behavior can be interpreted as social distance. Non self-disclosure and retreat into a gay circle of intimate friends thus can lead to a weakening of social ties with non-gay friends, and a consequent loss of social capital (Sun, Farrer, and Choi 2006, 6).

Confronted with the choice between the tongzhi world and the mainstream world, some tongzhi such as Xiao Liu unequivocally renounced the tongzhi world and joined the mainstream world. In the postsocialist market economy where money and jobs determine a person's success, Xiao Liu coped with the pressure by eliminating his tongzhi-ness—the obstacle to his path to success, which would be marked by his incorporation into the mainstream.

PERFORMING MASCULINITY

Performing as a "normal" man in public is another strategy for tongzhi to evade stigma. In postsocialist China, a normal masculine man is socially recognized as a heterosexual, a boyfriend, a husband, and a father. Following this norm, tongzhi in my research take on these social roles and put on a masculine performance—evading symbols of stigma associated with femininity and flaunting desires for women, as well as maintaining distance from other tongzhi—to pass as heterosexual and reject tongzhi-ness.[3]

A proliferation of research has explored the issue of performing masculinity (Bradley 2013; Buiten and Naidoo 2013; Cunningham et al. 2013; Hatfield 2010; Migliaccio 2009; Tivers 2011; Yow-Juin Wang 2012). Researchers (Coltrane 1994) have argued that hegemonic masculinity, or the dominant ideology of masculinity, is perceived as the quality of men in power. This hegemonic masculinity is upheld as the ideal that men in general approximate, emulate, and strive for. There are myriad ways in which men strategically perform masculinity, such as enacting physical strength, being self-reliant, taking risks, exerting control over women, and exhibiting fearlessness and aggression (Courtenay 2000; Serrant-Green, McLuskey, and White 2008; T. Zheng 2006, 2009a, 2009b, 2012). Those who adhere to the ideal are rewarded with greater access to social resources (Connell 1995; Kendall 1999; Migliaccio 2001, 2009; Mirande 1997; Sargent 2001).

Two of the ways in which a man performs masculinity to achieve the hegemonic ideal are described next. The first is to act stoically—both physically and emotionally—to show that he is unhurt, unshackled, and in control of his emotions and situations (Collison and Hearn 2005; Kaufman 1992; Kimmel 1996; Migliaccio 2001). The second is to avoid behaviors associated with femininity, such as displays of expressive intimacy in friendships. Migliaccio (2009, 239), in his study of men's friendships, argues that "doing friendship is doing gender"; that is, men's friendship is part of a masculine performance wherein men enact behaviors such as being

dispassionate, avoiding expressiveness, and having instrumental relationships to conform to masculine expectations.

Tongzhi in my research also perform masculinity to meet expectations of a "normal" masculine man. As research has pointed out, assimilation to the hegemonic masculine ideal means refraining from behaviors that are associated with women, such as expressive affections in
friendships (Connell 1995; Kimmel 1996; Migliaccio 2009). Likewise, for
tongzhi in my research, performing masculinity necessitates the erasure
of visible symbols of femininity that are identified by tongzhi as easily
giving away their tongzhi-ness. They differentiate prestige symbols from
stigma symbols that could cast doubts on their "passing" endeavors.
These "feminine" stigma symbols include but are not limited to piercing
ears, carrying handbags on the shoulder, carrying big handbags (according to tongzhi, only women carry big handbags; men carry small wallets
or small bags around their waists), swinging buttocks while walking,
wearing tight shirts or tight jeans, speaking in a high pitch or in a coquettish way, having tongzhi friends, two men exchanging roses, and hanging
pin-ups of handsome men next to the bed. These signs, according to the
tongzhi, give away their identity and discredit their claim to be "normal"
heterosexuals.

Visible manifestations of behaviors that are considered as too feminine
not only invite discrimination from the mainstream world but also are derided and ridiculed as "too C (sissy)" in the tongzhi world. This is another
indication of how the power of the postsocialist heteronormative discourse
impinges on the narratives in the tongzhi community. Many tongzhi favor
men who look and act masculine *(nanren wei)* and denigrate men who act
like women. They constantly invoke the derogatory term "too C" to disparage and mock men who behave like women. This means that tongzhi
have to take special precautions to jettison these stigma symbols and to
talk, speak, act, and gesture in a masculine fashion not only in public but
also within the tongzhi community.

A similar phenomenon occurred in the 1970s and 1980s gay community in the United States, in which gay men were pressured to adhere
to hegemonic masculine ideals through the "relentless repudiation of
femininity"; by doing so they would debunk the construction of their
image as failed men (Levine 1998, 13). In his research with the gay community in New York in the 1970s and 1980s, Levine points out that performing a hegemonic "macho" man in lieu of a "failed" man increased a
man's attractiveness to other gay men who subscribed to the hegemonic

masculine ideal. He introduces the term "gay clone" to capture gay men's cloning of hegemonic masculine ideals through refuting passivity and rejecting displays of affection and emotion.

For tongzhi in my research, passing as heterosexual also means exhibiting strong interest and desires for beautiful women. Xiao Tan shared an apartment with his colleagues in the city. When I visited his apartment, I noticed that large photos of beautiful female singers and movie stars hung next to his bed. Knowing that he was not interested in women, I conveyed my surprise. He laughed and responded, "Those are just a cover-up so that my roommates will not be suspicious of me." He then let out his mischievous smile and, pointing at the small, nearly unnoticeable photos of handsome boys hanging beneath the gigantic photos of the women, said, "These pictures are the ones I am really looking at every day. The women's pictures help hide these handsome boys that I truly appreciate."

In addition to demonstrating a desire for women and effacing feminine ways of carrying the self, tongzhi also do not want to be seen with other tongzhi in public.[4] While performing masculinity in public and managing the information they convey about themselves, tongzhi have to consider with whom they want to be seen. Perceptions of a person are usually shaped by the person she or he is with, because the underlying assumption is that people who are alike tend to socialize together. Hence, if a tongzhi's companion voluntarily exhibits stigma symbols such as acting feminine, his behaviors can reveal both of them as tongzhi and subject both to suspicion and stigma. For instance, Xiao Wen met a tongzhi online and told him where he worked. The next day, that tongzhi came to his workplace to look for him. He said, "I didn't expect him to come at all! I was petrified when I saw him because I was worried that his behaviors would raise my colleague's suspicion. I immediately took him outside and talked to him. I told him that people were watching and that he needed to be extra discreet in his words and behaviors not to give away his tongzhi identity." Any weakness his online friend displayed could potentially betray both of them.

In public, tongzhi couples not only need to perform masculine behaviors and avoid feminine behaviors but also have to remain distant from each other. Xiao Chen and Xiao Lin had been a couple for about six months. One time, the three of us were riding the bus together to go to the shopping mall. I was seated while Xiao Lin and Xiao Chen were standing next to each other. In the midst of our talking and laughing, Xiao Chen suddenly changed his expression. In a quiet and nervous tone, he said he saw his colleague in the back seat. He then immediately moved to another location and stood far away from Xiao Lin, facing in the opposite direction. He remained there until his colleague got off the bus. Normally the couple loved me to tag along whenever they rode a bus, walked on the street, or shopped in the mall because my presence drew people's attention away from the stigma symbol and made them relaxed in public. However, in this case when his colleague was nearby, he completely cut off communication with his boyfriend because he was uncertain about his maintenance of emotional distance and his enactment of masculinity in the presence of his boyfriend.

On Chinese Valentine's Day,[5] Xiao Chen bought two movie tickets for lovers' seats (*qinglv zuo*—this movie theater offers theater rooms for couples only, wherein each sofa can seat only two people. They are called "lovers' seats" or "couple's seats"). He and his boyfriend thought the movie would be shown in a big hall, but when they walked in, both were astounded to discover that the small room seated only twenty people. Every sofa could seat only two people, and everyone was in clear view of one another. All the lovers sitting on the sofa were heterosexual. Seeing this situation, the two immediately backed out and dared not walk back in. They hid in a corner where Xiao Chen handed his boyfriend the rose he bought for him. His boyfriend immediately pushed the rose away, red-faced with anger and embarrassment. In the end, they decided to wait in the corner until the lights went off. As soon as the room grew dark, Xiao Chen walked into the hall first, and his boyfriend followed. Instead of sitting up straight on the lovers' seat, both slouched to prevent people from seeing them. When the movie finished, both waited until everyone left before they stood up and walked out. As they exited the theater, Xiao Chen tried to pull his boyfriend toward the elevator, but his boyfriend pushed him away and walked to the escalator because he did not want people to see two men entangled together.

Similarly, in other public places such as the street and malls, Xiao Chen and his boyfriend consciously reject signs that could be conceived as stigma symbols. Xiao Chen said to me, "When I walk on the street with my boyfriend, I dare not be close to him. We have to walk, talk, and dress like normal men and maintain a distance from each other." When the three of us shopped in the mall, Xiao Chen bought himself and his boyfriend a set of what they called "lovers' outfits" (*qinglv zhuang*). It was the same outfit, but in different colors—one was gray and the other was white. I thought they would both look good in white. At my suggestion, both of them looked terrified and immediately said, "No, no, and no. Wearing the same color would be too obvious and ostentatious. People would start noticing us. It's better to wear different colors."

Another tongzhi couple worked at the same company where they carefully maintained a physical distance and a performance of masculinity on a daily basis. Indeed, they paid special heed not to walk close to each other or appear friendly to each other. One of them said to me, "We have to act like normal men and do business like normal men. When no one is around, we talk privately *(qiaoqiao hua)*. As soon as someone comes in, we immediately separate from each other. We dare not even give each other a simple look, let alone joke with each other."

Performing masculinity means not only carrying the self in a masculine way and sustaining a physical distance with other men but also taking on social roles as a "normal" man. Almost every tongzhi I encountered in my research had either a girlfriend or a wife and thus enjoyed the social role of a boyfriend or a husband. Some tongzhi availed themselves of websites that matched them with lesbians who were willing to form fake marriages. By entering into a fake relationship or a fake marriage *(xingshi hunyin)* with either a lesbian or a heterosexual woman, tongzhi could use it as a cover to mask their tongzhi identity and be integrated into society as a boyfriend, a husband, or a father while continuing underground sexual activities with tongzhi partners.

My interactions with the wives and girlfriends of the men in my research revealed that generally it was the women who initiated the romantic relationships and pursued the men. According to the men, they agreed to establish the relationships to conform to gendered expectations of men, even though they were not interested in the women. Some men told the women about their tongzhi identity, but most did not. Those women who were informed by the men told me that the men were either confused or had gone astray because of the adverse influences of other men. The women told me that it was only a short-term obsession, a predicament that would eventually be changed and overcome by their overwhelming love and meticulous care of the men in marriage.

Xiao Yan had been dating his girlfriend for a couple of years. He said, "I try very hard to hide it [his tongzhi identity] from my girlfriend. I dare not get piercings. I dare not put my handbag on my shoulder. My girlfriend complains that those behaviors make a guy look like a woman. I save all my normal friends' contact numbers in one software system, and all my tongzhi friends' contact numbers in another. When my tongzhi friend calls, I need to put in a password before I can accept phone calls or text messages." It so happened that one time these two software systems were not working and a text message came in without a request for a password. His girlfriend saw the message and asked him, "What's this?" Terrified of making her suspicious, he had to lie and act calm.

To many tongzhi, establishing a heterosexual family and fathering a child represent not only a performance of masculinity but also a fulfillment of social and family responsibilities. Reflecting traditional Confucian values, many tongzhi consider it selfish to only think of their own happiness and disregard social and family responsibilities (see also Miège 2009). For instance, Xiao Cheng noted, "We shouldn't be selfish. We should bear the responsibility to continue the line. We should think about our parents." In consideration of their parents, the majority of the tongzhi in my research dared not reveal their identity to them and were prepared to marry and father a child down the road. Xiao Tan said, "Of course I can never tell my parents. My father would break my leg if he knew I was this kind of person. There is no way that I would say anything to them even when I am ready to enter the casket" *(jinle guancai ye buneng shuo)*.

Tongzhi in my research reported an immense amount of fear of failing in their daily performance of masculinity and passing as a heterosexual. Indeed, they warned me not to mention or talk about the subject of tongzhi in public because it would make them feel awkward and uncomfortable. The incessant dread of being discovered and discredited put a strain on their mental state. Living in such constant fear may exact a high psychological price—"a very high level of anxiety, in living a life that can be collapsed at any moment" (Goffman 1959, 87). In China, it was estimated that 35 percent of self-identified tongzhi had felt a strong desire to commit suicide, and 9 to 13 percent had attempted suicide (X. Su 2009).

Despite what can be an intolerable strain on tongzhi's mental state, tongzhi find no other alternative but to continue their performance of masculinity in order to seek legitimacy in the dominant culture and achieve acceptance by the mainstream world. Embedded in this performance of masculinity are not only the erasure of tongzhi identity and performance of masculinity in public but also self-criticism and self-censorship in the tongzhi community.

SELF-CRITICISM

According to Goffman (1959), stigmatized individuals spatially partition their world into forbidden, civil, and back places. The first place is forbidden or out of bounds where exposure means expulsion. The second place is civil where there is an illusion of acceptance of their differences—"where persons of the individual's kind, when known to be of his kind, are carefully, and sometimes painfully, treated as if they were not disqualified for routine acceptance, when in fact they somewhat are." The third place is a back place where persons of their kind "stand exposed" and do not need to conceal their stigma (p. 81). The back place can be voluntarily or involuntarily created by these individuals themselves.

The back places for tongzhi include but are not limited to the local AIDS organizations, cruising areas in the park, tongzhi bars, tongzhi bathhouses, and online chat rooms. These places make them feel safe and reassured because only tongzhi work in the organizations, gather in those places, chat online, or are permitted entrance. At least there they do not need to worry about running into a straight person. These places also enable tongzhi to know each other personally while also keeping themselves anonymous. As illustrated in the last chapter, these places help form a community where tongzhi who share the same stigma can provide each other with moral support, advice about romantic relationships, methods to cope with their parents' pressure to marry, and the comfort of feeling "at home, at ease, accepted as a person who really is like any other normal person" (Goffman 1959, 20).

However, at the same time, in these back places, tongzhi criticize aspects of the tongzhi community that they find problematic and unsatisfying. In this section, I unpack these criticisms that target the promiscuous, overly superficial, and financially driven tongzhi community.

Almost everyone I talked to expressed their dissatisfaction with the tongzhi community's obsession with appearance. Xiao Fang said, "In the online tongzhi chat rooms, when you start chatting with someone, they first say hi and then immediately ask how big your thing [penis] is and request a video chat so that they can see your body and face." Jia said, "Among tongzhi, the first thing they ask about is the size of your penis when erect and not erect, your looks, your age, your height, your weight, your waist size, and your body shape. All of this information is about your appearance. As long as you feel good about the person's looks, you can take that person home at night. This is completely different from heterosexual relationships that prioritize interests, hobbies, tastes, and other things." They showed me online tongzhi chat rooms where it was customary to provide a formula of weight/height/waist size/penis size/dead or alive ("dead" means that the penis stays the same size despite erection, and "alive" means it changes sizes). After exchange of this information, the two parties would initiate a video chat to confirm all the size information before setting up a time and a place to hook up.

In addition to the obsession with appearance and looks, the popularity of 419 (symbolizing one-night stands), group sex, and casual sex is another pivotal criticism in the tongzhi group. I was told that online chat posts were filled with the phone numbers of tongzhi looking for 419 and group sex. (The term "419" is another appropriation of the English language, which, like the use of the term "gay," reflects tongzhi's desire to emulate the success of the Western gay movement; at the same time, it serves as a secret code allowing them to communicate with each other without revealing their homosexuality). Many tongzhi complain that almost all tongzhi relationships start with sex, go through love, and end in friendship. In a tongzhi relationship, it is almost required that partners give each other permission to have casual sex outside the relationship. Although some tongzhi couples agree to meet and engage in group sex, many tongzhi express feelings of disgust and disenchantment with the promiscuity of the tongzhi group. It seems that these criticisms really express the ambiguity felt by most tongzhi about what the mainstream regards as an illicit activity.

Complaints about the paramount role of sex in both romantic and workplace relationships proliferate in local grassroots organizations. Xiao Fang, who worked for one of the AIDS organizations, felt irate that members in his organization "slept with each other and turned the office into a hotel for casual and random sex." As he related to me, the director of his organization hired his ex-boyfriend Ben to work in the organization, and because of their sexual history, the director disregarded Ben's "unacceptable behaviors in the office."

For example, the office was furnished with a bed for employees who did not have living accommodations, and Ben often brought strangers to the bed to engage in casual sex. When Xiao Fang came to work in the morning, he was often disgusted to find condom packages in the garbage and tainted spots left on the sheets. He complained that the office no-sex policy was a farce because the director turned a blind eye to Ben's behavior in the office. He declared that the mess left in the office after sex was disrespectful to him as an employee: "The office is turned into a hotel for employees to sleep with each other. If they cleaned up their mess and hid it from me, it would be fine."

Xiao Fang also felt appalled that employees bedded each other. As he related to me, as soon as his director's boyfriend returned to his faraway hometown to see his parents during the Chinese New Year, the director immediately turned to his ex-boyfriend Ben and cohabited with him. At the same time, Ben engaged in casual sex with other tongzhi's boyfriends. Xiao Fang said to me, "I met a friend online who is currently studying in the United Kingdom. He told me that his boyfriend is studying at a university in Dalian. When we were chatting online, I told him that I caught Ben sleeping with a guy in the office and I sent him that guy's online chat room number. He immediately texted me back, saying that that online chat room number was his boyfriend's."

Although the messy sexual liaisons in his organization dismayed Xiao Fang, he also felt disheartened and resentful that, because he was considered overweight and undesirable by the tongzhi group, he had been unable to find anyone who was willing to have 419 or group sex with him. Since Xiao Fang entered the tongzhi circle, he had been confronted by the harsh reality that appearance is the determining factor for relationships or sexual encounters within it. Categorized as "fatty" by the community, he had experienced the full taste of bitterness after many painful failures in his own attempts to engage in 419 or group sex with other tongzhi. His alienation from the tongzhi group and awareness of heterosexual relationships that did not prioritize looks grew as he came to realize the emphasis put on appearance among the other tongzhi.

Other tongzhi often invoke, with deep feelings, the positive model of long-term heterosexual relationships as contrasted to fleeting and superficial tongzhi relationships. As they contend, pressure from society, family, and friends makes heterosexual relationships difficult to break, whereas the underground nature of tongzhi relationships makes them difficult to maintain. They attribute the disloyalty to the lack of social constraints and to men's nature to conquer and pursue new partners. Xiao Min said, "Heterosexual sex is holy because it's for reproduction, but tongzhi sex is just a game. To men, it's unimaginable to have sex with only one person. It's like eating one dish for one's whole life. Eventually you are fed up with it" *(ni si le)*. As many tongzhi assert, among married heterosexuals, marriage is a tool to keep society secure and stable, and both the child and the marriage preclude the couple from pursuing extramarital affairs. Among tongzhi however, such constraints are lacking, so sexual pursuits become easy and relationships became short-lived.

This self-castigation is ironic given the growing prevalence of extramarital affairs in contemporary China. In my earlier work, I studied extensively the sexual infidelities of middle-class Chinese businessmen (T. Zheng 2009a, 2009b). Romanticizing heterosexual relationships as everlasting and loyal and disparaging tongzhi relationships as transient and dishonest reflect tongzhi's disdain of the tongzhi subculture and affirmation of the mainstream culture as the ideal.

Even in the back places many tongzhi express their validation of the heterosexual norm. Indeed, they divide themselves into two groups, labeling one group as "normal" because its members are in a heterosexual marriage and the other group as "abnormal" due to their inability to marry heterosexually. During my research, many tongzhi expressed to me their yearnings to live a "normal" life through heterosexual marriage. As Xiao Pan stated, "Some guy's tongzhi-ness is not too serious *(qingdu de)*. After they marry, they can learn to be normal and lead a normal life. So these tongzhi can have a chance to change back to normal. Others however, will be abnormal their entire life." Xiao Jiang said that he belonged to the group that could not lead a normal life; hence he felt miserable because he was unable to fulfill a man's responsibilities to continue the lineage or reproduce, as ordained by society and family. Xiao Jiang and tongzhi like him lamented that others had a family to return to at the end of the day, but they would be "painfully living like a monster," destined to be old and lonely in the future. Addressing themselves as "abnormal" *(bu zhengchang)*, "pervert" *(biantai)*, "immoral," and "psychologically distorted" *(xinli jixing)*, they expressed to me their wishes to be "normal."

Indeed, the self-shame is so intense that some tongzhi even join the mainstream in reviling tongzhi in public. Xiao Han, for instance, said if one person knew his tongzhi identity, he felt the whole world knew it and despised him. He said, "Being a tongzhi is something that is so unspeakably shameful *(jianbude ren de dongxi)* that I would have no place to hide my face if it were exposed." In public he always denounced and condemned tongzhi-ness. When he was at home spending time with his relatives, one of his relatives looked at him and said, "You look like a homosexual." He immediately turned angry and responded, "What are you talking about? Are you kidding me? How can I be an abnormal pervert *(biantai)*? Do you really think I am an abnormal pervert? You really hurt me."

Yet, when the mainstream world vilified and demonized his own group, Xiao Han felt distraught because of his complicity in the victimization of himself and the group.[6] As we have seen, to prove that he was not a homosexual, he felt compelled to demean and disparage the very group of which he was a member. Goffman would have us understand his defensive response as a "direct expression of his defect" and see "both defect and response as just retribution for something he . . . did, and hence justification of the way" he was treated (Goffman 1963, 6). If self-criticism was a rescue strategy in public to ward off stigma and prejudice and seek integration into the mainstream, then self-shame in private was an internalization of the hegemony of postsocialist heteronormativity.

Tongzhi's self-criticisms also include the charge that the community is too obsessed with financial gains. As illustrated in the last chapter, local grassroots AIDS organizations not only ran a wide array of activities for tongzhi to socialize and mingle but also engaged in HIV prevention activities, HIV testing, and other HIV-related services. Although the organizations appeared activist in nature, employees of the organizations constantly complained to me that people who work there are financially driven and do not really care about the activist work on behalf of tongzhi.

According to the employees, fighting for resources and dividing up those resources are the true goals of the nationwide AIDS-related and tongzhi-related meetings they attended on behalf of their organizations. Many employees of grassroots organizations perceived the nature of the work not as activism, but as an enterprise intended to claim resources and maximize profits *(lizi dangtou)*. Complaints abounded about tongzhi's financial greed in these organizations. For instance, a director of an organization complained to me that his so-called volunteers charged a ridiculous amount of money for simple work such as filling out forms. In another organization where I volunteered, an employee, Xiao Ling, told me that many people in this line of work held a mercenary attitude and saw profit as the only goal of their work *(weili shitu)*. I was working with Xiao Ling in his organization in 2005, and two years later when I contacted Xiao Ling again, he told me that many employees had left to set up other organizations so that they could apply for money themselves to run their own projects while faking invoices for reimbursements.

Xiao Han stated that, in this line of work, everyone did it for money. "Who would do it without money? Only hypocritical people would say money is not important. Our leader embezzled a large amount of the funding." To shield his embezzlement from the funding source, the director would bring in a stack of fake invoices every month and ask the employees to sign them. Xiao Han said that he and the other employees were exhausted from faking so many different signatures on all the invoices.

A lot of the money the director embezzled, according to Xiao Han, was supposed to be awarded to each employee for every tongzhi he recruited to complete an HIV test, as well as to each tongzhi who was brought in. Xiao Han observed the director filling his own wallet with that money. At a nationwide conference, the director complained that it was too much trouble to submit invoices for every expenditure. The funding source reaffirmed that the money was not intended for him and he did not have any right to claim it. The director remained quiet but continued to have his employees sign fake signatures on fake invoices. At times, the director would tell them, "I bought these things for my personal use. Let's just say that these purchases are for work and submit these invoices."

In another grassroots organization, employees also had to sign large numbers of fake invoices every month, the reimbursements of which went into the pocket of the leader of the organization. Many tongzhi who worked in these organizations felt disenchanted and disillusioned. Some left and joined the mainstream workforce. Others remained in the organizations and treated the work only as a source of income.

CONCLUSION

In his work on hydroelectric politics in northwest Yunnan, Ralph Litzinger (2007) explores the ways in which urban-based activists there used the media and allied with transnational river activists in Southeast Asia to contest the government's large-scale hydroelectric dam project on the Nu River. Litzinger contends that this "transregional and transnational activism" was made possible by the newly gained "mobility of capital, goods, people and ideas, as well as activist connections" (284). He argues that this new form of "local, regional and transnational collective actions" to challenge the state portend real social change in the near future (299).

Whereas northwest Yunnan's activists in Litzinger's research galvanized transnational organizations to pressure the Chinese state and combat social injustice, tongzhi in my research cover up their sexual identities and fail to formulate an open-identity social activist group. Indeed, as this chapter shows, the power of postsocialist heteronormativity seeps into the everyday realities of tongzhi's life, overshadowing transnational media about gay rights, and thwarting potential collective actions. It is through tongzhi's erasure of their own identity because of their desire to be "normal" and their ambivalence toward their own group that this power of postsocialist heteronormativity predominates.

Although tongzhi congregate in cruising areas and work at local AIDS organizations, they keep their real names, home addresses, and workplace information confidential from each other. They are cautious and discreet for fear of possible blackmail or disclosure of their tongzhi identity to their family and colleagues. Relationships are usually superficial. The weak ties and lack of solidarity among them create an environment that is not conducive to organized protests.

Aspiration for membership in the dominant culture also weakens their solidarity. As illustrated, onstage, tongzhi seek legitimacy through assimilation into the dominant culture. Embedded in this assimilating process is not only the erasure of tongzhi identity but also an expressed desire to lead a "normal" life through marriage and by reviling tongzhi in public. The need to mask their tongzhi identity and pass as heterosexual in public necessitates their unwillingness to take any daring steps. Many do not frequent tongzhi bars and bathhouses for fear of endangering their anonymity. It is in the imminent danger of marginalization from the exposure that postsocialist heteronormativity deploys its power.

This yearning to be normal seems to be deeply seated, even when tongzhi appear to accept their identity. The story of the transformation of Xiao Liu's parents from rejecting to accepting his tongzhi identity is illustrative. It was broadcast on online websites, newspapers, and TV stations. Xiao Liu's parents were interviewed by multiple media venues and invited to speak at universities such as Fu Dan University in Shanghai. When the father first learned that his son was a tongzhi, he was so outraged and angry that he not only took up a knife in an attempt to kill his son but also bought a barrel of gasoline with the intent to murder the entire family by burning them. The parents gradually accepted their son and bought a house for him and his boyfriend. They not only helped take care of the tongzhi bar that their son opened, which was closed after a year and a half because of numerous police crackdowns, but also participated in tongzhi activities. They now run the first nationwide tongzhi parents' hotline to help parents accept and recognize their tongzhi children and their children's tongzhi partners. The parents were heralded by tongzhi as the father and mother of all tongzhi in China. *damn.*

Yet even in such an ideal story, the yearning to be normal is still present. Xiao Liu told me that despite all the public rhetoric by his parents in the media, from time to time, his parents still ask him, "Why can't you be normal? What's wrong with you?" With these words, he let out a helpless smile. Not long after we talked, Xiao Liu decided to leave everything behind him and traveled to the south, where he became a monk at a Buddhist temple.[7]

In most cases, self-shame and self-negation lead to an ambivalent attitude toward the group, which undercuts their collective solidarity. On the one hand, a tongzhi feels some alienation from his own group as he perceives the tongzhi community suffused with people who are unable to hide their tongzhi-ness. On the other hand, the same tongzhi also feels some alienation from the mainstream when caught in the continuous process of inventing, remembering, and keeping up with lies and new techniques of concealing information about himself. "Whether closely allied with his own kind or not, the stigmatized individual may exhibit identity ambivalence when he obtains a close sight of his own kind behaving in a stereotyped way, flamboyantly or pitifully acting out the negative attributes" (Goffman 1959, 107). In brief, he can "neither embrace his group nor let it go" (112). *lonely :(*

This ambivalence is conducive to the oscillation of "affiliation cycles" in tongzhi's identification with and participation in the tongzhi community (Goffman 1963, 38). Tongzhi feel torn between their attachment to their own group and to the mainstream world. When tongzhi's self-criticisms coalesce with their acceptance of the heteronormative discourse, it marks a decline in their identification with the tongzhi community and an increase in their identification with the mainstream. When tongzhi offer each other advice on how to cope with romantic relationships and how to fend off parents' pressure to marry, it marks an increase in their identification with the tongzhi community and a decline in their identification with the mainstream. In a nutshell, degrees of affiliation and identification with their own group and the mainstream fluctuate.

The potential consequences of collective protests also impede their actions. If the ultimate political goal of such protests is to remove stigma from the label of tongzhi, they might subject individuals to further stigmatization while only benefiting the next tongzhi generation. Engaging in collective action as tongzhi is tantamount to publicizing their stigmatized identity and leaving them vulnerable to further discrimination. Organized protests would amplify the differences between the tongzhi group and the mainstream, deepening the alienation between them and negating their day-to-day efforts to integrate into society. Moreover, as researchers have shown, in postsocialist China, the frequent use of armed police and espionage services down to the county level constitutes a formidable bulwark against organized protests (Perry and Selden 2000). For instance, the state managed to stymie attempts to organize labor resistance nationally and to isolate local protests (Davis 2000; Lee 2007). The tongzhi might pause before pursuing any attempt to organize protests on their own behalf if they considered the state's response to these recent labor protests. It is clear that any perceived threats to state authority will be dealt with harshly in China.

CHAPTER 7

Safe Sex among Men

Condoms, Promiscuity, and HIV

One hot summer afternoon, I accompanied twenty-four-year-old Ken and Ken's boyfriend Chen to the local CDC so that Ken could be tested for HIV. After the first test, Ken was asked by the physician to be tested a second time. He was then taken to a separate room for a fifteen-minute talk. Chen and I waited anxiously, worried that something was wrong. We discussed the issue and decided to search the building for a physician with whom to consult. Finding one, we asked him what would happen if our friend was found to be HIV positive. The physician said the CDC would record his name, birthplace, and current address; ask doctors in his birthplace to get in touch with him; and designate a hospital for his routine physical. The physician also underscored that our friend should be careful not to get a fever or a cold because of his compromised immune system.

After this conversation, we walked back to the waiting room, where we saw Ken exiting the room where he had been counseled. Looking distraught and despondent, Ken did not utter a single word. We did not say anything either. After we left the CDC, Ken broke the silence and said he did not want to live any more. He wanted to commit suicide. He also complained that AIDS did not have a cure, but cancer did.

By that time both Chen and I knew for sure that Ken had tested positive for HIV. While I was trying to calm Ken down by sharing my knowledge about HIV, Chen said that being Ken's boyfriend, he was certain he was positive too, because they did not use condoms in their relationship. Chen then asked if Ken had sex with his ex while they were together. Ken said yes. Chen asked how many times. Ken said he did not know. Chen said, "My God, you can't even remember how many times? So many times? Yet you never used condoms? You're so stupid! Why didn't you use condoms? Is it because you love him?" Ken said yes.

To help Ken cope with the situation, we traveled to the local AIDS NGO to ask its director for further advice. The director commented that the test result could be a false positive and suggested that Ken be tested a third time to confirm the finding. He then inquired if Chen had noncondom sex with Ken, and with an affirmative answer from Chen, he asked Chen to get tested as well. He also told Ken that he did not need to tell those he had sex with about his positive status because people were selfish beings and he just needed to worry about his own safety.

On our way back, Chen commented that he had never thought he or any of his friends would ever get AIDS. Ken said to me, "This is really unfair. I only had a couple of 419s [one-night stands] throughout the entire year. I was not promiscuous *(luan)* like others who constantly had 419s. I only did it [had sex] with people I had known for a while or with whom I had a relationship. I was not promiscuous, but I hit the target *(zhongbiao)*. Others were promiscuous but did not get it. Why me? Why did it happen to me who was not promiscuous?"

A few days later Ken told me that a man he had previously had sex with sent him a text, saying: "You have harmed me really badly." The man said he had tested HIV positive. Ken told me that he was at a loss as to what to do, because he had had sex with others while he was with Chen. After contemplating it for a while, he said he would follow the NGO director's advice and not tell any of his previous or future sexual partners about his HIV status.

When Ken visited the designated hospital for tests, he was given access to an online HIV-positive group with about fifty members. Ken came home and logged onto the online group under a fake name. Ken chatted with someone for a while and they became friends. Later on when Ken asked for that man's phone number, he was astounded to find that it was our friend Wu's number. Ken said to me, "Wu pretended so skillfully that I had no clue that he was positive!" Wu, Chen, Ken, and I had been hanging out in the park every night. Wu, like Ken, was a white-collar employee working in a local company. When AIDS NGO volunteers approached him for an HIV test in the park, Wu responded that he would get tested in the near future. "OK," he said, "I'll get tested—just a little blood—no big deal!" Neither Ken, Chen, or me had any idea that Wu had been positive a long time before we saw him make that promise to the volunteer.

In 2008, among infectious diseases, HIV was the leading cause of mortality (Meng et al. 2010). Unprotected sexual activities were reportedly common among the ten to twenty million men who were having sex with men in China (Gao and Wang 2007; Huan et al. 2013; Liu et al. 2012; Muessig et al. 2010; Wong et al. 2009). As mentioned in chapter 5, the frequency of unprotected sex was borne out in the increase in the rate of new infections through homosexual contact from 12.2 percent in 2007 to 32.5 percent in 2009 (Ren and Xing 2010; UNAIDS 2010).

Research on HIV/AIDS and other STDs has been conducted primarily from the perspective of the discipline of public health using quantitative research methods such as survey results and questionnaire responses. Categorizing certain groups as high-risk groups or high-risk populations, these researchers have used a rational choice model of human behavior that attributes high-risk behavior to personal choice and a lack of medical knowledge (Choi et al. 2003, 2004; He et al. 2006; Wang and Ross 2002; Wang et al. 2001a, 2001b; Zhang et al. 2000).

There has been little research on the social logic of tongzhi's decisions about condom use or the underlying sociocultural and political context that shapes tongzhi's risks for socially transmitted infections (STIs) and HIV. Through contextualizing tongzhi's sexual practices and condom use, this chapter fills that gap; it explores the cultural logic behind tongzhi's decision making about condom use, thereby illuminating the social mechanism that fuels the risks for HIV and STIs. My research suggests that factors such as perceptions of condoms and the nature of relationships exert as strong an influence on decision making as risk assessment. This is not to suggest that health education is unimportant, but it does indicate that education must be sensitive to the social circumstances of its beneficiaries. I argue that previous research failed to provide a means of implementing health education agendas in a socially effective way.

My research departs from the public health paradigm in asserting that the social positioning of tongzhi in a constrictive environment informs and shapes their sexual behaviors and condom use. More specifically, I reject public health researchers' mechanistic assumptions inherent in the rational choice model and argue that the sociocultural and political context in which tongzhi are embedded shapes their sexual behaviors. In so doing, I emphasize the social and cultural dimensions of disease transmission as the catalyst that produces high-risk health behaviors (Baer, Singer, and Susser 1997; Farmer 1999, 2006; Farmer, Connors, and Simmons 1996; Farmer, Lindenbaum, and Good 1993; Lindenbaum 1997, 1998; Parker 2001; Schoepf 1991, 1995, 2001, 2007; T. Zheng 2009b). I contend that a full understanding of the complexity of decision making about condom use is necessary to devise a culturally efficacious HIV intervention.

This chapter investigates the underlying complexities and nuances of tongzhi's decisions about condom use. Decisions about condom use are inextricably intertwined with the social positioning of tongzhi, which operates within the parameters of a system of power in postsocialist China[1] (Kaufman and Meyers 2006; Shao 2006; Yip 2006). Sociocultural and political factors and power relationships are the most important factors in tongzhi's decisions about condom use in the era of HIV/AIDS in postsocialist China.

POLICE HARASSMENT AND CULTURAL STIGMA

My research showed that cultural stigma and police harassment affect condom use among tongzhi. Police harassment—specifically the use of condoms as evidence that those arrested had engaged in sex work—often limits the provision of condoms at entertainment places and circumvents safe sexual practices. This practice of using condoms as evidence is in direct violation of current laws. The 2006 Law on AIDS Prevention (Wen 2006) clearly stipulates that police are not allowed to use condoms as evidence and that condoms should be provided or made accessible by business proprietors at public places. The most recent State Council 2012 Proposal (Office of State Council 2012) further stipulates that condoms should be made available at public places and that proprietors should strive to promote their use.

The police arrests and forced closure of entertainment places, which link condoms with sex work, reveal a discrepancy between current laws on paper and their implementation. I was told that several bathhouses were closed down on the charge of "providing sex work" based on the evidence that used or unused condoms were found. Some business owners were averse to condom distribution by local AIDS NGO volunteers for fear of the same charge by the police: They often prevented AIDS NGO volunteers' outreach work at their businesses. As I was told, the fear was legitimate, especially for owners who had not been able to consistently submit cash bribes to officials, because police did perform arrests, impose exorbitant fines, or close down businesses after finding used or unused condoms as evidence for sex work.[2]

Among tongzhi in my research, fear of police arrest based on the evidence of condoms is one of the factors leading to unsafe sex.[3] As discussed in chapter 4, police regularly patrol tongzhi bathhouses, bars, and parks.

During my research they closed down several local tongzhi bars and tong-zhi bathhouses and raided others—arresting, detaining, and heavily fin-ing the guests. On arrest, tongzhi were usually compliant in paying hefty fines to avoid identity disclosure and public shame. Fines and shakedowns were therefore common motives for police to vigorously pursue what was labeled as either sex work or promiscuous sexual behaviors that disrupt-ed social order. In this precarious environment, some sexual activities took place in a quick fashion in public parks or public toilets. Tongzhi who engaged in random sex in the park were so frightened by possible police patrols that they were often in too much a hurry to put on condoms.

As I have shown in the preceding chapters, a stigmatizing and hostile environment fuels tongzhi's practice of stealthy and surreptitious sex. Whereas in public they have wives and girlfriends, in private they meet in an array of venues such as online chat rooms, bathhouses, bars, and parks to engage in one-night stands (419s), threesomes (3p), or group sex *(qun pi)*. In the opening vignette of this chapter, when Ken was diagnosed as being HIV positive, he was a married man with a wife and a newborn baby. Their survival in society required that he lead a double life. To avoid loss of jobs, loss of family, loss of reputation, and social expulsion, tongzhi have no recourse but to seek out hidden places such as bathhouses to satisfy their needs.

The clandestine, secretive nature of sexual relationships and the fluid and erratic nature of romantic relationships often lead to risky sexual be-haviors. Despite the fact that they had wives or girlfriends, throughout my research tongzhi told me that they always felt lonely and sexually repressed. They felt compelled to look for random sex to release sexual pressures and receive temporary physical satisfaction. Although some did form roman-tic relationships, cultural stigma and social pressure usually made it hard to sustain them. Living a double life also often kept them from develop-ing a serious, conjugal relationship. As a result, underground, risky sexu-al behaviors to achieve instant physical gratification were often pervasive at places such as bathhouses.

Bathhouses are the ideal places for clandestine, random sex, especial-ly in winter times when it is too cold to meet in the park. The following is a description of one of the local bathhouses that I visited.

This bathhouse was located in the center of the city. My friend Ming and I arrived at the address and saw a nondescript building with no indi-cation that it was a business; there was only a long flight of cement stairs leading to the basement. The stairs were so rough and steep that I had to exercise caution walking down. The walls on both sides of the stairs were dirty and flaky, covered with graffiti. It took a while for us to reach the bottom, where we saw an entrance right in front of us leading into the bathhouse. As Ming walked through the entrance, he bumped his head on the ceiling, which was very low. He let out a loud cry of pain. We walked in.

A good-looking young man was sitting at the front desk. Behind him was printed the name of the bathhouse. Around him artificial decorations of green leaves and red flowers were hanging from the ceiling. The entrance area had cement floors and unpainted walls.

As we approached the front desk, the young man riveted his eyes on me, watching my every move and looking me up and down. Not turning his eyes elsewhere, he asked Ming if I was a woman or a man in drag (*fancuan*). Ming told him that I was a woman. He immediately responded that women were not allowed in the bathhouse. Ming requested to see the manager.

A few minutes later, the manager appeared from the back door. As soon as he saw Ming, he greeted him enthusiastically. Ming and the manager had known each other for years and were good friends. Ming explained to the manager my identity as a researcher and requested my entry into the bathhouse. He told the manager that the tongzhi in the bathhouse would simply regard me as a man in drag, a commonplace in the community. He also assured the manager that he would accompany me the entire time and that we would not cause any trouble. After his explanation and assurance, the manager allowed us to enter.

Immediately on entering the bathhouse we were surrounded by romantic music and steamy air. Men with towels covering their lower bodies were walking by. At the other end of this room was a dark room for uninhibited sex. Nothing could be seen in the dark room. Inside, there were around twenty cubes separated by curtains, with each cube having space for two people. In many of the cubes, 0s lay on the beds inside, waiting for 1s. When a 1 came in, he touched a 0's rectum and started sex. While a 1 usually touched the other's rectum to indicate that he was a 1, a 0 usually touched the other's penis to indicate that he was a 0. Group sex was also common. In the absence of liquid lubricants, it was customary for men to use saliva to help with the penetration.

Almost no one used condoms in oral sex in the bathhouse, and a number of men did not use condoms in penetrative sex. Although quantitative research shows that 30 percent of the men in bathhouses do not use condoms in penetrative sex (Beijing AIDS Institute 2012), my research suggests that the number could be higher due to self-reporting errors. My informants had seen in the bathhouses that many men who did use condoms took them off in the middle of sex. Quantitative research that relied on self-reporting could miss a significant number of these men who did engage in noncondom risky sex but thought they did not because they started out with condom-use safe sex.

Although reasons for not using condoms were diverse,[4] men in my research cited fear of police and social stigma as two of the reasons for risky sexual practices. The director of the local AIDS NGO I volunteered for encountered police raids in a bathhouse during his outreach work in 2008 and witnessed men being arrested and taken away by the police. Social stigma is also one of the main barriers in testing for HIV because it could lead to identity exposure (Choi et al. 2006). Faced with social stigma, police arrests, and an antagonistic environment, many tongzhi lack the desire to live a long life because a long life means a longer duration of social suffering and psychological pain. Many young men told me that they plan to overdose on pain medication and commit suicide when they reach the age of forty or fifty. In the words of one of my informants, "Tongzhi only live for today and don't think about tomorrow. If they catch the virus [HIV], in ten to fifteen years they'll be fine. So it doesn't matter, as they want to kill themselves down the road anyway." The careless, nonchalant attitude toward life is inexorably linked to the adverse environment that instills fear and duress in the men's lives. Indeed, according to the existing research, at least 30 percent of tongzhi ruminated about suicide (Yu 2010).[5]

Cultural stigma also hinders HIV-positive tongzhi from disclosing their HIV-positive status to sexual partners, thus exposing other tongzhi to a high risk of HIV infection. As shown in the beginning vignette, Ken was advised by the local AIDS NGO director not to publicize his positive status to his previous or future sexual partners. Ken took his advice. In his post-test sexual encounters with other men, he never revealed his status. After Ken tested positive, we also learned that Liang, a close friend of ours, had kept his positive status from us and from his sexual partners, which were many because he was into group sex. My informant Gan, an NGO volunteer, also told me of an experience he had in his outreach work. Five men who had met online had engaged in group sex without condoms. The next day three of these five men bumped into each other at the hospital designated for HIV-positive patients; they were there to have their white blood count tested. Gan was accompanying one of these three men. Seeing each other at the hospital, these three men realized that all of them were HIV positive. They felt so embarrassed that they tried to avoid each other in the hospital.

CONDOMS AND 1S AND 0S

My research showed that 1s often possess the power to decide on condom use, and if a 0 likes a 1, a 0 will comply and engage in risky sex. As illustrated in chapter 3, the identities of 1s and 0s are shaped and determined by culturally idealized masculine and feminine qualities. A 1 takes on the male role, which is associated with aggression and control, whereas a 0 takes on the female role, which is associated with passivity and submission.

In general, men in my research complained about the discomfort of condom use. I was told that because a 0's exterior [of the rectum] was tight yet the interior was loose, the condom pulled 1's penis *(bei zhuai)* and made the head of the penis feel blocked *(bei dingzhu)* by the tip of the condom. In their words, "it was just not comfortable" *(bu shufu).*

0s told me that the discomfort was especially acute during their first same-sex act. When they first entered the tongzhi circle, their rectums were tight, because they were not used to same-sex acts; condom use could exacerbate that pain. As time went by, even after they became used to same-sex acts, I was told by some 0s that condoms made them feel uncomfortable when the rectums were too dry or when they "were not in the mood" *(meijinru zhuangtai).* At those times, when friction induced pain, they would sometimes request that 1s not use condoms.

Some 1s in my research asserted that it is rare for 1s to get HIV, but it is common for 0s to do so. As they explained to me, 0s had a higher infection rate because they harbor sperm inside, suffer wounds and lacerations, and bleed from the rectum. This belief that it is difficult for 1s to be infected discouraged some 1s from wearing condoms.

Others believed that it was pure luck, not condom use, that rendered men either diseased or free of disease. If the man has good luck, whatever he does, he will not get the disease [HIV]. He could do it ten times a week without getting the disease. However, If the man has bad luck, he could do it only once in ten years but get the disease. In their words, "it was completely chance" *(dian).*

Some 1s considered condoms contrary to the essential nature of sex. Sex, as they explained, is spontaneous and impulsive. The nature of sex is antithetical to the thinking, preparations, and caution required when wearing a condom. To quote one of my informants, "Sex is an uncontrollable act of the moment. When I cannot help myself *(qingbuzijin)*, I forget about using condoms. All I want is absolute pleasure *(shuang)*. Condoms are in the way to my experience of complete pleasure *(linli jinzhi)*. I forget everything." Xiao Lin even claimed that during the time it would take to stop to put on the condom, he would "have already completed sex and obtained physical pleasure" *(you daitao de shijian yijing zuowanle)*!

In the situation where 1 strives for full physical pleasure, 0's obedience to 1 is analogous to the wife's obedience to her husband. When 0 likes 1, he is bent on doing anything to satisfy his desire, including not using a condom. This was especially true, as I was told, among 0s who have low self-esteem about their own body types and appearance. For instance, Xiao Dan, because of his weight problem, had a difficult time finding sexual partners. When he finally found a 1 for a hookup, he did everything to satisfy 1's taste and make 1 achieve his uttermost pleasure. In the process, he disregarded his own health by not using a condom.

As I was told, in a sexual encounter, 0 might ask 1 to use a condom. If 1 refused, 0 would submit if he were interested in 1. However, 0 might refuse if he was not so desirous of 1. For instance, Xiao Chen, a 0, told me, "0 usually would do anything, including not using condoms, to please the 1 he likes. However, if he doesn't like the 1, it would be a different story."

In an interview, Xiao Jen, a 0, shared with me his wish to please the 1 whom he liked: "I liked a guy I met at the park, and he took me to his apartment. During sex, I felt extreme pain—after all, it was my first sexual experience. He asked how I felt; I said I felt pleasure. He asked how much pleasure; I answered: 'As much pleasure as you feel.' In fact, the entire time I was about to die of pain. But in my mind, I wanted the 1 I liked to feel as much pleasure as possible. Oh, yes, he didn't use a condom."

Another 0, Xiao Ye, also recounted his submission to the 1 he liked in his last sexual encounter:

1: I don't have a condom—looks like we're going to do it without a condom.

XIAO YE: Not very good, right? Do you have anything *(ni youshi ma)*?

1: No, I don't have anything *(wo meishi).* Let's not use it.
XIAO YE: OK.

In this dialogue, Xiao Ye appears passive, worried about hurting 1's feelings and bent on pleasing him. Instead of asking 1 if he had any STDs or HIV, Xiao Ye softens the question by asking if 1 "has anything." Hearing 1's negative response to the question, Xiao Ye immediately submits to 1's insistence on not using a condom.

To prevent possible infections as a result of not using a condom, 0s usually resort to sitting on the toilet afterward in an effort to expunge the virus or bacteria. Xiao Han, a 0, recounted his last sexual experience to me:

> I didn't know he wasn't wearing a condom when he penetrated me. Later, as he was doing me, I touched his penis in the back, and realized he wasn't using a condom. I didn't want to continue. He strongly asserted that he wasn't going to use the condom, and continued doing me. I complied, but requested that he not ejaculate inside of me. However, he ignored my request and did ejaculate inside of me. Afterwards, I washed myself and sat on the toilet to expel the semen. I believed that if there was any virus or bacteria, it could be expelled from my body.

Although strategies such as expunging viruses from the body and examining the other party's genital areas may not be effective, 0s such as Xiao Han and Xiao Ye risk their physical health for the promise of romance and love with the men they like. Indeed, during my fieldwork, some casual sex partners did become boyfriends, with the 0s assuming the attributes and traits of a culturally compliant female to please the men they liked. Their cultural embodiment of an obedient female became a positive aspect of their identity that they hoped could be appreciated by the men they relished. In other words, their desire to be intimate and emotional with potential boyfriends exceeded their fear of disease. Acting otherwise could potentially jeopardize their opportunities to continue or develop a future relationship with the men who appealed to them. However, when the men they were with were not to their liking, they would be more assertive about condom use, considering the sex act to be casual sex without the potential for romance.

CONDOMS AND PROMISCUITY

To many men in my research, condoms signify promiscuity and lewdness. Tongzhi perceive condoms not as a means to protect against disease, but as a sign that someone is promiscuous and therefore is not desirable as a long-term partner. Condom use, instead of symbolizing responsibility and nondisease, is conceived as just the opposite—as a sign of irresponsibility, promiscuity, and even disease.

For example, my informant Xiao Sun, after chatting online with a man for a while, decided to meet him. Xiao Sun then followed his new friend to his apartment where he saw five condoms lying on a desk. Xiao Sun said to me, "As soon as I saw the condoms, I knew that he often took different men back home." Xiao Sun felt sad that he was just one of the guys being brought there. The next time when he visited his friend, he saw that there was only one condom left. The change in the number of condoms further confirmed his belief that his friend was promiscuous and often had sex with random men. The condoms on the desk, to Xiao Sun, epitomized his friend's licentiousness and promiscuity, that he was just one of many sexual partners his friend had.

Two other informants of mine, Wen and Fang, had met at the park. Wen told me that when he first saw Fang, he walked two laps around the park before summoning the courage to talk to him. Wen thought he was not as good-looking as Fang and was happily surprised by Fang's positive response. They walked to a peaceful place and talked a while. Afterward, both of them decided to go to a hotel together.

At this time, Fang suggested that Wen purchase a condom. Wen replied, "Don't worry—I've got one!" He showed Fang that he had both the lubricant and condoms ready in his pocket. Unbeknownst to Wen, Fang reacted to seeing Wen's condoms this way: "He's very promiscuous *(luan)*. Look—he's got everything [condoms] prepared wherever he goes! It means that he is looking for sex whenever he goes to a place. He's always prepared to have sex. He's a playboy with an unfaithful heart" *(hua)*.

Because men generally seek partners whom they believe to be safe and use condoms with those whom they consider unsafe (Tavory and Swidler 2009; Watkins 2004), negotiation of condom use is subject to the assessment of sexual partners, and decisions on condom use influence the development of the relationship. Two of my informants, Lan and Ming, met through an online chat room. When they had sex the first time, Ming asked Lan, "Are you promiscuous? If you're promiscuous, then use a condom. If you're not promiscuous, then you don't need to use a condom." Lan recalled, "I thought, if he isn't afraid, what am I afraid of? So I didn't use a condom." Thereafter they entered a romantic relationship. Ming continued asking Lan not to use condoms in the relationship: "You're not promiscuous, so you don't need to use it."

Lan was confronted with two choices given by his sexual partner, who later became his boyfriend. Each choice not only had a moral implication about his character, his moral being, and his health status but also had a profound effect on the development of their relationship. If Lan chose to use the condom, he would relay a message to his partner that he was promiscuous and diseased or that he did not trust his sexual partner. His condom use would undercut the possibility of forming a romantic relationship with his partner. If Lan chose not to use the condom, he would establish himself as reliable and clean. The choice would have a deep bearing on their relationship. damn

In the end, Lan chose not to use condoms to show that he was not unsafe and that he trusted his partner. This choice heightened intimacy, enhanced the seriousness of the relationship, and cemented his connection to Ming. It not only confirmed to Ming that the relationship was something special and different from others but also consolidated a subsequent romantic relationship with him. In this sense, noncondom use laid the foundation for a meaningful sexual encounter.

The association of condoms with promiscuous partners is so powerful that it shapes the ways men read each other's behaviors related to condoms and prompts men to reject their use. Men such as Ming, Fang, and Xiao Sun rely on both questions and judgment to determine who is clean and who is promiscuous. They take precautions against diseases by making questionable judgments about who is clean and who is not. The presence of condoms on the desk relayed a message to Xiao Sun that the user was unsafe, morally dubious, and untrustworthy. The fact that Wen carried condoms in his pocket everywhere suggested to Fang that Wen was always prepared to have sex, also a sign of promiscuity and unfaithfulness. Ming's question to Lan whether he was promiscuous was the fulcrum on which condom use would be decided.

In addition to these myriad judgments and outright questions, men also gauge the safety of partners in other ways before deciding whether to use a condom. My research showed that men decide that a person is "clean" if he looks handsome and clean or does not have any abnormal growth in the rectum or genital area. They will use condoms when they do not trust their sexual partners, when they believe their sexual partners have had a plethora of other sexual partners, or when they believe that their sexual partners are leading a promiscuous lifestyle. The assessment of sexual partners as promiscuous or not plays a significant part in decisions about whether and when to use condoms, and that assessment is highly influenced by their attraction to their potential partners.

In her research on young Norwegian gay men, Middelthon (2001) notes that they consider condom use a sign of their ability to control risk and a prerequisite for taking full pleasure in the sexual encounter. The absence of a condom and the fear of infection could limit their ability to fully enjoy the sexual encounter. In that context, condoms are reassuring signs that indicate the user is a reliable man who practices safe sex (Middelthon 2001). Unlike with young Norwegian men, use of condoms for some tong-zhi does not indicate to the partner that the one initiating sex is safe and disease free because he practices safe sex. Rather, use of condoms gives away to the partner that the other is sexually active, has many sexual part-ners, and is promiscuous and diseased. The partner then feels that because he is only one of many, the person initiating sex treats their sex as casual and trivial and will move on to someone else after him. In short, the part-ner does not feel valued or treasured. Using condoms, in this case, indi-cates not only the user's promiscuity but also the diminishing value of the partner, because health concerns are given prominence over emotions.

CONDOMS, FAMILIARITY, AND LOVE

In the vignette that opens the chapter, Ken stated that the reason he did not use condoms with his ex was because he loved him. In the preceding section, Lan, by not using condoms, described how he was able to begin a romantic relationship with his sexual partner. In both stories, the act of not using a condom became a symbol of love and facilitated the develop-ment of a relationship with love and intimacy.

Indeed, men in my research consistently shared stories that illustrate the association between noncondom use and romantic relationships and familiarity. My informant Xiao Fan, for instance, had sexual relations with a friend for three months. He explained to me that the relationship was purely sexual between two best friends, so they did not call each other *bf* (boyfriend). However, they thought condoms were unnecessary because they were always with the same person and they were familiar with each other. So they never used condoms during the relationship.

Although Xiao Fan and his friend did not consider their three-month sexual relationship to be a romantic one, their familiarity with each other was sufficient for them to abjure condom use. In this case they subordinated rational considerations of health to cultural understandings about familiarity and friendship. Jettisoning condoms—the vehicle against infection—was crucial in proving their mutual trust with each other and the difference in their relationship from that of a hookup with a stranger.

Another informant of mine, Xiao Meng, was thirty-eight years old when I met him. At that time, he was in a romantic relationship with twenty-four-year-old Xiao Chen. When they met in the park, Xiao Meng had already been married for ten years. They called each other *bf* (boyfriend). Having been together for a long time, Xiao Meng said they had gotten tired of each other sexually. However, because they still had feelings for each other, they continued the relationship.

Xiao Meng did not use condoms in the relationship because they had known each other for a while. In addition, he contended that his boyfriend was not the promiscuous and messy *(luanqibazao)* type, so there was no need to use condoms. His boyfriend only hooked up with wealthy men a couple of times a month, and each time he could earn a couple of hundred yuan. He himself engaged in one-night stands only several times a month. Because neither he nor his boyfriend belonged to the promiscuous and messy kind, they believed that they did not need to use condoms.

Even though Xiao Meng and his boyfriend engaged in one-night stands several times a month, and his boyfriend was also involved in commercialized sexual relationships with wealthy men, neither of them considered their behaviors as "promiscuous" or "messy." Because Xiao Meng and his boyfriend knew each other, they believed that neither of them belonged to the social category of the diseased, immoral, and devious. By categorizing each other as "not messy" and not belonging to that social group, they found no reason to use condoms. Indeed, it was familiarity and love between Xiao Meng and his boyfriend that trumped the reality that both of them conducted unsafe sexual practices. Once again, they linked condoms to unfamiliarity, moral decay, and disease (see also Kane and Mason 1992).

Stories similar to these highlight the intricate, complex ways in which condom use signals the nature of a relationship, pinpointing the symbolic link between familiarity, love, and noncondom use. This argument aligns with the existing literature on heterosexuals that demonstrates that non-condom use among steady partners may function as a sign of trust (Holland et al. 1991; Hollway 1989; Kippax et al. 1990; Willig 1995; Worth 1989). Two men who are strangers may engage in assessments and calculations of health risks and negotiate condom use. However, two men who are friends or lovers may halt such rational calculations as cold or unwarranted, despite the potential dangers they face. To cement a relationship or friendship, one may need to have emotions take precedence over emotionless calculations and caution about risks. In a love relationship, belief or trust of sexual partners can be irrational, rather than based on their sexual behaviors or social or personal characteristics. Through noncondom use, men like Xiao Meng express and enact love and trust of their partners.

As illustrated, familiarity and love are often an important basis on which men judge who is safe and who is unsafe. Because sexually transmitted diseases are often associated with moral decay and the problems of "the other" who are deviant and contaminated, men believe that their sexual partners whom they are either familiar or in love with are moral and safe (see also Kane and Mason 1992). Condom use is deemed necessary with strangers, but not with friends or lovers, because condoms signify the absence of intimacy and trust. Familiarity or a love relationship renders health risk assessments inappropriate, which are construed a sign of a loveless, emotionless relationship. In the words of one of my informants, "When you know the person, it's likely that you don't use condoms. You know that this person isn't messy (*luan*—promiscuous). If you don't know the person, you're more likely to use condoms as you don't know if this person's messy or not."

Noncondom use, inextricably linked with love and familiarity, serves as a vehicle to either establish or affirm a relationship. Because condom use is associated with promiscuity and disease (see also T. Zheng 2009b), using condoms in a loving relationship can potentially raise suspicions of disloyalty and infidelity, which runs the risk of calling into question the exclusiveness and feelings of attachment between the two parties (Holland et al. 1991; Ingham, Woodcock, and Stenner 1991; Sobo 1995).[6]

In this sense, safe sex is, ironically, unsafe, because it potentially challenges a relationship. Sobo (1995), in her study of ethnic women in

Cleveland, Ohio, reveals the social and cultural reasons underlying noncondom use in committed relationships. As Sobo (1995) illustrates, noncondom sex allowed the women to feel gratified and happy about their lives. To the women, condom use was associated with extramarital affairs and denoted nonexclusiveness, mistrust, and a failure of the relationship. Noncondom use, in contrast, conveyed trust, honesty, and commitment. Women actively employed condom-less sex to prove to themselves that their men did not stray sexually and that they were wise in judging men and selecting male partners. Noncondom use was a psychosocial strategy for the women to feel not only wise but also accomplished in achieving the American dream of faithful monogamy. Women gained status and self-esteem by presenting to others their loyal, honorable, and perfect relationships. In this sense, noncondom use was paramount in confirming the women's worth and value in a committed, stable, and monogamous conjugal relationship.

The connection between noncondom use and a caring, satisfying relationship resonates with men in my research. Men in romantic relationships or who are familiar with each other often abandon condom use to express their love, convey their trust, and enjoy intimacy with each other. Indeed, they construe noncondom use as a sign of intimacy and the stability of a relationship. As I was told, even in their relationships with their girlfriends, they never use condoms because their girlfriends ask them not to. In both the same-sex and heterosexual relationships that many men engaged in simultaneously, noncondom use constitutes a crucial indicator of the long-term, loving, and monogamous relationship.

YIN-YANG, STEAM HEAT, AND DRUGS

In addition to the earlier mentioned reasons for noncondom use, men in my research related to me other reasons such as yin-yang, steam heat, and drugs.

The men told me that condoms blocked their absorption of yin and yang during sex and thus hindered the process that benefited men's health. According to Chinese Taoist philosophy, yin is negative, dark, passive, cold, wet, and feminine, and yang is positive, bright, active, dry, hot and masculine. Yin and yang interact with each other to influence health. Sexual fluids of semen and vaginal secretions are considered sources of primordial vitality, and their exchange has the power to either augment or diminish either party's life (Furth 1992, 1994). Sex strengthens yang and replenishes yin by absorbing yin and yang from sexual partners—thereby enhancing potency, transcending body limitations, and defeating the entropy of age to achieve immortality (Furth 1994).

In classical China, men were taught to cultivate the body and strive for longevity and youthful appearance in old age through manipulations of yin and yang. Men were advised to absorb yin and replenish yang from concubines and prostitutes and use that replenishment to impregnate their wives and attain immortality. Men were also advised to boost their original Qi [energy force] by absorbing women's breast milk, saliva, and vaginal secretions. Various techniques were recommended to men to attain the utmost yin from female partners and thereby strengthen their yang and slow down the aging process. These techniques included sexual postures, choice of sex partners, and adjusting sexual practices according to seasonal changes, dates, and timing of the day. For instance, it was believed that men were able to absorb the maximal yin from female partners by retaining their penises in the women's vaginas as long as possible and appropriating the female red vital essence for themselves (Furth 1994).

My research showed that vestiges of the Taoist ideology survive and are manifested in some tongzhi's beliefs. I was told that an exchange of semen and vaginal secretions is crucial for men to bolster their own health. Condoms are an impediment that interrupt and block this exchange, hence hampering the process to cultivate the body and improve health.

One of my informants, Xiao Shan, told me,

> I have to have sex with both men and women so that it can keep my yin and yang balanced. If there's too much yang in me, I would become wild, unruly, and violent *(yeman)*. If there's too much yin in me, I would start acting like a woman. Right now I belong to the middle as I adjust them [yin and yang] well *(tiaohe de hao)*. If I have sex with a quite feminine 0 such as Lily [our friend who is a 0], it's OK. However, if he is more masculine and man-like *(yemen)*, then I'll need to have sex with a female sex worker *(xiaojie)* to balance it. This way I can take turns to absorb both yin and yang.

Like Xiao Shan, other men in my research contended that it is beneficial to their health for their flesh to touch their partners' flesh during sex.

The goal of sex is to achieve a balance between yin and yang through absorbing yin and yang from both men and women without obstacles such as condoms to impede the process. 0—a man who acted like a woman—is believed to harbor more yin than yang. The extra amount of yin is blamed for precipitating his female-like behaviors. Exchange of sexual fluids with a 0, according to Xiao Shan, would normalize the supply of yin in his body. However, exchange of sexual fluids with a man who is masculine would result in superfluous yang in his body. Copulation with a female, in this case, would yield an overabundance of yin to offset the surplus of yang. The consequential balance of yin and yang would nourish his body and buttress his health.

Although some men cite this aspect of Chinese Taoist ideology to account for their noncondom use, other men invoke parts of traditional Chinese medicine to explain why they do not use condoms in bathhouses. These men believe that heat and steam have the power to expand cells in the body, expunge toxins, and cleanse the body. In the words of Xiao Ming, "It's OK not to wear condoms in bathhouses. The heat in the bathhouses functions to purge the body of toxins. As the body swells, toxins are expelled in the process. So when you have sex there, you can't contract the AIDS virus or other diseases."

Chinese traditional medicine identifies toxins as substances that interfere with and damage bodily functions (L. Yang 2011). These toxins are said to originate from both inside and outside of the body and have accumulated and been built up in our bodies since birth. They vary from the waste products in our bodies to the polluted air we breathed in or the pesticide residuals in the food we ate. Chinese traditional medicine believes that these toxins compromise our immune system and impair our health. Hence it is crucial to eliminate them and cleanse the body through various avenues.

Traditional Chinese medicine identifies heat, steam, or sauna therapy as one of the most effective vehicles to flush toxins out of the body (L. Yang 2011). Heat or steam through sauna therapy is said to flush out toxic metals, toxic chemicals, chronic infections, and other blockages in the body. The detoxification process nourishes the skin, increases blood circulation, heightens metabolism, and relaxes tendons—ultimately slowing down the aging process, strengthening the immune system, and obstructing infiltration by viruses and bacteria into the body.

Some men in my research, as avid believers in Chinese traditional medicine, rejected condom use in bathhouses, believing that the therapeutic effect of heat and steam prevent infections. Indeed, business owners of bathhouses and sauna places avail themselves of the detoxification theory and actively advertise it in their businesses. During my visits to a few bathhouses and sauna venues, I saw the medicinal effect of heat and steam therapy described, imprinted, and engraved on the walls of steam rooms, reminding consumers of its advantages and benefits for the body.

Drug use is another factor that can lead to noncondom use. My research showed that some men injected or took soft drugs such as ketamine, ecstasy, and crystal methamphetamine, which stimulated them so much that they would abjure condom use during sex. Injection of these drugs is called "skating" *(liu bing)*. This term is used not only because the Chinese pronunciation of "skating" is similar to the pronunciation of "crystal methamphetamine," but also because the experience under the influence of the drug is as exhilarating and stimulating as skating.

Some men coax others into noncondom sex by offering them drugs so they can experience skating. While skating, as I was told, judgment is so impaired that men crave only the thrill of ejaculation. One of my informants, Xiao Lan, for instance, was offered skating by a stranger at a tongzhi bar. The skating experience was so stimulating that he stayed awake the entire night and had noncondom sex with the stranger. Another informant of mine was offered skating by a man he chatted with online. Later, my informant met with this man and his friend, and the three of them had noncondom group sex. The ecstasy experienced in skating replaced any health concerns about condom use.

CONCLUSION

Although public health epidemiological studies emphasize the importance of individual responsibility based on appropriate medical knowledge in the decision to use condoms, my research found that rational decision making was prevented by a number of political, social, and cultural factors that were enacted as structural violence (Lorway, Reza-Paul, and Pasha 2009; Nguyen 2003). Researchers define poverty, power, and social exclusion as forms of structural violence that catalyze the social vulnerability of groups and individuals (Farmer et al. 1996; Parker 2001; Parker, Easton, and Klein 2000).[7] My research showed that these political, social, and cultural factors play a critical role in shaping tongzhi's high-risk sexual behaviors and susceptibility to HIV and STIs.

Political factors such as police harassment, police arrests, and a hostile environment fuel high-risk sexual behaviors and limit condom use. As illustrated, the discrepancy between current laws and the police practice of using condoms as evidence for sex work is one of the factors leading to noncondom use. On the one hand, tongzhi seek secretive, underground sexual encounters through various routes such as online chat rooms, bathhouses, and parks to evade possible arrest and social ostracism. On the other hand, HIV-positive tongzhi feel compelled to keep their status a secret from sexual partners, once again to protect themselves from social expulsion. In so doing, they put other tongzhi at risk for HIV infection.

Sociocultural factors such as condoms being seen as symbols of promiscuity, infidelity, and the antithesis of love also curtail condom use in sexual encounters. As demonstrated in this chapter, condoms signify lewdness and promiscuity. Negotiation of condom use is subject to the assessment of sexual partners. Carrying condoms at all times and having condoms on the desk evince a person's promiscuity, untrustworthiness, and moral decay. Use of condoms also convinces the partner that the person is sexually active with many sexual partners and is possibly diseased. Other ways of judging partners' moral character also determine condom use. The association of condoms with promiscuous partners shapes the ways in which men gauge each other and hinders trust in their partners' moral character, causing them to forgo condom use. Noncondom use, in turn, enhances intimacy and paves the way for a romantic relationship.

Condom use thus defines the nature of a relationship. As shown in the chapter, the presence of familiarity and love deems condom use unnecessary and unwarranted. Intimacy, love, and friendship trump heartless, cold calculations of health risks; these emotions are expressed, displayed, and enacted through noncondom use. Because sexually transmitted diseases and HIV are often connected with immorality and deviance, friends and lovers who are moral and safe are also construed to be disease free and risk free. Whereas a request to use condoms can generate suspicions of infidelity and distrust and endanger a relationship, noncondom use is a means to seal a relationship as committed and close.

Power relationships between 1s and 0s further complicate the issue of condom use. As illustrated, 1s usually make the decision whether to use condoms. The gender dynamics between 0s as playing the female role and 1s as playing the male role bestow 1s with certain powers and prerogatives, such as making decisions about condom use. If 0 likes 1, 0 would likely defer to 1 and accept noncondom use to keep 1 happy and satisfied, in the hope of an ensuing romantic relationship. In enacting a culturally submissive femininity to please men, 0s risk their physical health for the promise of romance and love with the men they like. The desire for intimacy, in this case, trumps the desire for health. They are unwilling to put a potential romantic relationship at stake by asking their partners to use condoms. However, if they do not favor their partners, they would confront them and be assertive about condom use, because they consider it to be one-time casual sex only without the potential for romance.

Condom use is further impeded by Taoist ideology, Chinese traditional medicine, and drug use. As shown, some men believe that the yin-yang exchange through sex is enhanced without the obstacle of condoms. To them, it is beneficial to strike a balance between yin and yang through extracting yin and yang from both men and women without using condoms, which obstruct the process. Others believe that condoms are unnecessary in bathhouses because the steam heat prevents infections by viruses and bacteria. This belief originates from Chinese traditional medicine, which identifies heat, steam, or sauna therapy as one of the most efficacious conduits through which toxins can be removed and expelled from the body and encroachment of viruses or bacteria can be terminated. What results is a cleansed body with a strong immune system. In addition to these two beliefs, drug use is an impetus for noncondom use.

Through investigating tongzhi's sexual behaviors related to condoms and examining the micro-processes through which condoms were not used, this chapter has explored the underlying structural factors that increased tongzhi's vulnerability to HIV and STI transmission. As shown, these structural factors impinge on and shape the decision-making process of tongzhi, which in turn, has repercussions on their bodies and health.

Maybe Not Marriage

A Future Free of the Closet

Xiao Lin, one of my key informants, was twenty-five years old. Both his parents and grandparents were waiting for him to get married and give birth to a son, because his brother's wife had just had a girl. The pressure on his shoulders was so heavy that he felt as though he was carrying all his family members' expectations everywhere he went.

Xiao Lin had a girlfriend but had been putting off proposing to her, even though his girlfriend had been proactive in pushing the relationship further. Several times when we were together, she sent him text messages asking him to cohabit with her. She also told him about other guys who said that they loved her—a strategy to make him feel a sense of urgency. To which Xiao Lin responded, "If you like them, go ahead and be with them." His girlfriend complained, "Why can't you be a bit jealous?"

Xiao Lin asked me what he should do because he did not like her at all. He also said his girlfriend was jealous of me, suspecting that he was interested in me and that I was the one who got in the way of their relationship. He had to reassure her that it was not the case.

Faced with his girlfriend's proposal, Xiao Lin was in a dilemma. He told me that his conscience told him not to marry her because he would be eaten up by feelings of guilt, as he was not able to give her the kind of happiness that she deserved from a heterosexual husband as time went by. Yet at the same time, his sense of family responsibilities overshadowed his conscience and urged him to marry her. Wrestling between the conflicting responsibilities toward her and toward his parents, Xiao Lin felt the only way out of this heart-wrenching situation was to put off his decision, which he did.

Tired of waiting indefinitely, his girlfriend called his parents, telling them that she suspected their son was a homosexual. That phone call made his parents so upset and so hurt that both felt sick and were hospitalized for two months.

Before receiving that phone call, Xiao Lin's parents had been asking him why he was not married. His father said to him, "You are already twenty-five years old. How come you're still not married? What's wrong?" His mother also asked him, "What kind of woman do you want? Don't be too particular about who's going to be your future wife. As long as there's someone, you should go ahead and get married." To these questions and admonishments, he always responded that he did not have a good job, nor had he yet purchased an apartment. A good job and an apartment, as he told his parents, were prerequisites for a marriage.

After his parents were hospitalized, his mother called him; part of their anguished conversation is shown next:

MOTHER: What's homosexuality?

XIAO LIN: I'm not a homosexual. Don't listen to her nonsense.

MOTHER: How do you correct it? If you have it, do correct it.

XIAO LIN: OK, if I have it, I'll correct it.

MOTHER: How shameful it is to have this kind of malady *(mao bing)*! What're you going to do with your life having this malady?

XIAO LIN: Don't imagine things, ma.

MOTHER: Long time ago your brother mentioned that he felt you weren't normal. He felt you had an illness. Is there any medicine for this illness?

XIAO LIN: [silent]

MOTHER: We're worried about you. As long as you're not married, we're worried.

XIAO LIN: Let's stop talking about this, ma.

MOTHER: Do you have a girl you like?

XIAO LIN: No.

MOTHER: Marry Hua [his girlfriend] then. You're so old! Wouldn't it be great to get married? You'll have someone to cook for you and wash clothes for you. Then we'll no longer need to worry about you. Otherwise who'll take care of you? You'll feel so great with marriage—why don't you marry?

XIAO LIN: It's OK as long as I am happy, right?

MOTHER: If you don't correct it, you'll harm your family as well as other people. We're afraid that you do have the illness. That [illness] is not good for you.

XIAO LIN: Ma, I assure you that I'll definitely get married.

Every time he saw the worried looks of his parents, Xiao Lin said he was on the verge of crying. Seeing his parents suffer from worrying about him broke his heart. To fulfill his filial responsibility (Ikels 2004; Miège 2009), Xiao Lin said to me that he would marry his girlfriend when he reached thirty and then would find a boyfriend after marriage. That would satisfy his parents, his girlfriend, and his own needs. He lamented that he would spend much of his life with the wrong person, whom he did not love. He also felt deeply guilty toward his girlfriend because he knew that he would ignore her psychologically and physically in the marriage, which could be unbearable for her.

Like Xiao Lin, many tongzhi around the age of twenty-five feel the pressure to marry. However, they are able to put it off with the excuse that they lack a decent job or an apartment. However, when tongzhi hit the age of thirty, they are perceived in a different light. Considered as adults, they are expected to have financial independence and to establish a family. Failure to meet these social expectations invites increasing suspicion and mounting derision and disdain.

Today in China, researchers (L. Nan 2012) estimate that more than 90 percent of male tongzhi will marry heterosexual women or female tongzhi. The term "sham marriage" *(xingshi hunyin)* is used to describe a legal marriage between a male and female tongzhi for mutual benefit. A proliferation of sham marriage dating websites for male tongzhi to meet female tongzhi and set up marriages indicates its popularity. The purpose of a sham marriage is to satisfy the demands of families, relatives, and society, while enabling the partners to continue engaging in same-sex relationships. Seamless as the plan is, couples often find themselves embroiled in conflicts springing from financial and emotional involvements with parents and relatives, such as arguments about the costs of family visits and responsibilities for caring for elderly parents.

Although some tongzhi choose sham marriages, the majority of tongzhi in my research, such as Xiao Lin, either had already married heterosexual women or were going to marry their heterosexual girlfriends while continuing to engage in same-sex relationships. Almost all the wives of tongzhi in my research were unaware of their husbands' sexual orientation; the few who did know were firm believers that their husbands would change. In China, it is estimated that sixteen million wives of tongzhi *(tong qi)* are currently living in "loveless" and "sexless" marriages (F. Xing 2012). Some tongzhi in my research related to me that they had never had sex with their wives. Recent research has shown that wives of tongzhi often suffer physically and psychologically in such marriages: One woman who was married to her husband for forty years never had sex, and it was not until she was sixty-seven years old that she learned that her husband was a tongzhi; a woman in a nine-year marriage had never experienced a kiss or a hug from her tongzhi husband and was surviving on antidepressants to cope with her loneliness (F. Xing 2012, 107).

A recent suicide of a wife of a tongzhi drew much attention in the media. In 2012, Hongling Luo, a thirty-one-year-old professor at Sichuan University who held a Ph.D., jumped off a thirteen-story apartment building to end her life as the wife of a tongzhi, dying instantaneously (B. Gu 2012). It was reported that before her marriage, her husband had lied to her, telling her that his sexual orientation was bisexual, which she believed. After marriage, her husband suddenly turned cold toward her. He was seldom home and rarely had sex with her. Feeling distraught, Luo confronted him and asked if he was indeed a tongzhi. To her question, he insisted that he was bisexual and that he married her because he loved her. He also rejected her request for divorce. Once again, Luo trusted him. It was reported that, since their marriage, Luo had been supplying him with half of her own monthly salary because he was unemployed. Afraid that half of her monthly salary was not enough for him, Luo also handed him her savings bank account and never asked him how he spent the money. A year later, Luo looked at his smartphone log and discovered he had been engaging in same-sex liaisons since their wedding. It showed that he had been using the iPhone she bought him to contact men, using the money she gave him to buy his male lovers presents, and engaging in video-chat sex with men in the apartment she rented. Yet her husband again rejected her requests for divorce. Falling into a depression, she was put on antidepressants. Before her suicide, she wrote this on Twitter: "If possible, I indeed hope one day same-sex marriage can be implemented in China. That way, even though we are unable to change some people's selfish nature, maybe it can avoid many tragedies?"

Sincere as Luo's plea for same-sex marriage was, tongzhi told me that, even if same-sex marriage were legalized in China, they would not marry their male lovers. Online blogs echoed this sentiment; for example, one read, "Honestly, should our country pass same-sex marriage laws and allow same-sex marriages, most tongzhi would not come out of the closet" (F. Xing 2012, 213). Choosing heterosexual marriage because of pressure from parents and society, however, has not only led to suffering and pain for their wives but also created guilt and misery among the tongzhi themselves. Many tongzhi in my research, for instance, not only suffer daily gnawing guilt toward their wives but also suffer the distressing tension of living double lives. As a result, as mentioned earlier, it was estimated that 35 percent of self-identified tongzhi have felt a strong desire to commit suicide and that 9 to 13 percent had attempted suicide (X. Su 2009).

In 2008, twenty-eight-year-old tongzhi novelist Nan Kang, learning that his lover of seven years had married a woman, committed suicide by throwing himself into the Xiang River. In 2013, another tongzhi, Sun Moyang, a twenty-nine-year-old graduate of Zhejiang University, committed suicide by jumping off a twenty-one-story apartment building. His tongzhi identity was accidentally discovered by his mother when she accessed his computer, at which point he was compelled to come out of the closet. His mother attempted to change his tongzhi identity by spending every single night interrogating, instructing, and educating him. Seeing that it did not work, she then galvanized all the relatives to join the battle. Thereafter, every day of his life was filled with numerous phone calls and visits from his relatives, who swore at him, criticized him, and admonished him. Faced with mounting intolerable pressure, he launched into a nine-day hunger strike. However, the hunger strike had no impact on his family's attitude toward him. He finally chose suicide and ended his life.

Statistically, more tongzhi than wives of tongzhi have committed suicide. However, media coverage of and social reactions to the suicide of tongzhi pale immensely in comparison with those to the suicide of wives of tongzhi. Of the three incidents just described, the suicide of Luo, a wife of a tongzhi, received nationwide mainstream media coverage through vehicles such as movies, TV shows, magazines, newspapers, and major news websites. However, the two tongzhis' suicides only received media attention from tongzhi-related websites. The little media coverage of tongzhi suicide has had little impact on society as a whole.

In contrast, the suicide of Luo incited an uproar in society. Online comments expressed indignant resentment toward the "deceitful, selfish and callous" tongzhi and a sympathy for the "kind, innocent, and gentle" wives of tongzhi (Qing 2013). Indeed, the suicide of Luo caused such a stir that the Beijing People's Court and several Sichuan lawyers recommended three changes to the marriage law (Haifu Li 2013; Y. Zi 2013). The first change is to render revocable a marriage between a heterosexual person and a tongzhi who has concealed his or her same-sex orientation before marriage; the current law stipulates a lack of emotional connections between two parties as the benchmark for divorce. The next two changes concern financial arrangements—allocating little or none of the communal possessions to the tongzhi who "has viciously concealed his/her same-sex orientation and deceived the other party into marriage" and stipulating that, in the event of the death of the heterosexual party as a result of the deceit, the dead party's relatives have the right to demand financial compensation from the tongzhi (Haifu Li 2013; Y. Zi 2013). Indeed, Luo's parents did sue Luo's tongzhi husband in court, demanding financial compensation of 650,000 yuan.

Like the Beijing People's Court and these Sichuan lawyers, society in general has accorded to wives of tongzhi an overwhelming amount of sympathy and support. Whereas wives of tongzhi are referred to as "innocent victims," tongzhi are depicted as selfish perpetrators pursuing their own goals at the expense of their wives' happiness (Bian 2012). In the current social milieu of consistent heteronormativity and the recent unprecedented social support of wives of tongzhi, tongzhi lose both ways: They are not only pressured by society and parents to marry heterosexually but also are condemned, denounced, and possibly sued in court for doing so. Faced with even more obstacles and antagonism, tongzhi are forced to find a way to adapt to this increasingly more hostile environment.

In linking sexuality with state power, socioeconomics, and cultural practices, this book demonstrates that the Chinese tongzhi are caught in a constant tension and paradox—both contesting and embracing normality to negotiate and carve out a legitimate space for themselves in the rapid social and economic transformations taking place in postsocialist China. As we have seen, liberalization after the Maoist era created a space for tongzhi in China, albeit not a comfortable space. Whereas decriminalization has made it somewhat safer to be a tongzhi, the arbitrary actions of the police and the power of continuing social prohibitions and cultural constraints make it difficult for tongzhi to live their lives openly. In fact, tongzhi are often forced to lead double lives, conforming outwardly to social norms while covertly rebelling and living as tongzhi. Unlike in the West where, since the Stonewall movement, gays have asserted their right to practice a gay lifestyle, in China, tongzhi adopt the dominant moral ideal of heterosexuality and aspire to membership in the dominant culture; in so doing, they recognize their own marginal status and are reluctant to engage the state and society in asserting their sexual rights.

This has resulted in a schizophrenic existence that is not only personally frustrating but also dangerous, particularly with regard to HIV/AIDS and other sexually transmitted diseases. On the one hand, tongzhi conform to social norms and cultural constraints by entering heterosexual marriages and pursuing material wealth as a means of avoiding stigma and becoming "normal" postsocialist subjects; however, what I call "economic normalization" falls short of a political strategy because it perpetuates a market personhood rather than a political subject pursuing recognition of same-sex-attracted people's rights. On the other hand, tongzhi rebel against social norms by covertly living tongzhi lives under the cover of either heterosexual or sham marriages and by appropriating the mainstream discourse to refute and defy social prejudice and resignify tongzhi-ness. As members of a marginalized population, in their struggle for both social survival and individual happiness, their conformity and rebellion paradoxically undercut the goals they aspire to reach, perpetuate social prejudice against them, and thwart the activism they purport to do.

I began my fieldwork with several key questions in mind. Most basically, what is the situation of male homosexuals in postsocialist China, and what is their attitude toward their own condition? More specifically, what is their approach to social and political activism? What is their vulnerability to sexually transmitted diseases, and how do they navigate this danger? Answering the most general of these questions required opening the door to their perception of their own condition/lifestyle as a necessary first step to understanding their approach to society, politics, and disease.

This book makes a major contribution to the study of tongzhi in several ways. My study was conducted in Dalian in northeast China, an area where this kind of research has never been conducted before; it thereby contributes to the overall picture of the changing anthropology of homosexuality in this large and diverse country.

This book rejects the theory of "Western homogenization" by suggesting that the activism of Chinese tongzhi does not follow the pattern established in the West, in which gay men have organized politically and insisted on their place in the social and political mainstream. In contrast, Chinese tongzhi are reluctant to come out of the closet and to demand rec-

ognition of their sexual orientation as normal. They are active collaborators with the state, rather than antagonistic opponents of the state. Their
aspiration to be part of the dominant culture and their ambivalence toward their own group weaken their collective solidarity. There is a conflict between their desire to emulate the global and their subservience to
the local.

This book makes a contribution in illuminating the intersection
between gender, sexuality, and the nation in postsocialist China. On the
one hand, it demonstrates the ways in which distinctive gender roles are
considered crucial in safeguarding the security of the nation in postsocialist China. More specifically, it shows how gender is used to control
sexuality and how a strong manhood and proper male gender roles are
deemed critical in reviving and strengthening the nation in the rapid
social and economic transformations taking place in postsocialist
China. Homosexuality is considered a peril to the security of the nation
because it reflects powerlessness and inferiority, reminiscent of the colonial past when China was defeated by the colonizing West and plagued by
its image as the Sick Man of East Asia.

On the other hand, this book affirms that the 1 and 0 identities are
formed as a result of the local cultural system and economic and social
transformations in the postsocialist era. Unlike Western gay identities that
obscure gender and accentuate sexuality, gender difference is pivotal
to tongzhi's identities: 1s and 0s differ from each other as two different
gendered identities, rather than assuming a common identity based on
the same sexual orientation.

This book accentuates the role gender plays in constructing same-sex
identities and foregrounds a new cultural system of gender and power that
underlies tongzhi's sexuality. It shows how 1s and 0s create a new, alternative hegemonic gender system through reworking and reconfiguring the
heterosexual norms in innovative ways. As a result of 1s' and 0s' paradoxical conformity to and subversion of the heterosexual norm, the alternative hegemonic gender system is in constant flux, undergoing continuous
negotiations, contentions, and challenges that render it both repressive and
liberating.

This book also highlights the impact of social class, economic wealth,
and political ideology on same-sex identities, sexual practices, and career
choices in an increasingly stratified postsocialist China. Eschewing the
monolithic, unified model of Chinese tongzhi, this book links sexuality

with class, socioeconomics, and politics through highlighting the internal differences in the tongzhi population and the ways in which diverse sexual practices and identities are shaped by and enact hierarchies of social class, economic stratification, and political orientation.

More specifically, on the one hand, this book illustrates the ways in which the rift created by class results in a community replete with conflict and dissent in a society with increasing social inequalities. On the other hand, it demonstrates how tongzhi's embrace of the neoliberal ideology not only perpetuates and solidifies state power contingent on consumerism but also reproduces and normalizes the dominant state ideology that good state subjects are heterosexuals driven by economic interests.

This book makes a major contribution to queer studies not only through a grounded study of tongzhi's lived experiences but also by emphasizing the politics of difference and providing a political economic analysis of sexuality. It demystifies a unitary, monolithic category of Chinese tongzhi who share a universal experience in same-sex behaviors. It demonstrates that Chinese tongzhi are a multilayered group with variegated and disparate experiences, shaped by hierarchies of social class and economic differences in a socially stratified postsocialist society.

Through shedding light on the ways in which sexual practices are informed by and perpetuate social inequality, economic stratification, and the legitimacy of the Chinese state, the political economic analysis of sexuality in the book highlights the relationships between state polity, socioeconomics, and cultural practices.

This book provides an alternative to the public health paradigm in the study of HIV/AIDS and explores the ways in which diseases are social processes shaped by social relations and cultural factors. Debunking public health studies' emphasis on individual responsibility predicated on accurate medical knowledge, this book illustrates the ways in which rational decision making is curtailed by political, social, and cultural factors that are enacted as structural violence.

More specially, this book unravels the linkage between decisions about condom use and the social positioning of tongzhi within a system of power in postsocialist China. It demonstrates the ways in which political factors such as police harassment, police arrests, and a hostile environment fuel high-risk sexual behaviors and circumvent condom use. As a result of the incongruity between current laws and police practice, tongzhi have sought clandestine, underground sexual encounters to avoid possible arrest and social ostracism. Sociocultural factors such as power relationships between 1s and 0s and the symbol of condoms as promiscuity, infidelity, and the antithesis of love also cripple condom use in sexual encounters.

Through investigating the underlying complexities and micro-processes of decisions about condom use, this book pinpoints the kind of structural factors that increase tongzhi's vulnerability to HIV and STI transmission. It contributes not only to the development of HIV/AIDS research and intervention policies but also to anthropological inquiries on sexuality, gender, and HIV/AIDS.

I want to end this book on a positive note. Recent reports have shown that more tongzhi are beginning to stand up and claim their sexual rights in big cities such as Beijing, Shanghai, and Guangzhou. In Beijing, for instance, a tongzhi couple broadcast their wedding live via Twitter, although it was disrupted by the son of one of the couple who smashed the tables and drove away the guests (Han 2013). In Shanghai, lawyer Zhou Dan (2009) came out of the closet and has written books on the topic of tongzhi. In Guangzhou, about one hundred family members of tongzhi appealed for legalization of same-sex marriage in a public letter (Han 2013). In 2014, a male tongzhi, Xiao Zhen, filed a lawsuit in a Beijing court against both a Chongqing therapy clinic for its claimed cures for homosexuality and the major search engine company in China—Baidu Company—for its dissemination of advertisements for cures for homosexuality. Xiao Zhen claimed that he was guaranteed a cure for his homosexuality by a clinic with a payment of 30,000 yuan. The first hour-long treatment cost 500 yuan and involved electric shock of his body on sexual arousal. Later he decided to sue both the clinic and the search engine company, demanding an apology and a compensation fee of 14,299 yuan to cover the financial loss and psychological damage he suffered. This lawsuit, which was scheduled to open in a Beijing court on July 31, 2014, was the first legal case in China that involved a therapy clinic's claim to cure homosexuality. During the investigation, the Beijing People's Court discovered that the therapist in the therapy center had falsified his certificate as an advanced therapist. The verification process proved that his certificate was fake. The court also declared that the shock therapy is beyond the purview of psychological therapy and that homosexuality is not a mental illness. However, the court rejected Xiao Zhen's charges against the therapy center for the psychological damage and the search engine company for the dissemination of advertisements for the cure of homosexuality. In the verdict released on December 19, 2014, the court ruled that the therapy center apologize to Xiao Zhen on its website homepage for forty-eight hours and pay 3,500 yuan to Xiao Zhen to cover his financial loss (L. Zhou 2014). Both Xiao Zhen and his lawyer believe that this lawsuit had a positive impact on the change of public opinions on homosexuality and on the protection of tongzhi rights (W. Du 2015). Reports such as these show that, although the path is a difficult one, at the end of the path there is a gleam of hope.

Acknowledgments

I would like to extend my sincere thanks to all the tongzhi, money boys, tongzhi bar and tongzhi bathhouse owners, and local people who shared with me their experiences, thoughts, and feelings. Without their support and contributions, conducting the fieldwork for this book would have been impossible.

Over the years of my research and writing, I became greatly indebted to my professors, colleagues, and friends. I owe special thanks to my advisors at Yale—Helen Siu, Deborah Davis, William W. Kelly, and Harold W. Scheffler—for their generous mentorship and supportive encouragement of my professional development both during my study there and after I graduated: Without their support I would not be where I am today. My advisors always had a great deal of faith in me and offered me helpful professional advice. Professor Helen Siu invited me to Yale to deliver talks about parts of the book and provided invaluable feedback on the material, and Professors Deborah Davis, William Kelly, and Harold Scheffler sent me articles and materials related to Chinese tongzhi and Western homosexuality. Their generous mentorship, continuous inspiration, and precious advice have shaped who I am today as an anthropologist and a scholar. I thank them for having taught me, supported me, and encouraged me more than they could realize, for which I am forever grateful.

I also thank my professor, mentor, and friend Jack Wortman for being a constant source of intellectual and emotional support. He has consistently mentored me in every aspect of my life—emotional, professional, and academic. Whenever I need someone to talk to, he is always there for me. He not only listens to me patiently but also provides me with helpful and wise advice on problems and issues in my life. Over the years I have relied on his advice to resolve both professional and emotional issues. His wealth of knowledge and his insights have helped me understand myself, my cultural roots, and my internal conflicts. I thank him for guiding me through my life. I also thank him for being a tireless and generous advisor who not only has helped me correct the language of this book but also has inspired and stimulated me intellectually. My debts to him and to my advisors can never be repaid.

My thanks also go to Marc Blecher and Ralph Litzinger for their continuous inspiration, unwavering support, and encouraging, incisive, and constructive comments that have helped improve the quality of the book. I thank Marc Blecher for sending me relevant materials on the subject matter as food for thought. I am grateful to Ralph Litzinger for keeping me updated on stimulating issues happening in China.

Thank you to Erik Bitterbaum, president of SUNY Cortland, for his continuous support of my professional development and for his help in providing me grants to present parts of the book at various conferences. Thank you to Provost Mark Prus, Dean Bruce Mattingly, and Amy Henderson-Harr, director of Research and Sponsored Programs, for their unwavering support. Amy Henderson-Harr has helped me not only to prepare grant applications but also to secure IRB approval for all my research projects, without which I would not have been able to complete the fieldwork and finish the manuscript on time. My thanks also go to my dear and respected colleagues, Herbert Haines and Sharon Steadman, for their generous encouragement and support over the years.

My special gratitude goes to Vanessa Fong, Mayfair Yang, Federico Varese, Jun Jing, Wanning Sun, Mark Selden, Xin Liu, Douglas Feldman, Susan Brownell, Susan Dewey, and Gregory Mitchell for their consistent support and encouragement. I thank Robin McNeal, Connie Shemo, Dorothy Ko, Douglas Feldman, and Susan Dewey for having invited me to Cornell University, SUNY Plattsburgh, Columbia University, SUNY Brockport, and the University of Wyoming for campus-wide talks on this project. My thanks also go to Dave Grass, who has not only supported me emotionally but also has filled my life with happiness and joy. His curiosity about life and his role as a stimulating intellectual interlocutor have helped me better understand American culture.

I would like to extend my special gratitude to my editor at the University of Minnesota Press, Jason Weidemann, for his enthusiasm about my project, for his careful reading of my manuscript, for his comments that have helped improve the manuscript, and for his expertise and support in guiding me through the book preparation, review, contract, and production process.

Notes

Introduction

1. The featherball, called a JianZi in Chinese, typically has three to five feathers fixed into a rubber sole or plastic disc. There are two forms of playing featherball. The first is called Circle-Kick: three to eight players use upward kicks to keep the featherball from touching the ground. The second is called Duel Kick: two players kick the featherball like shooting soccer balls to each other. During play, various parts of the body are used; mostly the feet. The objective is to keep the featherball from touching the ground.

2. Tze-lan Deborah Sang, in her study of the Chinese translation of Western sexology terms in Republican China during 1912 and 1949, contends that the characters of *tongxing'ai* (same-sex love) were adopted and borrowed from the Japanese *doseiai*, which was coined in Japan by Japanese intellectuals in their translation of European sexology at the end of the Meiji (1868–1912) and early Taisho (1912–25) periods (Sang 2003, 278). However, agreeing that the Chinese discourse on homosexuality narrowed after the 1920s, Sang argues that *tongxing'ai* was still not signified as an identity or personhood, but as "an intersubjective rapport" (2003, 297, 292–93).

3. The Gay and Lesbian Awakening Day, created by the Taiwan Institute of Gay and Lesbian Studies in 1995, also became a hallmark day for Chinese gays and lesbians to gather and advocate against social prejudice on campus.

4. Organizations also observed the international project of the AIDS Memorial Quilt. They published online information about the 1983 AIDS Memory Wall, explaining that its purpose was to commemorate the dead and respect every life on earth. They prepared their own memory walls lit by candles, naming the motif of this event in China as "witnessing"—striving to mobilize society to partake in AIDS prevention work. Through participations in these international events, grassroots organizations hoped to increase public concern about AIDS issues and support for AIDS-infected individuals.

   On International AIDS Day, some organizations staged events to encourage people to eat with and hug AIDS patients. This represented yet another strategy to disseminate knowledge about AIDS and dismantle prejudice against AIDS patients (X. Ma 2010; Yifei Zhang 2010).

   Some organizations invited American and French activists and scholars to discuss issues concerning community building and gay relationships. Others staged events such as gay film festivals and queer literature forums, inviting authors and translators of queer-related books to discuss queer literature and the queer voice in current discourse.

5. Mayfair Yang observes that, although post-Mao China is the fastest-growing capitalist economy in the world, those who study gender must pay heed to the state as well as to the market economy, because the state still plays the most important role in Chinese economic development. Yang quotes Manuel Castells in asserting that the post-Mao state still regards "economic development . . . not [as] a goal but a means" to state power (1999, 36).

6. Boellstorff (2007b) points out that the terms "lesbian and gay" miss many categories such as bisexual and transgendered and that the term "LGBT" also misses categories such as intersexed.

7. This viewpoint aligns with poststructuralists' and 1980s feminists' arguments that the politics of difference is constructed by the interwoven configurations of race, ethnicity, and class (Kristeva 1982; Lacan 1968; Moore 1994). Feminists in the 1980s debunked the fixed category of "women" and illuminated the social hierarchies and differences within the category produced by race, class, ethnicity, nationality, and sexual orientation (Alcoff 1988). For instance, Pratt (1984) highlights how her skin color and lesbian identity led to her different experiences as a woman. Allison (1994) narrates how her low-class identity as "white trash" and her denigrated identity as a lesbian shaped her experiences as a woman. Stoler (1995) differentiates the experiences of European women from those of the Javanese women who were exploited to maintain the Dutch colonial regime. Mohanty (1991) also points to a hierarchy between white women and women of color in which Western feminists portray women of color as subjugated and sexual objects, without a voice and in the shadow.

8. Mitchell (2011) discusses how affluent Western gay sex tourists rationalize their tourism as beneficial for the economy and the gay rights movement. Chasin (2001) unravels the relationship between a new niche market and gay and lesbian consumers emerging in the United States and examines the intersections between the gay and lesbian press, advertising, boycotting, and the mechanisms of funding the gay rights movement. Halperin and Traub (2010) critique homonormativity as a proud social identity and explore shame and embarrassment in gay history as a new way to examine lesbian and gay culture. Warner (1999, 22) interrogates the ideal image of homosexuals that excludes "queers, sluts, prostitutes, *trannies,* club crawlers, and other lowlifes." Puar (2007) interrogates homonormative ideologies that reproduce social inequalities along the lines of race, class, and nation. Dean (2009) examines non-homonormative behaviors of abandoning condom use and embracing unprotected sex of barebacking to illuminate this non-homonormative subculture.

9. At the time of this writing, six yuan = one U.S. dollar.

10. This personal story previously appeared in T. Zheng (2013).

1. A Cultural History of Same-Sex Desire in China

1. *Nanfeng* (male-mode or male-love) was another very common expression to depict homoerotic relationships.
2. It was recounted that in the Northern Dynasties (A.D. 386–535), a famous scholar Chen Chien, because of his large penis, caused intercourse to be very painful for his sexual partner—the sixteen-year-old boy Zi Gao (Ruan 1991). To endure the pain, Zi Gao bit on the bed covers so hard that he destroyed the covers. When asked if he was hurt, Zi Gao responded, "My body is yours. I am loved by your love; even death is worthy."
3. In the story, Wen Di was extremely generous toward his male favorite Deng Tung, who became the richest man of his time. Deng Tung displayed his loyalty toward Wen Di by using his mouth to dry out Wen Di's skin blister. Wen Di dressed down his son for his son's refusal to do it. After his son took over the reign, he retaliated against Deng Tung, who died of starvation.
4. The literati displayed far more interest in homoerotic pleasure than the other social classes (C. Wu 2004). Throughout Chinese history, it was the literati who exerted an influential impact on the trends of cultural fashion.
5. During the late Ming Dynasty, the life path of young boy actors and catamites was usually a pitiful one. These young boys were feminized and treated as sexual objects for the enjoyment and fantasies of elite men (C. Wu 2004). Because the dominating man in the homoerotic relationships enjoyed prestige and higher social status, the dominated one, like women, was relegated to a lower status and social stigma (Sommer 2002). Unlike women who could be taken as concubines, catamites faced rejection as they aged. Although a few managed to purchase an official position, most during the late Ming era were abandoned. Stories depicted them as beggars who usually died at an early age (C. Wu 2004).
6. E. Chou (1971) showed that the male lover Ho Shen of Emperor Chien Lung was rewarded with the role of prime minister.
7. These guidebooks were called in Chinese *hua pu* (flower book), with the connotation of "prostitute book." They appeared during the Ming Dynasty, became extremely popular during the Qianlong (1735–96) period, and lasted throughout the end of the nineteenth century (C. Wu 2004).
8. Translated Western authors included Magnus Hirschfeld, Havelock Ellis, Iwan Bloch, Richard von Krafft-Ebing, Sigmund Freud, and Edward Carpenter (Kang 2009). Through citations and translations, the medical framework of normality versus deviation in Ellis's theory became the hegemonic view in China during the 1920s (Kang 2009; Sang 2003).
9. Information in this paragraph is drawn from Cui Zi'en's speech at the screening of his movie *To Tongzhi* at Cornell University on October 26. Please also see Y. Yang (2009).

10. Lydia Liu (1993) demonstrates that the creation of the feminine third-person pronoun "ta" opened a new space to discuss gender power relationships.

11. Foucault (1978, 112) theorized a transformation from an "alliance"—"a system of marriage, of fixation and development of kinship ties, of transmission of names and possessions"—to sexuality that was based on biological difference.

2. Popular Perceptions of Homosexuality in Postsocialist China

1. Bourdieu and Margolis have argued that the power to name, to define a social identity and to ascribe characteristics to that identity is a political power. The "rights and needs" of particular individuals are established through the naturalized differences between the identities (cited in Moore 1994).

2. Gupta and Ferguson (1997, 13) point out that the subject is not simply affected by changing schemes of categorization and discourses of difference but is actually constituted or interpellated by them.

3. It was reported that the transmission rate in Guangzhou was more than 8 percent in 2009 and the national transmission rate was 4.9 percent in 2008 (F. Chen 2008; N. Ji 2011).

4. The article pointed out that 60 percent of homosexuals in an investigation did not use condoms during sex (M. You 2005). AIDS experts, as reported, contended that it was extremely difficult to ask homosexuals to have a stable sexual partner or to reduce sexual partners. In addition, highly frequent unprotected oral sex also exposed this group to a high risk of getting HIV.

5. It was said that homosexuality epitomized society's moral degradation because it could lead to tolerance of group sex, incest, human-animal sex, and the extinction of humans (C. Qiao 2005). It was claimed that ancient Rome was destroyed by such moral degradation (C. Qiao 2005). Homosexuality was also described as despicable (S. Bao 2008). In another media article (M. Da 2008), it was said that to a normal Chinese person, homosexuality was a disease: "When they refuse to be cured, they are no different from those who run around soccer playground naked, attached to a tag that reads 'proclivity to expose sexual organs.'"

6. A media article related a story that a man from Qingdao was refused medical care by local doctors beause of his homosexual identity. The man said that the doctor cared for many prostitutes and drug users but not him. The doctor said to him, "Aren't you ashamed of yourself? What are your kind of people going to do in society?" He knelt down in front of the doctor seeking help, but the doctor refused (Chai 2005).

7. The adults were urged to look for the antidote: "What you need to remember is that corrections take a long time. So you must have sufficient psychological preparation and exert continuous efforts" (H. Wu 2011).

8. It was said that the Doppler machine was imported to help identify the reasons for problems in sexual functioning.

9. At a homosexual bar, Zhang befriended a man who arranged for him to work in his company and live in his home. Zhang later on found that he had a new boyfriend, so Zhang quarreled with him. As a result, Zhang was fired and asked to move out. Zhang opened his door with a duplicate key and stole his computer and printer and asked for compensation of 8,000 yuan for a break-up fee.

10. One story described a new residential community in Wenzhou in which scores of "mysterious," well-dressed men entered and exited a suite (X. Lan 2006). The police raided the suite one night and discovered that it was a homosexual club where prostitution took place. Forty members took saunas in the living room and then lay on the sofa resting and watching TV. If they liked other members, they would pay 30–60 yuan and enter a suite. The report cited law professor Zhang Jinsong, who said that homosexual clubs seriously damaged social morality (X. Lan 2006). Another story related a skirmish between a woman and her boyfriend that disclosed the crime of her boyfriend who had paid a male prostitute he met online for sex (M. Liu 2005). In the last story, it was reported that homosexual websites were filled with photos of male prostitutes and sexual transactions they helped to arrange (N. Zheng 2003). Through investigation, the reporter noted that 80 percent of the men in the online chat room were engaging in sexual transactions.

11. "Fake women" is a role created by Japanese ACG (animation, comics, and games).

12. A Japanese movie, *Born for Myself,* recounted a story of a man with "a gender impediment" who was in love with his boyfriend and, after painful struggles, decided to go through a transgendered surgery (J. Xia 2010). Chongqing counselor Hu Hui told the reporter that this movie had a negative impact on kids by encouraging transgender identification.

13. This article attributes homosexuality to sexual liberation and material desires.

14. Lu Tu, the man who came out to reporters at a newspaper agency (Zhuang 2008), pointed out that many homosexual students could not find a job appropriate for them because of their feminine image.

15. Luo (2010) defined the future mainstream society as a society with a sound legal system, a masculine and militaristic spirit, and a patriotic and heroic sentiment. Without a strong military, the country can never be a strong nation: "A country is not strong until we retrieve the land neighbor countries have plundered from us." Luo reminded people that Communist Party founding generals sacrificed their lives for this land and this kind of militaristic spirit should be advocated.

16. The report stated that "the initiator was originally silent about the rampant fake-women disaster, but was dismayed at the sight of several fake-women high school students and finally decided to act" (Chong 2010).

17. Commercial interests were blamed for pushing the disappearance of manly traits. Articles pointed out that many men worked in "women's professions" such as stylists and makeup specialists. This, according to a Chongqing counselor, provided fecund soil for fake women (J. Xia 2010). Other authors contended that the phenomenon was a result of the profit-driven consumer society where fake women became stars to earn profits (P. Wang 2012).

18. Sun Yunxiao (2009) points out that boys' grades were lower, boys' advantages were not advanced, and boy's development was not guided.

19. Yifei Mu (2012) states that feminized education starts in nurseries and it is too late to start saving the boys in junior high. The seriously unbalanced gender ratio of teachers facilitates the cultivation of boys who lack manhood.

20. Authors claimed that another source was family education (Lu 2012).

21. Yifei Mu (2012) points out that parents dote on boys, following them everywhere until they scream in terror at the sight of a roach. These boys, according to the author, can only be tender leaves in green houses and will easily degrade into fake women.

22. Sun Yunxiao (2009) points out that boys need the discipline and supervision from fathers to learn how to be a man.

23. It was said that he liked to feel protected by other males and did not like females. He was ostracized for acting like a woman (D. He 2012).

24. It was noted that a boy would yearn for a masculine man and would therefore assume a female role in a homosexual relationship. Having a weak father leads to the boy's mistaken gender identification, and the imperfect mother affects the boy's understanding of the opposite sex: Such setbacks led the boy to pursue same-sex partners (D. He 2012).

25. Li and Wang (1992) point out that many homosexual men could get along with older women but are unable to relate to young and beautiful women because they feel in awe of these women.

26. Li and Wang (1992) contend that the reason that the youngest son tended to be a homosexual is because he usually did not like boys' activities that were risky and wild. It is difficult for a loner boy to relate to other boys.

27. In a media article (Lun 2005), a female homosexual, because of poor child-rearing experiences, self-identified as a male and was repulsed by her female identity and sexual organs.

28. The psychologist categorized her conduct as gender confusion because she felt disgusted by her female gender and female sex organs and emulated male dress codes (Wo 2006).

29. It was said that the father or mother's extramarital affairs would lead to the child's hatred of women or men (Zhuang 2008). In addition, extramarital affairs, same-sex sexual harassment, extreme curiosity, weak fathers and dominant mothers, and parents' neglect could also cause the child's homosexuality.

A media story told of a homosexual whose mother died young and he grew up with his father (M. Yi 2001). At the age of thirteen, he was sexually harassed by a grown-up male neighbor. That experience made him not interested in women and only interested in men.

30. Dr. Kong noted that many visitors were parents (Zhuang 2008).

31. It was noted that children would consider homosexuality normal and therefore join the homosexual group (Shen 2007).

32. Lu was married and tried every means to force himself to change, but was not able to do so. Later he divorced. In this report, Lu revealed that after he married and had a child, he was afraid that his child was also a homosexual (Zhuang 2008).

33. Haijiao Pan (2009) contends that the lack of resistance to making same-sex friends led children to transplant their emotional needs to same-sex friends and mistake themselves as homosexuals.

34. Others argued that adversity education to train boys' tenacity and perseverance should be instilled in boys too (Lu 2012).

35. Commentators also argued that more male teachers should be teaching in nursery schools (D. Gu 2012).

36. In China, schools are usually given a number to name them.

3. The 1s and the 0s

1. Herdt (1994) depicts the initiation rituals in the Sambia Highland wherein boys offer fellatio to older men and ingest their semen through a ritual cycle to enter the social identity of manhood. It is believed that semen is finite and that boys have to continue ingesting semen to build enough storage for reproduction when they reach the age to marry.

2. Chapter 2 is an example of how the meanings of same-sex practices were shaped and dictated by the local cultural contexts in the diverse eras in Chinese history.

3. Sinnott (2004) also depicts that *toms* and *dees* in female same-sex relationships in Thailand do not share a common identity, but are distinguished from each other by their gender difference.

4. Let me emphasize that these discriminatory comments about women were made by same-sex-attracted men in my research. As noted, they were a testament to their gender ideology characterized by gender asymmetry and gender hierarchy.

5. Carillo (1999) finds that Mexican culture marks distinct masculine traits from feminine traits. As he states, the vast majority of Mexicans believes that gay men, especially those in working-class communities, are feminine. Caceres and Rosasco (1999) also contend that some working-class gay men exhibit traditional feminine roles. Klein (1999) discusses that in Brazil, *travestis* transform their bodies to meet the ideal standards of femininity.

6. The *Hijras* community in India offers another example of such a population (Hall and O'Donovan 1996).

7. It is important to note that despite his boyfriend's financial support of him, Xiao Sun did not harbor any love or passion for his boyfriend.

8. Such stories were ubiquitous throughout my fieldwork. It is impossible to cite even a fraction of the stories I have gathered from the fieldwork. Here I listed four representative ones.

9. Ogasawara (1998) discusses what she calls the "informal power" wielded by office ladies on their male superiors at a major Tokyo bank office. She argues that women's power in the workplace is neither coincidental nor transient, but inscribed in the structures of workplace male dominance. This research complicates the simplistic and monolithic approach of oppressed women and powerful men.

10. For this kind of resistance, please also see Scott (1990) and Hall and O'Donovan (1996). Hall and O'Donovan portray how the marginalized Banaras *Hijras* in India subvert the gender asymmetry within their society (i.e., by appropriating it for their own benefit. They manipulate the socially constructed cultural and ideological meanings embedded in the Hindi linguistic gender forms to maintain their solidarity, assert their social identity (female forms), and attain a "distance" and "emphatic power" (male forms).

11. Interviews with male clients in karaoke bars reveal an internalization of culturally prescribed sex roles in their sexual beliefs (T. Zheng 2009b). More specifically, men believe that they are driven by biologically spontaneous, natural, and overpowering sexual desires that are intrinsic to men. Although they agree that sexual desires can be pernicious and destructive to society, they argue that sexual desires should not be controlled because they are natural. Interviews with women, however, show that women define sex as a culmination of affections and love rather than as fulfilling natural sexual desires.

12. I have been in close contact with both of them since 2006.

13. Moore (1994, 82) has argued that the resistance does not need to be "discursive, coherent or conscious." She contends that if one cannot resist outside the dominant discourse or structure, one can at least displace oneself within it.

14. Butler (1993) argues that this "theatrical agency" makes legible the weakness and instabilities of the heterosexual normative. She points out that social constructs of sex necessitate repeated citations and perpetual efforts to enforce the norms. The very fact that this reiteration is necessary indicates that the norms are incomplete and unstable. As Butler states, "It is the *instabilities*, the possibilities for rematerialization, opened up by this process that mark one domain in which the force of the regulatory law can be turned against itself to spawn rearticulations that call into question the hegemonic force" (2). This instability, as Butler contends, will eventually lead to the "crisis" of the production of the norms (10).

4. The Normal Postsocialist Subject

1. Ogasawara (1998), in her work on male superiors and female office workers, argues similarly that power imposes constraints and limits, whereas disadvantage can provide opportunities.
2. Chinese tongzhi have translated the English term "out of closet" directly into Chinese.
3. According to Xiao Liu, the leader is thirty-eight years old.
4. Pollak (1986) discussed similar practices among gay men in Germany. He believed that most gay men lived a life in which emotions were separated from sexual activity.
5. In Shenzhen, permanent "citizens" hold local urban household registration cards, known as "blue cards," and the intermediary category between permanent and temporary residence is categorized as the "blue chop," introduced in 1995 (Wong and Huen 1998, cited in Kipnis 1998).
6. Such inequality has not been reduced despite the gradually changing household registration system. In the late 1980s, some provinces started selling "blue cards" or "blue seals" to migrant workers. This intermediary category between the permanent and temporary residence was created during the national austerity drive (1988–91) when migrants were desperately seeking protection from expulsion and local governments were desperately raising their own development funds (Wong and Huen 1998; Woon 1999).
7. See Davis 1995; Honig 1992; Kipnis 1998; Jiwo Ng 1998; H. Yan 2008.
8. Money boys usually move around from job to job to protect themselves and to gain more clients. Research on money boys in South China supports their mobile nature (Kong 2011b).

5. Organizing against HIV in China

1. Work units here include companies, agencies, and organizations.
2. In addition to tongzhi, the English term "gay" is often used to denote same-sex identity. Some of my respondents indicated to me that because this English term was not well known by ordinary Chinese, using it was a way to disguise their sexual identity. My respondents also perceived Western gay men as having achieved much greater progress, evidenced by the Stonewall movement and legalized gay marriage (see also D. Murray 2000).
3. This label disruption can also be found in the early gay movement in the United States. In his research on U.S. AIDS activism, Gamson (1989, 1995) argues that gay activists used societal labels to dispute them and used their abnormality and expressions of gay identity to challenge the process by which this identity was and is defined.

4. These statistic have been quoted by many gay-related magazines, e-mail lists, and websites. *Our Voice Newsletter* is a bimonthly publication on issues related to the gay community, HIV-positive community, and the MSM grassroots organizations. This publication is sponsored by the Ford Foundation and run by the Chinese AIDS Infected Community.

5. HIV/AIDS prevention work in NGOs generally includes but is not limited to health consultation, blood testing, outreach to bathhouses and entertainment places to hand out condoms and education booklets, peer education, health training, and hotline consultation.

6. In the NGOs for which I volunteered, every employee and every volunteer were tongzhi.

7. The clinic charges 2,010 yuan up front and 200 yuan for each therapy session.

8. MSM is the expression suggested by U.S. health authorities at the end of the 1990s.

9. Chinese National Day is observed each year to commemorate the founding date of the People's Republic of China in 1949 by the Chinese Community Party.

6. Embracing the Heterosexual Norm

1. Goffman (1963, 19) asserts that a stigmatized person exhibits a split between virtual and actual identity, and this split can fragment the person's social identity, cutting the person off from society and from him- or herself.

2. Goffman (1959, 99) asserts that people who pass need to maintain distance with "normals" to avoid slip-ups.

3. To control or guide others' impression, as Goffman states (1963), a person usually needs to change his or her appearance and manner.

4. This "with" relationship can potentially communicate social information about a person: "To be 'with' someone is to arrive at a social occasion in his company, walk with him down a street, be a member of his party in a restaurant, and so forth. The issue is that in certain circumstances the social identity of those an individual is with can be used as a source of information concerning his own social identity, the assumption being that he is what the others are" (Goffman 1953, 47).

5. The Chinese Valentine's Day falls on July 7 in the lunar calendar when, according to the legend, goddess Zhi Nu can reunite with her earthly lover Niu Lang.

6. Goffman asserts, "He will suffer feelings of disloyalty and self-contempt when he cannot take action against 'offensive' remarks made by members of the category he is passing into against the category he is passing out of—especially when he himself finds it dangerous to refrain from joining in this vilification" (1959, 87).

7. Based on his life story, Xiao Liu's novel, titled *Tragic Story of Boys in Dalian*, was published on tongzhi websites and heralded as "classical." It is an intense love story between two men who were forced by their parents to marry women. After their

separation, their untold sorrow and agony grew unbearable. A year later when they finally met again, one of them committed suicide in front of his lover. His lover, having then lost the will to live, told the police that he was the killer. He was then executed. On request, they were buried together. Xiao Liu wrote, "Since we are not allowed to love each other alive, let us be together after death!"

7. Safe Sex among Men

1. Research has shown that China's epidemic is closely associated with social and economic inequality, especially in the realms of gender, rural-urban residence, and poverty. For instance, in rural China, China's twenty-year underinvestment in rural health has taken a toll on urban unemployed and rural migrants in the city (Saich 2000). It has also resulted in poor-quality public medical care and inadequate health personnel and facilities in rural areas (Yip 2006, 186).

2. In Hangzhou, for instance, media reports about the closedown of a tongzhi bathhouse highlighted used condoms in both photos and videos to indicate the association between sex work and condoms (Junyong Wang 2008).

3. My research finding is corroborated by the research conducted by the Beijing AIDS Institute (2012).

4. For instance, men in their fifties told me that they had never used condoms their entire lives and that condoms made them lose their erection.

5. It is important to recognize how attitudes toward suicide in China differ from attitudes in the West. In the West, it is common to refer to suicide as "an act of cowardice." In China, it is often considered an honorable solution to a difficult dilemma.

6. Condom use, by placing the self or the partner in the unsafe, promiscuous category, can potentially damage mutual trust in the relationship. Whereas noncondom use makes the men feel that their relationships are committed, close, and intact, condom use can jeopardize a loving relationship by posing threats and attacking the foundation—trust—of a romantic relationship.

7. As Parker notes, risks of AIDS "can never be fully understood without examining the importance of issues such as 'class,' 'race' or 'ethnicity' and the other multiple forms through which different societies organize systems of social inequality and structure the possibilities for social interaction along or across lines of social difference" (Parker et al. 2001, 169).

Bibliography

Adam, Barry. 1986. "Age, Structure, and Sexuality: Reflections on the Anthropological Evidence on Homosexual Relations." In *Anthropology and Homosexual Behavior*, ed. Evelyn Blackwood, 19–33. New York: Haworth.

Ai, Wen. 2007. "Tanfang Taiyuan Tongxinglian Quan Shenghuo, Nanxing Longxiong Chuan Nvzhuang Miyou" (Among Taiyuan homosexual group, men have breast augmentation and wear women's clothes). *Shanxi Xinwen Wang* (Shanxi News), March 27, 3.

Alcoff, Linda. 1988. "Cultural Feminism vs. Poststructuralism: The Identity Crisis in Feminist Theory." *Signs* 13, no. 3: 405–36.

Alford, Lacey. 2010. *The Great Firewall of China: An Evaluation of Internet Censorship in China*. Düsseldorf: VDM Verlag Dr. Müller.

Allison, Dorothy. 1994. *Skin: Talking about Sex, Class, and Literature*. Ann Arbor, MI: Firebrand Books.

Altman, Dennis. 1996a. "On Global Queering." *Australian Humanities Review*, July 2. http://www.australianhumanitiesreview.org/archive/Issue-July-1996/altman.html.

———. 1996b. "Rupture or Continuity? The Internationalisation of Gay Identities." *Social Text* 14, no. 3: 77–94.

———. 1997. "Global Gaze/Global Gays." *GLQ: A Journal of Gay and Lesbian Studies* 3: 417–36.

An, Ed. 2011. "China's HIV/AIDS-Infected Population Estimated at 780,000." *Xinhua Wang* (Xinhua Net), November 29. http://news.xinhuanet.com/english2010/china/2011-11/29/c_131277694.htm.

Anagnost, Ann. 2004. "The Corporeal Politics of Quality (suzhi)." *Public Culture* 16, no. 2: 189–208.

Anderson, Benedict. 1983. *Imagined Communities: Reflections on the Origin and Spread of Nationalism*. London: Verso.

Appadurai, Arjun. 1996. *Modernity at Large: Cultural Dimensions of Globalization*. Minneapolis: University of Minnesota Press.

Baer, Hans A., Merrill Singer, and Ida Susser. 1997. *Medical Anthropology and the World System*. Westport, Conn.: Bergin & Garvey.

Bai, Mu. 2001. "Zhongguo Tongxinglian Diaocha Baogao" (A report of Chinese homosexuals). *Baimu Yiyao* (Baimu Medicine), October 4. http://www.100md.com/Html/Dir0/11/80/65.htm.

Baidu. 2006. "Zhuanzai Wenzhang" (Posted articles). *Baidu Wang* (Baidu Net), February 20. http://tieba.baidu.com/f?kz=84791566.

Bao, Daniel. 1993. "Invertidos Sexuales, Tortilleras, and Maricas Machos: The Construction of Homosexuality in Buenos Aires, Argentina, 1900–1950." *Journal of Homosexuality* 24, no. 3/4: 183–219.

Bao, Hongwei. 2010. "'We Who Feel Differently': LGBTQ Identity and Politics in China." The University of Sydney, June 14, 1–9. http://wewhofeeldifferently.info /files/WWFD_Hongwei_Bao.pdf.

Bao, Shi. 2008. "Tongxinglian—Ni Youshenmo Zhide Jiaoxiao De" (Homosexuals—what are you yelling about?). *Tianya Shequ* (Skyline Community), September 24. http://www.tianya.cn/publicforum/content/free/1/1432137 .shtml.

Barlow, Tani. 1994. "Theorizing Woman: Funu, Guojia, Jiating." In *Body, Subject and Power in China*, ed. Angela Zito and Tani E. Barlow, 253–90. Chicago: University of Chicago Press.

Beemyn, Brett, ed. 2013. *Creating a Place for Ourselves: Lesbian, Gay, and Bisexual Community Histories*. New York: Routledge.

Beijing AIDS Institute, ed. 2012. *Tongzhi Yulechangsuo de Anquantao Shiyong Qingkuang* (Condom use at tongzhi entertainment places). Beijing: Beijing AIDS Institute.

Besnier, Niko. 1993. "Polynesian Gender Liminality through Space and Time." In *Third Sex, Third Gender: Beyond Sexual Dimorphism in Culture and History*, ed. Gilbert Herdt, 285–328. New York: Zone Books.

———. 2002. "Transgenderism, Locality, and the Miss Galaxy Beauty Pageant in Tonga." *American Ethnologist* 29, no. 3: 534–66.

Bian, Zhe. 2012. "Tongqi Bi Tongzhi Geng Yinggai Bei Guan Ai" (Wives of tongzhi should be more cared for than tongzhi). *Sohu Xinwen* (Sohu News), July 5, 946. http://news.sohu.com/s2012/dianji-946.

Bing, Shui. 2006. "Jilu: Yigetongxinglian Aizibing Ganranzhe de Shengcun Zhuangtai" (Record of a homosexual AIDS patient's existence). *Meiri Shangbao* (Daily Commercial Newspaper), September 3, 4.

Blackwood, Evelyn. 1998. "Tombois in West Sumatra: Constructing Masculinity and Erotic Desire." *Cultural Anthropology* 13, no. 4: 491–521.

———. 2005. "Gender Transgression in Colonial and Postcolonial Indonesia." *Journal of Asian Studies* 64, no. 4: 849–80.

Blackwood, Evelyn, and Saskia Wieringa, eds. 1999. *Female Desires: Same-Sex Relations and Transgender Practices across Cultures*. New York: Columbia University Press.

Bo, Shi. 2012. "Ta Guandian: Tongxinglian Shuobaile Jiushi Xinli Biantai" (His opinion: homosexuals are perverts). *301 Jiankang Wang* (301 Health Net), October 12. http://sex.301jk.com/xxl/nxxxl/201009/196261.html.

Bo, Si. 2012. "Congxiao Yufang Tongxinglian" (Preventing homosexuality from childhood). *Yanyuan Bosi Xinli Zixun Zhongxin* (Yanyuan Bosi Counseling Center), August 9. http://www.pkuboss.com/CN/xinlizixun_1001.html.

Boellstorff, Tom. 1999. "The Perfect Path: Gay Men, Marriage, Indonesia." *GLQ: Journal of Gay and Lesbian Studies* 5, no. 4: 475–510.

———. 2004. "Zines and Zones of Desire: Mass-Mediated Love, National Romance, and Sexual Citizenship in Gay Indonesia." *Journal of Asian Studies* 63, no. 2: 367–402.

———. 2005. *The Gay Archipelago: Sexuality and Nation in Indonesia*. Princeton, N.J.: Princeton University Press.

———. 2007a. *A Coincidence of Desires: Anthropology, Queer Studies, Indonesia*. Durham, N.C.: Duke University Press.

———. 2007b. "Queer Studies in the House of Anthropology." *Annual Review of Anthropology* 36: 17–35.

Boudieu, Pierre. 1977. *Outline of a Theory of Practice*. Cambridge: Cambridge University Press.

———. 1990. *The Logic of Practice*. Cambridge: Polity Press.

Bradley, Kym. 2013. "(Re)presentations of (Hetero)sexualized Gender in *Two and a Half Men*: A Content Analysis." *Journal of Gender Studies* 22, no. 2: 221–26.

Brook, Timothy, and B. Michael Frolic. 1997. *Civil Society in China*. London: M. E. Sharpe.

Brown, Wendy. 2005. *Edgework: Critical Essays on Knowledge and Politics*. Princeton, N.J.: Princeton University Press.

Brownell, Susan. 1995. *Training the Body for China: Sports in the Moral Order of the People's Republic*. Chicago: University of Chicago Press.

Buiten, Denise, and Kammila Naidoo. 2013. "Constructions and Representations of Masculinity in South Africa's Tabloid Press: Reflections on Discursive Tensions in the *Sunday Sun*." *Communication: South African Journal for Communication Theory and Research* 39, no. 2: 194–209.

Bullough, Vern L. 1976. *Sexual Variance in Society and History*. New York: Wiley.

Butler, Judith. 1990. *Gender Trouble: Feminism and the Subversion of Identity*. New York: Routledge.

———. 1993. *Bodies That Matter: On the Discursive Limits of "Sex."* New York: Routledge.

Caceres, Carlos F., and Ana Maria Rosasco. 1999. "The Margin Has Many Sides: Diversity among Gay and Homosexually Active Men in Lima." *Culture, Health & Sexuality* 1, no. 3: 261–75.

Carillo, Hector. 1999. "Cultural Change, Hybridity and Male Homosexuality in Mexico." *Culture, Health & Sexuality* 1, no. 3: 223–38.

Carrier, Joseph. 1985. "Mexican Male Bisexuality." *Journal of Homosexuality* 11, no. 1/2: 75–85.

Casey, M. Boyden, ed. 2013. *Internet Censorship and Freedom in China: Policies and Concerns*. New York: Nova Science.

Chai, Jing. 2005. "Tongxinglian Ye You Ai, Shengming Benshen Bingwu Xiuchi" (Homosexuals have love, life itself has no shame). *39 Wang* (39 Net), August 22. http://www.39.net/aids/tongxing/xinli/125902.html.

Chamberlain, Heath B. 1993. "On the Search for Civil Society in China." *Modern China* 19, no. 2: 199–215.

Chan, Anita. 1993. "Revolution or Corporatism? Workers and Trade Unions in Post-Mao China." *Australian Journal of Chinese Affairs* (January 29, 1993): 31–61.

———. 1996. "The Changing Ruling Elite and Political Opposition in China." In *Political Oppositions in Industrializing Asia*, ed. Garry Rodan, 161–87. London: Routledge, 1996.

———. 1998. "Labor Standards and Human Rights: The Case of Chinese Workers under Market Socialism." *Human Rights Quarterly* 20, no. 4 (1998): 886–904.

———. 2001. *China's Workers under Assault: The Exploitation of Labor in a Globalizing Economy (Asia and the Pacific)*. New York: East Gate Books.

Chan, Anita, and Robert A. Senser. 1997. "China's Troubled Workers." *Foreign Affairs* 76: 104–17.

Chan, Kam Wing. 2010. "The Household Registration System and Migrant Labor in China: Notes on a Debate." *Population and Development Review* 36, no. 2 (June): 357–64.

Chan, Kam Wing, and Will Buckingham. 2008. "Is China Abolishing the *Hukou* System?" *China Quarterly* 195 (September): 582–606.

Chasin, Alexandra. 2001. *Selling Out: The Gay and Lesbian Movement Goes to Market*. New York: Palgrave Macmillan.

Chen, Feng. 2008. "Diaocha Faxian Zhongguo Nantongxinglian Aizibing Ganranlv Da 4.9%" (The AIDS transmission rate is 4.9 percent among male homosexuals in the survey). *Nanfang Ribao* (Nanfang Daily Newspaper), December 3, 4.

Chen, Liyong. 2003. *Feichang Gushi—Zhongguo Tongxinglian Qinggan Shilu* (Extraordinary stories: True stories of Chinese homosexual love). Beijing: Zhongguo Sanxia Publishing House.

Choi, Kyung-Hee, David Gibson, Lei Han, and Yaqi Guo. 2004. "High Levels of Unprotected Sex with Men and Women among Men Who Have Sex with Men: A Potential Bridge of HIV Transmission in Beijing, China." *AIDS Education and Prevention* 16, no. 1: 19–30.

Choi, Kyung-Hee, Hui Liu, Yaqi Guo, Lei Han, and Jeffrey S. Mandel. 2006. "Lack of HIV Testing and Awareness of HIV Infection among Men Who Have Sex with Men, Beijing, China." *AIDS Education and Prevention* 18, no. 1: 33–45.

Choi, Kyung-Hee, Hui Liu, Yaqi Guo, Lei Han, Jeffrey S. Mandel, and George W. Rutherford. 2003. "Emerging HIV-1 Epidemic in China in Men Who Have Sex with Men." *Lancet* 361, no. 9375: 2125–26.

Chong, Qing. 2010. "Weiniang Dangdao Wanchuwei? Chongqing Fanweiniang Lianmeng: Huanhui Yangguang Hao Erlang" (Fake women playing out of bounds? Anti-fake-women league in Chongqing calling for real men). *Shidai Xinbao* (Times Newspaper), July 5, 11.

Chou, Eric. 1971. *The Dragon and the Phoenix: The Book of Chinese Love and Sex*. New York: Arbor House.

Chou, Wah-shan. 2000. *Tongzhi: Politics of Same-Sex Eroticism in Chinese Societies*. New York: Haworth Press.

Christiansen, Flemming. 1990. "*Hu Kou* in China." *Issues and Studies* 26, no. 4: 23–42.

Cohen, Lawrence. 1995. "The Pleasures of Castration: The Postoperative Status of Hijras, Jankhas, and Academics." In *Sexual Nature/Sexual Culture*, ed. Paul Abramson and Steven Pinkerton, 276–304. Chicago: University of Chicago Press.

Cohen, Myron. 1993. "Cultural and Political Inventions in Modern China: The Case of the Chinese 'Peasant.' " *Daedalus* (Spring): 151–70.

Collison, David, and Hearn, Jeff. 2005. "Men and Masculinities in Work, Organizations, and Management." In *The Sage Handbook of Men and Masculinities*, ed. Cornell Raewyn, Jeff Hearn, and Michael Kimmel, 289–310. London: Sage.

Coltrane, Scott. 1994. "Theorizing Masculinities in Contemporary Social Science." In *Theorizing Masculinities*, ed. Harry Brod and Michael Kaufman, 39–60. Thousand Oaks, CA: Sage.

Connell, Raewyn. W. 1995. *Masculinities*. Berkeley: University of California Press.

Courtenay, Will H. 2000. "Constructions of Masculinity and Their Influence on Men's Well-Being: A Theory of Gender and Health." *Social Science & Medicine* 50: 1385–1401.

Cui, Jie, and Xiao, Shuijin. 2012. "Nanjing 'Zhengqi Ba' Zuzhi Nanqingnian Maiyin An" (Nanjing 'Zhengqi Bar' organized male youth prostitution). *Jiancha Ribao* (Jiancha Daily), February 7, 4.

Cunningham, Sheryl, David Domke, Kevin Coe, Anna Fahey, and Nancy Van Leuven. 2013. "Accruing Masculinity Capital: Dominant and Hegemonic Masculinities in the 2004 Political Conventions." *Men and Masculinities* 16, no. 5: 499–516.

Currier, Ashley. 2012. *Out in Africa: LGBT Organizing in Namibia and South Africa*. Minneapolis: University of Minnesota Press.

Da, Lin. 2006. "Bandao Chenbao Fabu Qishi Tongxinglian de Wenzhang, Dalian Lianhe Xinli Zhensuo Shoulian Qiancai Pohuai Tongzhi" (*Baodao Morning Daily* publishing prejudiced articles against gays, Dalian Lianhe Psychology clinic accumulating money and damaging gays). *Gay Online Email List*, February 17.

———. 2010. "Some Gay Men's Self-Uncleanness Causes Increase of Social Prejudice." *Gay Online Email List*, September 28.

Da, Ming. 2008. "Tongxinglian, Qingbuyao Zai Wangluo Youxi Li Chuxian" (Homosexuals, please do not appear in Internet games). *Baidu Wang* (Baidu Net), September 25. http://q.yesky.com/thread-17546824-1-1.html.

Dai, Xiao. 2008. "Xiaoyuan Tongzhi Suxingri" (Campus gay awakening day). *Gay Online Email List,* December 2.

Dalian Metropolitan City Government. 2009. "Dalian Hukou Zhengce Document" (Dalian Document of Household Registration System). Dalian: Dalian Public Security Bureau.

Danlan. 2006. "Zhuanzai Wenzhang" (Posted articles). *Danlan Wang* (Danlan Net), February 17. http://www.danlan.org/dispArticle_6515.htm.

Davis, Deborah. 1995. "Introduction." In *Urban Spaces in Contemporary China,* ed. Deborah Davis et al., 1–27. Washington, D.C., and Cambridge: Woodrow Wilson Center Press and Cambridge University Press, 1995.

———, ed. 2000. *The Consumer's Revolution.* Berkeley: University of California Press.

Dean, Tim. 2009. *Unlimited Intimacy: Reflections on the Subculture of Barebacking.* Chicago: University of Chicago Press.

Dehesa, Rafael de Ia. 2007. "Global Communities and Hybrid Cultures in Early Gay and Lesbian Electoral Activism in Brazil and Mexico." *Latin American Research Review* 42, no. 1: 29–51.

D'Emilio, John. 1983. "Capitalism and Gay Identity." In *Powers of Desire: The Politics of Sexuality,* ed. Ann Snitow, Christine Stansell, and Sharan Thompson, 100–113. New York: Monthly Review Press.

Dikotter, Frank. 1995. *Sex, Culture, and Modernity in China.* London: Hurst & Company.

Dou, Lao. 2010. "Response to Arrests of Gay Men." *Gay Online Email List,* September 28.

Du, Weijie. 2015. "Yiding Yao Youren Zhanchulai" (Someone must stand out). *Nanfang Zhoumo* (South Weekend), February 5, 2.

Du, Xianghong. 2007. "Qufenhao Tongxingyilian Yu Tongxinglian" (Distinguishing same-sex attachment from same-sex love). *Zhongguo Xuesheng Wang* (Chinese Students), August 6. http://www.fzsex.fj.cn/409.html.

Dutton, Michael. 1998. *Streetlife China.* Cambridge: Cambridge University Press.

Dynes, Wayne R., and Stephen Donaldson. 1992. *Homosexuality and Government, Politics and Prisons.* New York: Routledge.

Elliston, Deborah. 1995. "Erotic Anthropology: 'Ritualized Homosexuality' in Melanesia and Beyond." *American Ethnologist* 22, no. 4: 848–67.

———. 1999. "Negotiating Transnational Sexual Economies: Female Mahu and Same-Sex Sexuality in Tahiti and Her Islands." In *Female Desires: Same-Sex Relations and Transgender Practices across Cultures,* ed. Evelyn Blackwood and Saskia E. Wieringa, 230–52. New York: Columbia University Press.

Epps, Brad. 1995. "Proper Conduct: Reinaldo Arenas, Fidel Castro, and the Politics of Homosexuality." *Journal of the History of Sexuality* 6, no. 2: 231–83.

Epstein, Steven. 1987. "Gay Politics, Ethnic Identity: The Limits of Social Constructionism." *Socialist Review* 17 (May–August): 9–54.

Evans, Harriet. 1993. *Sexual Citizenship: The Material Construction of Sexualities*. London: Routledge.

Fang, Gang. 1995. *Homosexuality in China* (Tongxinglian zai zhongguo). Jilin: Jilin Renmin Publishing House.

Farmer, Paul. 1999. *Infections and Inequalities: The Modern Plagues*. Berkeley: University of California Press.

———. 2006. "A Biosocial Understanding of China." In *AIDS and Social Policy in China*, ed. Arthur Kleinman, Joan Kaufman, and Tony Saich, x–xxii. Cambridge, Mass.: Harvard University Asia Center.

Farmer, Paul, Margaret Connors, and Janie Simmons, eds. 1996. *Women, Poverty, and AIDS: Sex, Drugs, and Structural Violence*. Monroe, Maine: Common Courage.

Farmer, Paul, Shirley Lindenbaum, and Mary-Jo Delvecchio Good. 1993. "Women, Poverty, and AIDS: An Introduction." *Cultural Medical Psychiatry* 17, no. 4: 387–97.

Farrer, James. 1998. *Opening Up: Youth Sex Culture and Market Reform in Shanghai*. Chicago: University of Chicago Press.

Fi, Ling. 2007. "Daxuesheng Tongxinglian Zhong Nannan Tongzhi Shi Nvnv Tongzhi de 2.24 Bei" (Among college students male homosexuals are 2.24 times more than female homosexuals). *Jiangsu Wang* (Jiangsu Net), June 24. http://news.jschina.com.cn/gb/jschina/society/node25884/node28168/node 28174/node28176/userobject1ai1555170.html.

Foucault, Michel. 1977. *Discipline and Punish: The Birth of the Prison*. New York: Pantheon Books.

———. 1978. *The History of Sexuality*, vol. 1: *An Introduction*. Trans. R. Hurley. New York: Random House.

———. 1984. *The History of Sexuality*, vol. 2: *The Use of Pleasure*. Trans. R. Hurley. Harmondsworth, Middlesex: Penguin.

———. 1988. *Technologies of the Self: A Seminar with Michel Foucault*. Amherst, Mass.: University of Massachusetts Press.

Freccero, Carla. 2006. *Queer/Early/Modern*. Durham, N.C.: Duke University Press.

Fu, Jing. 2009. "Tongxinglian Qunti Aizibing Fangzhi Mianlin Tiaozhan" (Challenges faced by homosexual group in HIV/AIDS prevention). *Zhongguo Ribao* (China Daily Newspaper), October 18.

Furth, Charlotte. 1988. "Androgynous Males and Deficient Females: Biology and Gender Boundaries in Sixteenth- and Seventeenth-Century China." *Late Imperial China* 9, no. 2: 1–31.

———. 1992. "Chinese Medicine and the Anthropology of Menstruation in Contemporary Taiwan." *Medical Anthropology Quarterly* 6, no. 1: 27–48.

———. 1994. "Rethinking Van Gulik: Sexuality and Reproduction in Traditional Chinese Medicine." In *Endangering China: Women, Culture, and the State,* ed. Gail Hershatter, Christina K. Gilmartin, Lisa Rofel, and Tyrene White, 125–46. Cambridge, Mass.: Harvard University Press.

Fuss, Diana. 1989. *Essentially Speaking: Feminism, Nature and Difference.* New York: Routledge.

Ga, Lao. 2007. "Cunzai de Liliang" (The power of existence). *Gay Online Email List,* February 12.

Gamson, Joshua. 1989. "Silence, Death, and the Invisible Enemy: AIDS Activism and Social Movement Newness." *Social Problems* 36, no. 4: 351–67.

———. 1995. "Must Identity Movements Self-destruct? A Queer Dilemma." *Social Problems* 42, no. 3: 390–407.

Gao, M. Yun, and Shuguang Wang. 2007. "Participatory Communication and HIV/AIDS Prevention in a Chinese Marginalized (MSM) Population." *AIDS Care* 19, no. 6: 799–810.

Gao, Yanning, ed. 2006. *Tongxinglian Jiankang Ganyu* (Interventions of homosexual health). Shanghai: Fudan University Publishing House.

Gay Men Health Forum. 2009a. "Zhongguo Nantong Jiankang Luntan Jiu Fuyang Shijian Zhi Weishengbu Ji Guojia CDC de Jianyi" (The Chinese gay men health forum proposes suggestions to the national CDC and the hygiene ministry regarding the Fuyang incident). *Chinese Gay Men Health Forum,* November 29.

———. 2009b. "Guojia CDC Jiji Dafu Zhongguo Nantong Jiankang Luntan de Jianyi" (National CDC positively responds to the suggestions posed by Chinese gay men health forum). *Chinese Gay Men Health Forum,* November 30.

Geyer, Robert. 2002. "In Love and Gay." In *Unofficial China in a Globalizing Society,* ed. Perry Link, Richard P. Madsen, and Paul G. Pickowicz, 251–74. Lanham, Md.: Rowman & Littlefield.

Godelier, Maurice. 1986. *The Making of Great Men: Male Domination and Power among the New Guinea Baruya.* New York: Cambridge University Press.

Goffman, Erving. 1959. *The Presentation of Self in Everyday Life.* New York: Anchor Books.

———. 1963. *Stigma: Notes on the Management of Spoiled Identity.* Englewood Cliffs, N.J.: Prentice-Hall.

Goldstein, Donna. 2003. *Laughter Out of Place: Race, Class, Violence, and Sexuality in a Rio Shantytown.* Berkeley: University of California Press.

Goldstein, Joshua. 2007. *Drama Kings: Players and Publics in the Re-Creation of Peking Opera, 1870–1937.* Berkeley: University of California Press.

Goodkind, Daniel, and Loraine A. West. 2002. "China's Floating Population: Definitions, Data and Recent Findings." *Urban Studies* 39, no. 12: 2237–50.

Graham, Sharyn. 2003. "While Diving, Drink Water: Bisexuals and Transgender Intersections in South Sulawesi, Indonesia." *Journal of Bisexuality* 3, no. 3/4: 233–47.

Gramsci, Antonio. 1995. *The Prison Notebooks of Antonio Gramsci*. New York: International Publishers [copyright 1971].

Green, James N. 1999. *Beyond Carnival: Male Homosexuality in Twentieth Century Brazil*. Chicago: University of Chicago Press.

Gu, Bo. 2012. "Nvboshi Luo Hongling Tiaolou Zisha: Pu Nvboshi Luo Hongling Zishaqian de Tongqi Shenghuo" (Female Ph.D. Luo Hongling jumped off building and committed suicide: Her life as a wife of a tongzhi exposed). *Sichuan Xinwen*, July 18, 3.

Gu, Dening. 2012. "Qianjiao Baimei de Weiniangtuan Zheshe Nansheng Weiji" (A crisis of manhood is reflected by coquettish fake-women league). *Huanqiu Shibao* (World Times), April 10, 4.

Gui, Shixun, and Liu Xian. 1992. "Urban Migration in Shanghai, 1950–88: Trends and Characteristics." *Population and Development Review* 18, no. 3: 533–48.

Gupta, Akhil, and James Ferguson. 1997. "Culture, Power and Place." In *Culture, Power, Place: Explorations in Critical Anthropology*, ed. Akhil Gupta and James Ferguson, 1–32. Durham, N.C.: Duke University Press.

Hall, Kira, and Veronica O'Donovan. 1996. "Shifting Gender Positions among Hindi-Speaking Hijras." In *Rethinking Language and Gender Research*, ed. Janet Bing, Victoria Bergvall, and Alice Freed, 223–66. London: Longman.

Halperin, David M., and Valerie Traub, eds. 2010. *Gay Shame*. Chicago: University of Chicago Press.

Han, Xu. 2013. "Chinese Homosexuals Propose Legal Marriage" (Zhongguo Tongxinglian Tichu Hefa Jiehun Suqiu). *Xinhua Wang* (Xinhua Net), March 4. http://gb.cri.cn/27824/2013/03/04/6011s4038408.htm.

Hatfield, Elizabeth Fish. 2010. "'What It Means to Be a Man': Examining Hegemonic Masculinity in *Two and a Half Men*." *Communication, Culture & Critique* 3, no. 4: 526–48.

He, Daifu. 2012. "Tongxinglian Haile Wode Hunyin" (Homosexuals harmed my marriage). *Xingyixue Zhensuo* (Sex Clinic), 313. http://www.xyx120.cn/txlhw.htm.

He, Qun, Ye Wang, Peng Lin, Yongying Liu, Fang Yang, Xiaobing Fu, Yan Li, Baoshan Sun, Jie Li, Xixi Zhao, Jeffrey Mandel, Sheila Jain, and Willi McFarland. 2006. "Potential Bridges for HIV Infection to Men Who Have Sex with Men in Guangzhou, China." *AIDS Behavior* 10: S17–S23.

He, Weiwei. 2009. "Nishi Tongxinglian Weishenmo Hai Quwo?" (Why do you marry me knowing you are homosexual?). *Yi Wang* (Yi Net News), September 4. http://news.e23.cn/content/2012-04-05/2012040500981.html.

Herdt, Gilbert. 1994. *Guardians of the Flutes*, vol. 1: *Idioms of Masculinity*. Chicago: University of Chicago Press.

Hershatter, Gail, and Emily Honig. 1988. *Personal Voices: Chinese Women in the 1980s*. Stanford: Stanford University Press.

Heze Yangguang Xing Nan Huiguan (Heze Sunshine Style Man's Club). 2013. April 24. http://www.hz.xsdtz.com/about.asp.

Hinsch, Bret. 1992. *Passions of the Cut Sleeve: The Male Homosexual Tradition in China*. Berkeley: University of California Press.

"HIV/AIDS Cases Rising in China." 2012. *Huffington Post*, November 28, 2. http://www.huffingtonpost.com/2012/11/28/hiv-aids-china-cases-rising_n_2203294.html.

Ho, Loretta Wing Wah. 2008. "Speaking of Same-Sex Subjects in China." *Asian Studies Review* 32: 491–509.

———. 2009. *Gay and Lesbian Subculture in Urban China*. London: Routledge.

Hoffman, Lisa. 2003. "Enterprising Cities and Citizens: The Re-Figuring of Urban Spaces and the Making of Post-Mao Professionals." *Provincial China* 8, no. 1: 5–26.

———. 2008. "Post-Mao Professionalism: Self-Enterprise and Patriotism." In *Privatizing China: Socialism from Afar*, ed. Li Zhang and Aihwa Ong, 168–81. Ithaca, N.Y.: Cornell University Press.

Holland, Janet, Caroline Ramazanoglu, Sue Scott, Sue Sharpe, and Rachel Thomson. 1991. "Between Embarrassment and Trust: Young Women and the Diversity of Condom Use." In *AIDS: Responses, Interventions, and Care*, ed. Peter Aggelton, 127–48. London: Falmer Press.

Hollway, Wendy. 1989. *Subjectivity and Method in Psychology: Gender, Meaning, and Science*. London: Sage.

Hong, Lao. 2007. "Jidian Qiang" (Memory wall). *Gay Online Email List*, September 10.

Honig, Emily. 1992. *Creating Chinese Ethnicity: Subei People in Shanghai, 1850–1980*. New Haven, Conn.: Yale University Press.

———. 2003. "Socialist Sex: The Cultural Revolution Revisited." *Modern China* 29, no. 2: 143–75.

Hu, Wei. 2008. "Hangzhou Zuidade Nantongxinglian Hanlincun Bei Chachu" (The biggest hangzhou male homosexual's hanlin village was closed down). *Zhongguo Chuang* (The Chinese Window), October 9, 4.

Hua, Wen. 2012. *Buying Beauty: Cosmetic Surgery in China*. Hong Kong: University of Hong Kong Press.

Huan, Xiping, Chun Hao, Hongjing Yan, Wenhui Guan, Xiaoqin Xu, Haitao Yang, Na Wang, Min Zhang, Weimin Tang, Jing Gu, and Joseph Lau. 2013. "High Prevalence of HIV and Syphilis among Men Who Have Sex with Men Recruited by Respondent-Driven Sampling in a City in Eastern China." *Asia Pacific Journal of Public Health* 27: 122–33.

Huang, Guosheng. 2006. "Tongxinglian Nanhai" (A homosexual boy). *Wenzhou Ribao* (Weizhou Daily), October 24, 14.

Huang, Philip. 1993. "Public Sphere/Civil Society in China?" *Modern China* 19, no. 2: 216–40.

Ikels, Charlotte, ed. 2004. *Filial Piety: Practice and Discourse in Contemporary East Asia.* Stanford: Stanford University Press.

Ingham, Roger, Alison Woodcock, and Karen Stenner. 1991. "Getting to Know You . . . Young People's Knowledge of Their Partners at First Intercourse." *Journal of Community and Applied Social Psychology* 1, no. 2: 117–32.

Jackson, Peter. 1999. *Lady Boys, Tom Boys, Rent Boys: Male and Female Homosexualities in Contemporary Thailand.* New York: Haworth Press.

Jankowiak, William. 2013. "Chinese Youth: Hot Romance and Cold Calculation." In *Restless China,* ed. Perry Link, Richard P. Madsen, and Paul Pickowicz, 191–212. Chicago: University of Chicago Press.

Jeffreys, Elaine. 2007. "Querying Queer Theory—Debating Male-Male Prostitution in the Chinese Media." *Critical Asian Studies* 39, no. 1: 151–75.

Ji, Chengcheng. 2012. "Shanghai Nanzi Zhongxue" (Shanghai Male Junior High School). *Sohu Jiaoyu* (Sohu Education), April 10. http://learning.sohu.com /20120410/n340222854.shtml.

Ji, Nan. 2011. "Guangzhou Nanxing Tongxinglian Aizi Ganranlv Gaoda 8%" (Male homosexual transmission rate is as high as 8 percent in Guangzhou). *Population Picture Book* (Renkou Huabao), October 17. http://202.116.0.132/onews. asp?id=838.

Ji, Zhe. 2006. "Hangcheng Jinnian Yi Faxian 16 Li Tongxinglian Aizibing Ganranlv Gao Zengzhang" (16 cases have been found in Hangzhou this year, an increase in HIV/AIDS transmission rate among homosexuals). *Sihai Xiongdi* (Brotherhood around the Country), December 2. http://www.boy532.com /show.aspx?&id=1757&cid=11.

Jia, Yicheng. 1997. "Fandui Quxiao Tongxinglian Zhenduan" (Against removal of diagnosis of homosexuality). *Jingshen Weisheng Tongxun* (Psychiatry News), August 1, 12–16.

Jian, Li. 2009. "Haizi Dele Tongxinglian Zenmo Ban" (What to do if a child gets homosexuality). *39 Jiankang Wang Shequ* (30 Health Community). June 1. www.39.net.

Jiang, Jin. 2009. *Women Playing Men: Yue Opera and Social Change in Twentieth-Century Shanghai.* Seattle: University of Washington Press.

Jiang, Nanyu. 2003. "Jiedu Quanguo Shouli Tongxinglian Jiufen de Sifa Tiaojie" (Interpreting the first homosexual dispute). *Sohu Xinwen* (Sohu News), November 12. http://news.sohu.com/01/02/news215480201.shtml.

Jiu, Cuo. 2008. "Tongxingjiande Shenmo Jiechu Hui Chuanran Xingbing" (What kind of sexual contact between same-sex can lead to transmission of STDs). *Sexual Health Net* (Xingjian kangwang), October 4. http://www.sexjk.com /Special/tongxing/20081004103343.html.

Johnson, Mark. 1997. *Beauty and Power: Transgendering and Cultural Transformation in the Southern Philippines.* Oxford: Berg.

Jones, Rodney H. 1999. "Mediated Action and Sexual Risk: Searching for 'Culture' in Discourses of Homosexuality and AIDS Prevention in China." *Culture, Health & Sexuality* 1, no. 2: 161–80.

Ju, Tong. 2009. "Beijing Tongxinglian Jianwen" (Experiences about homosexuals in Beijing). *64 Net* (64 Wang), September 21. https://64.71.141.144.

Kane, Stephanie, and Theresa Mason. 1992. "'IV Drug Users' and 'Sex Partners': The Limits of Epidemiological Categories and the Ethnography of Risk." In *The Time of AIDS: Social Analysis, Theory, and Method*, ed. Gil Herdt and Shirley Lindenbaum, 199–222. Newbury Park, Calif.: Sage.

Kang, Wenqing. 2009. *Obsession: Male Same-Sex Relations in China, 1900–1950.* Hong Kong: Chinese University of Hong Kong Press.

Kaufman, Joan, and Kathrine Meyers. 2006. "AIDS Surveillance in China: Data Gaps and Research for AIDS Policy." In *AIDS and Social Policy in China*, ed. Joan Kaufman, Arthur Kleinman, and Tony Saich, 47–74. Cambridge, Mass.: Harvard University Asia Center.

Kaufman, Michael. 1992. "The Construction of Masculinity and the Triad of Men's Violence." In *Men's Lives*, ed. Michael Kimmel and Michael Messner, 4–17. New York: Macmillan.

Kendall, Lori. 1999. "The Nerd within: Mass Media and the Negotiation of Identity among Computer-Using Men." *Journal of Men's Studies* 7, no. 1: 353–72.

Kennedy, Elizabeth Lapovsky, and Madeline D. Davis. 1993. *Boots of Leather, Slippers of Gold: The History of a Lesbian Community.* New York: Penguin.

Khan, Azizur Rahman, Keith Griffin, Carl Riskin, and Zhao Renwei. 1992. "Household Income and Its Distribution in China." *China Quarterly* 132 (December): 1029–61.

Khan, Azizur Rahman, and Carl Riskin. 1998. "Income and Inequality in China: Composition, Distribution and Growth of Household Income, 1988–1995." *China Quarterly* 154 (June): 221–53.

Kimmel, Michael. 1996. *Manhood in America.* New York: Free Press.

Kipnis, Andrew. 1998. "The 'Country' as a Foreign Country: Revising Household Registration Policy in the P.R.C." Paper read at the 97th Annual Meeting of American Association of Anthropology.

Kippax, Susan, June Crawford, Cathy Waldby, and Pam Benton. 1990. "Women Negotiating Heterosex: Implications for AIDS Prevention." *Women's Studies International Forum* 13, no. 6: 533–42.

Klein, Charles. 1999. "The Ghetto Is over, Darling: Emerging Gay Communities and Gender and Sexual Politics in Contemporary Brazil." *Culture, Health & Sexuality* 1, no. 3: 239–60.

Kleinman, Arthur, Yunxiang Yan, Jing Jun, Sing Lee, and Everett Zhang, eds. 2011. *Deep China: The Moral Life of the Person.* Berkeley: University of California Press.

Kong, Travis. 2002. "The Seduction of the Golden Boy: The Body Politics of Hong Kong Gay Men." *Body & Society* 8, no. 1: 29–48.

———. 2010. "Outcast Bodies: Money, Sex and Desire of Money Boys in Mainland China." In *As Normal as Possible: Negotiating Sexuality and Gender in Mainland China and Hong Kong,* ed. Yau Ching, 17–35. Hong Kong: Hong Kong University Press.

———. 2011a. *Chinese Male Homosexualities: Memba, Tongzhi and Golden Boy.* London: Routledge.

———. 2011b. "Transnational Queer Labor: The 'Circuits of Desire' of Money Boys in China." *English Language Notes* 49, no. 1: 139–41.

———. 2012. "Reinventing the Self under Socialism." *Critical Asian Studies* 44, no. 2: 283–308.

Kristeva, Julia. 1982. *Powers of Horror: An Essay on Abjection.* New York: Columbia University Press.

Kuer, Duli. 2010. "Quanguo Kuer Yingshi Yingzhan" (Schedules for queer movie exhibit around the country). *Gay Online Email List,* March 15.

Kulick, Don. 1998. *Travesti: Sex, Gender, and Culture among Brazilian Transgendered Prostitutes.* Chicago: University of Chicago Press.

Lacan, Jacques Marie Émile. 1968. *The Language of the Self: The Function of Language in Psychoanalysis.* Baltimore: Johns Hopkins University Press.

Lai, Weijian. 2006. "Shilianwangliao Bei Yinyou Cheng Tongxinglian" (Loss of love chat, tempted to be a homosexual). *27 Wang* (27 Net), February 9. www.xx27.net.

Lan, Se. 2006. "Tongxinglian Beishuai, Qiaozha Fenshoufei" (A homosexual is abandoned, blackmail breakup fee). *Huaxia Yiyao Jiankang Wang* (Chinese Medical Health Net), April 13. http://health.886120.com/594/2005-08-25/93608.shtml.

Lan, Xuan. 2006. "Jingfang Qudi Nantongxinglian Julebu" (The police shut down a male homosexual club). *Zhongguo Xinwen Wang* (Chinese News Net), April 13. http://health.886120.com/594/2005-08-24/92667.shtml.

Lan, Yang. 2008. "Tongxinglian Zhi Xiaodiaoyan" (Investigation on homosexuality). *Nongqing Zhongnan* (Affection for South China), July 29. http://www.ourznbbs.com/thread-186375-5-1.html.

Lao, Li. 2007. "Sun Haiying Wuju Re Zhong Nu" (Sun Haiying is fearless and arouses anger). *Sohu Yule* (Sohu Entertainment), August 16. http://yule.sohu.com/20070816/n251610650.shtml.

Lauretis, Teresa de. 1991. *Queer Theory: Lesbian and Gay Sexualities.* Bloomington: Indiana University Press.

Lee, Ching Kwan, ed. 2007. *Working in China: Ethnographies of Labor and Workplace Transformation.* New York: Routledge.

Levine, Martin. 1998. *Gay Macho.* New York: New York University Press.

Lewin, Ellen, and William L. Leap. 2002. "Introduction." In *Out in Theory: The Emergence of Lesbian and Gay Anthropology,* ed. Ellen Lewin and William L. Leap, 1–16. Chicago: University of Illinois Press.

Leznoff, Maurice, and William A. Westley. 1956. "The Homosexual Community." *Social Problems* 3, no. 4: 257–63.

Li, Bingqin, and David Piachaud. 2006. "Urbanization and Social Policy in China." *Asia-Pacific Development Journal* 13, no. 1: 1–24.

Li, Gang. 2010. "Beijing Zuidade Mou Tongzhi Jujide Beizhua" (Police arrests in Beijing's largest gay cruising area). *Gay Online Email List,* September 27.

Li, Haifu. 2013. "Chengdu Lvshi Shangshu: Weitongxinglian Pei'ou Qisu Lihun Lifa" (Chengdu lawyers petitioning for partners of tongzhi to file lawsuits of divorce). *Chengdu Shangbao* (Chengdu Business Newspaper), January 26, 8.

Li, Honggu. 2001. "Zhuanjia Jieshi: Tongxinglian Zhe Bushi Jingshenbing Bingren" (Expert's explanation: Homosexuality is not mental illness). *Sanlian Shenghuo Zhoukan* (Sanlian Life Weekly), March 28, 7.

Li, Rose Maria. 1989. "Migration to China's Northern Frontier, 1953–1982." *Population and Development Review* 15, no. 3: 503–37.

Li, Xiaoming, et al. 2007. "Stigmatization Experienced by Rural-to-Urban Migrant Workers in China: Findings from a Qualitative Study." *World Health and Population* 9, no. 4: 29–43.

Li, Xinyue. 2009. "Ruguo Fumu Shi Tongxinglian, Ni Cong Na Lai" (If parents are homosexuals, where do you come from?). *Dongbei Xinwenwang* (Northeast News), June 14, 2.

Li, Yinhe. 1998. *Tongxinglian Yawenhua* (Homosexual subculture). Beijing: Jinri Zhongguo Chubanshe (Today Chinese Publishing House).

———. 2006. "Regulating Male Same-Sex Relationships in the People's Republic of China." In *Sex and Sexuality in China,* ed. Elaine Jeffreys, 82–101. London: Routledge.

———. 2008. "Gongzhong Dui Tongxinglian de Taidu" (The public's attitude toward homosexuals). *Xuezhe Shequ* (Scholar's Community), October 30. http://www.china-review.com/sao.asp?id=20611.

———. 2009. *Tongxinglian Yawenhua* (Homosexual subculture). Inner Mongolia (Neimenggu): Neimenggu University Chubanshe.

Li, Yinhe, and Wang Xiaobo. 1992. *Tamen de Shijie—Zhongguo Nantongxinglian Qunti de Toushi* (Their world—an insider look of the Chinese male homosexual group). Beijing: Renmin Chubanshe (People's Publishing House).

Lim, Eng-Beng. 2005. "Glocalqueering in New Asia: The Politics of Performing Gay in Singapore." *Theatre Journal* 57, no. 3: 383–405.

Lin, Ming. 2012. "Shenmo Yuanyin Daozhi Tongxinglian Dilinghua?" (What reasons cause homosexuals in the low age group?). *Da Ai Wang,* January 4. http://www.bamaol.com/html/XLWZ/QGHY/TXLXL/488722012049593 7282.shtm.

Lindenbaum, Shirley. 1997. "AIDS: Body, Mind, and History." In *AIDS in Africa and the Caribbean,* ed. George C. Bond, John Kreniske, Ida Susser, and Joan Vincent, 191–94. Boulder, Colo.: Westview Press.

———. 1998. "Images of Catastrophe: The Making of an Epidemic." In *The Political Economy of AIDS,* ed. Merrill Singer, 33–58. Amityville, N.Y.: Baywood.

Litzinger, Ralph. 2007. "In Search of the Grassroots: Hydroelectric Politics in Northwest Yunnan." In *Grassroots Political Reform in Contemporary China,* ed. Elizabeth J. Perry and Merle Goldman, 282–99. Cambridge, Mass.: Harvard University Press.

Liu, Dalin. 2005. *Zhongguo Tongxinglian Yanjiu* (A study of Chinese homosexuals). Beijing: Zhongguo Shehui Chubanshe (Chinese Society Press).

Liu, Dalin, and Longguang Lu. 2005. *A Study of Chinese Homosexuals* (Zhongguo Tongxinglian De Yanjiu). Beijing: Zhongguo Shehui Publishing House.

Liu, Lydia. 1993. "Invention and Intervention: The Female Tradition in Modern Chinese Literature." In *Gender Politics in Modern China,* ed. Tani E. Barlow, 33–54. Durham, N.C.: Duke University Press.

Liu, Min. 2005. "Wangliao Jiejiao Nantongxinglian, Nvyou Chicu Baochu Tongxing Maiyin An" (Meeting male homosexuals via online chatting, girlfriend angered and exposing the case of homosexual prostitution). *Jinling Wanbao* (Jinling Evening Newspaper), July 15, 14.

Liu, Peng. 2012. "Weiniang Shangpin Kaishi Liuxing, Shangjia Cheng Xiaoliang Bucuo" (Fake-women merchandise begins to be popular, sales have been good). *Tianfu Zaobao* (Tianfu Morning Newspaper), January 28, 12.

Liu, Shusen, Lin Chen, Li Li, Jin Zhao, Wende Cai, Keming Rou, Zunyou Wu, and Roger Detels. 2012. "Condom Use with Various Types of Sex Partners by Money Boys in China." *AIDS Education and Prevention* 24, no. 2: 163–78.

Long, Da. 2010. "Caogen Zuzhi Fazhan, Ganwen Luzai Hefang" (Where is the road for grassroots organizations?). *Our Voice Newsletter* 23: 11–15.

Lorway, Robert, Sushena Reza-Paul, and Akram Pasha. 2009. "On Becoming a Male Sex Worker in Mysore: Sexual Subjectivity, Empowerment, and Community-Based HIV Prevention Research." *Medical Anthropology Quarterly* 23, no. 2: 142–60.

Lu, An. 2012. "Nanzi Zhongxue Jiudeliao Nansheng Weiji Ma" (Can a man's junior high school save a crisis of manhood?). *Lu An Xinhua JiaoYu* (Lu An Xinhua Education), April 5. http://luanpim.blog.edu.cn/2012/738647.html.

Luan, Xiaoting. 2006. "Same-Sex Emotional Attachment Alarming Parents." *Bandao Morning Newspaper* (Bandao Chenbao), February 16, 38.

Lun, Tan. 2005. "Shixian Jiaoju: Nudaxuesheng ba Tongxinglian Dangcheng Shishang?" (Focus: Do female university students regard homosexuality as a vogue?). *Tengxun Nuxing* (Tengxun Female), October 1. http://lady.qq.com/a /20051001/000014.htm.

Luo, Jinhai. 2003. "The Death of Repatriated Sun Zhigang." *Nanfang Dushibao* (South Municipal Newspaper), April 25, 2.

Luo, Yuan. 2010. "Taolun Shenmo Shi Weilai Zhuliu Shehui de Wenti" (On the future's mainstream society). *Huanqiu Shibao* (World Times), December 16, 6.

Ma, Qiusha. 2006. *Non-governmental Organizations in Contemporary China: Paving the Way to Civil Society?* New York: Routledge.

Ma, Xiao. 2010. "Yongbao HIV Yangxing Zai Guangzhou" (Embracing HIV positive people in Guangzhou). *Gay Online Email List*, December 1.

Madsen, Richard. 1993. "The Public Sphere, Civil Society, and Moral Community: A Research Agenda for Contemporary China Studies." *Modern China* 19, no. 2: 183–98.

Manalansan, Martin. 2003. *Global Divas: Filipino Gay Men in the Diaspora*. Durham, N.C.: Duke University Press.

Manderson, Lenore, and Margaret Jolly. 1997. *Sites of Desire/Economies of Pleasure: Sexualities in Asia and the Pacific*. Chicago: University of Chicago Press.

Mann, Susan. 2011. *Gender and Sexuality in Modern Chinese History*. New York: Cambridge University Press.

Martin, Biddy. 1997. *Femininity Played Straight: The Significance of Being Lesbian*. New York: Routledge.

Martin, Fran, Peter A. Jackson, Mark McLelland, and Audrey Yue, eds. 2008. "Introduction." In *AsiaPacific Queer: Rethinking Genders and Sexualities*, ed. Fran Martin, Peter A. Jackson, Mark McLelland, and Audrey Yue, 1–28. Urbana: University of Illinois Press.

Meng, Xiangdong, Allen F. Anderson, Lu Wang, Zhihe Li, Wei Guo, Zixuan Lee, Huixin Jin, and Yong Cai. 2010. "An Exploratory Survey of Money Boys and HIV Transmission Risk in Jilin Province, PR China." *AIDS Research and Therapy* 7, no. 17: 1–8.

Micollier, Evelyne. 2003. "HIV/AIDS-Related Stigmatization in Chinese Society: Bridging the Gap between Official Responses and Civil Society. A Cultural Approach to HIV/AIDS Prevention and Care." *UNESCO/UNAIDS Research Project* No. 20. Paris: UNESCO.

———. 2005. "Collective Mobilisation and Transnational Solidarity to Combat AIDS in China: Local Dynamics and Visibility of Groups Defending Sexual and Social Minorities." *Face to Face: Perspectives on Health* 7: 30–38.

———. 2006. "Sexualities and HIV/AIDS Vulnerability in China: An Anthropological Perspective." *Sexologies* 15: 192–201.

Middelthon, Anne-Lise. 2001. "Interpretations of Condom Use and Nonuse among Young Norwegian Gay Men: A Qualitative Study." *Medical Anthropology Quarterly* 15, no. 1: 58–83.

Miège, Pierre. 2009. "In My Opinion, Most Tongzhi Are Dutiful Sons!" *China Perspectives* 1: 40–53.

Migliaccio, Todd. 2001. "Marginalizing the Battered Male." *Journal of Men's Studies* 9, no. 1: 205–26.

———. 2009. "Men's Friendships: Performances of Masculinity." *Journal of Men's Studies* 17, no. 3: 226–41.

Mirande, Alfredo. 1997. *Hombres y Machos: Masculinity and Latino Culture*. Boulder, Colo.: Westview Press.

Mitchell, Gregory. 2011. "TurboConsumers in Paradise: Tourism, Civil Rights, and Brazil's Gay Sex Industry." *American Ethnologist* 38, no. 4: 666–82.

Mohanty, Chandra Talpade. 1991. "Under Western Eyes: Feminist Scholarship and Colonial Discourses." In *Third World Women and the Politics of Feminism*, ed. Chandra Talpade Mohanty, Ann Russo, and Lourdes Torres, 51–80. Bloomington: Indiana University Press.

Montgomery, Samantha A., and Abigail Stewart. 2012. "Privileged Allies in Lesbian and Gay Rights Activism: Gender, Generation, and Resistance to Heteronormativity." *Journal of Social Issues* 68: 162–77.

Moore, Henrietta. 1994. *A Passion for Difference*. Bloomington: Indiana University Press.

Mu, Yang. 2011. "Dalian Nanhai de Beiqing Gushi" (A tragic story of Dalian men). *Danlan Organization*, October 23. http://www.danlan.org/disparticle_37425_3_2.htm.

Mu, Yifei. 2012. "Nanzi Zhongguo Jiubuliao Nansheng Weiji" (Men's junior high school cannot save the crisis of manhood). *Hong Wang* (Red Net), April 5. http://hlj.rednet.cn/c/2012/04/05/2572363.htm.

Muessig, Kathry, Joseph D. Tucker, Bao-Xi Wang, and Xiang-Sheng Chen. 2010. "HIV and Syphilis among Men Who Have Sex with Men in China: The Time to Act Is Now." *Sexually Transmitted Diseases* 37, no. 4: 214–16.

Murray, Alison J. 2001. "Let Them Take Ecstasy: Class and Jakarta Lesbians." In *Gay and Lesbian Asia: Culture, Identity, Community*, ed. Gerard Sullivan and Peter A. Jackson, 165–84. New York: Harrington Park Press.

Murray, David. 2000. "Between a Rock and a Hard Place: The Power and Powerlessness of Transnational Narratives among Gay Martinican Men." *American Anthropologist* 102, no. 2: 261–70.

Murray, Stephen. 1992. "The 'Underdevelopment' of Modern/Gay Homosexuality in Mesoamerica." In *Modern Homosexualities: Fragments of Lesbian and Gay Experience*, ed. Ken Plummer, 29–38. London: Routledge.

Nan, Da. 2011. "Xiaonei 400 Xuesheng Xingquxiang Yichang" (400 college students have abnormal sexual orientation). *Jinling Wanbao* (Jinling Evening Newspaper), December 1, 7.

Nan, Lin. 2012. "Hongqi Zhitong" (The pain of wives of homosexuals). *Guangzhou Ribao* (Guangzhou Daily), February 13, 6.

Newton, Esther. 1979. *Mother Camp: Female Impersonators in America*. Chicago: University of Chicago Press.

Ng, Jason Q. 2013. *Blocked on Weibo: What Gets Suppressed on China's Version of Twitter*. New York: New Press.

Ng, Jiwo. 1998. *Jiazai Dajiale* (My Home Is in Dajiale). Hong Kong: Chinese University of Hong Kong.

Ng, Vivien. 1987. "Ideology and Sexuality: Rape Laws in Qing China." *Journal of Asian Studies* 46, no. 1: 57–70.

Nguyen, Vinh-Kim. 2003. "Anthropology, Inequality, and Disease: A Review." *Annual Review of Anthropology* 32: 447–74.

Ning, Bo. 2010. "Weishenmo Nanxing Tongxinglianzhe Yihuan Yangwei" (Why is it easy for male homosexuals to suffer impotence). 2010. *Ningbo Yiyuan Wang* (Ningbo Hospital Net), February 13. http://www.0574120.net/QuestionClassi fication/impotenceprematureejaculation/n93074105.html.

Office of State Council. 2012. *Aizibing Shierwu Xingdou Jihua* (AIDS Twelve Five Actions proposal). Beijing: Office of State Council of China.

Ogasawara, Yuko. 1998. *Office Ladies and Salaried Men*. Berkeley: University of California Press.

Ony, Shen. 2007. "Same-Sex Love at College: Alternative Emotions under Pressure" (Gaoxiao Tongxing Zhi Ai: Chongman Yali de Linglei Qinggan). *Xinhua Wang* (Xinhua Net), March 27. http://edu.qq.com/a/20070327/000066 .htm.

Ortner, Sherry. 1990. "Gender Hegemonies." *Cultural Critique* (Winter): 35–80.

Pan, Guangdong. 1946. *Xiangxinli Xue* (*Psychology of Sex: A Manual for Students* by Havelock Ellis). Beijing: Shangwu Yinshuguan.

Pan, Haijiao. 2009. "Zaolian Ye Keyi Biancheng Tongxinglian (Early love can be changed to homosexuality)." *39 Jiankangwang Shequ* (30 Health Community), June 10. www.39.net.

Pan, Suiming. 1995. "Homosexual Behaviors in Contemporary China." *Journal of Psychology and Human Sexuality* 7, no. 4: 1–17.

———. 1996. "Male Homosexual Behavior and HIV-Related Risk in China." In *Bisexualities and AIDS: International Perspectives*, ed. Peter Aggleton, 178–90. London: Taylor & Francis.

———. 1999. *Cun Zai Yu Hunag Niu: Zhong Guo Di Xia "Xing Chan Ye" Kao Cha* (Existence and irony: A scrutiny of the Chinese underground sex industry). Beijing: Qunyan Publishing House.

———. 2006. "Transformation in the Primary Life Cycle: The Origins and Nature of China's Sexual Revolution." In *Sex and Sexuality in China*, ed. Elaine Jeffreys, 21–42. London: Routledge.

Pan, Zhizhen. 2011. "Li Yinhe: Zhongguo Gongzhong Dui Tongxinglianzhe de Kuanrongdu Shenzhi Gaoyu Meiguo" (Li Yinhe: Chinese public's tolerance toward homosexuals exceeds the U.S.). *Xin Kuai Bao* (New Fast Newspaper), July 10.

Parker, Richard. 1999. *Beneath the Equator: Cultures of Desire, Male Homosexuality, and Emerging Gay Communities in Brazil*. New York: Routledge.

———. 2001. "Sexuality, Culture, and Power in HIV/AIDS Research." *Annual Review of Anthropology* 30: 163–79.

Parker, Richard, Delia Easton, and Charles H. Klein. 2000. "Structural Barriers and Facilitators in HIV Prevention: A Review of International Research." *AIDS* 14, Suppl. 1: S22–S32.

Parker, Richard, and John Gagnon, eds. 1995. *Conceiving Sexuality: Approaches to Sex Research in a Postmodern World*. New York: Routledge.

Parsons, Talcott. 1963. "On the Concept of Political Power." *Proceedings of the American Philosophical Society* 107: 232–58.

Perry, Elizabeth, and Mark Selden, eds. 2000. *Chinese Society: Change, Conflict and Resistance*. London: Routledge.

Pin, Dao. 2004. "Renshi Tongxing Lianqing" (Understanding homosexual relationships). *39 Wang* (39 Net), March 29. http://www.39.net/mentalworld/hlxl/artz /35689.html.

Plummer, Ken. 1992. "Speaking Its Name: Inventing Lesbian and Gay Studies." In *Modern Homosexualities: Fragments of Lesbian and Gay Experience*, ed. Ken Plummer, 3–28. London: Routledge.

Pollak, Michael. 1986. "Male Homosexuality." In *Western Sexuality: Practice and Precept in Past and Present Times*, ed. Philippe Aries and Andre Bejin, 40–61. York: Basil Blackwell.

Pratt, Minnie Bruce. 1984. "Identity: Skin, Blood, Heart." In *Yours in Struggle: Three Feminist Perspectives on Anti-Semitism and Racism*, ed. Elly Bulkin, Minnie Bruce Pratt, and Barbara Smith, 11–63. Brooklyn, N.Y.: Long Haul Press.

Prieur, Annick. 1998. *Mema's House, Mexico City: On Transvestites, Queens, and Machos*. Chicago: University of Chicago Press.

Puar, Jasbir. 2007. *Terrorist Assemblages: Homonationalism in Queer Times*. Durham, N.C.: Duke University Press.

Pun, Ngai. 2003. "Subsumption or Consumption? The Phantom of Consumer Revolution in Globalizing China." *Cultural Anthropology* 18, no. 4: 469–92.

———. 2005. "Global Production and Corporate Business Ethics: Company Codes of Conduct Implementation and its Implication on Labour Rights in China." *China Journal* (July): 101–13.

Pun, Ngai, and Chris King-chi Chan. 2008. "The Subsumption of Class Discourse in China." *Boundary 2: An International Journal of Literature and Culture* 35, no. 2: 75–91.

Qi, Cai. 2001. "Guitou Kongbu—Tongxinglian Qingxiang" (Penis terror—homosexual orientation). *Zhongguo Jiankang Wang* (Chinese Health Net), September 4. http://www.100md.com/html/dir0/13/06/74.htm.

Qiao, Cui. 2005. "Renting Tongxinglian Shi Shehui Daode Lunsang de Zhongyao Zhibiao" (Agreeing with homosexuality is an important index for social moral degradation). *Wode Wenxue Cheng* (My Literature City), March 9. http://blog.wenxuecity.com/myblog/3490/200503/4425.html.

Qiao, Dejian. 2005. "Nantongxinglian Gewuxia Jiqing Yongwen" (Male homosexuals dancing and passionate kissing). *Xibu Shangbao* (Western Commercial Newspaper), September 26, 15.

Qing, Mai. 2013. "Zhangfu Weizhuang Tongxinglian, Nvboshi Mingyun Tongqi Lu" (Husband pretends to be bisexual, female Ph.D. dies on the path of wife of tongzhi). *Baidu Tieba,* January 25. http://tieba.baidu.com/p/2120531862.

Rankin, Mary Backus. 1993. "Some Observations on a Chinese Public Sphere." *Modern China* 19, no. 2: 158–82.

Reddy, Gayatri. 2005. *With Respect to Sex: Negotiating Hijra Identity in South India.* Chicago: University of Chicago Press.

Reiss, Albert J. 1961. "The Social Integration of 'Queers' and 'Peers.'" *Social Problems* 9: 102–20.

Ren, Shaopeng, and Xing, Yali. 2010. "Zhengshi Tongzhi Zuzhi Vct Fuwuzhong De Wenti Yu Kunjing" (Face the problems and difficulties in MSM organization). *Our Voice Newsletter* 23: 15–16.

Rofel, Lisa. 1999. "Qualities of Desire: Imagining Gay Identities in China." *GLQ: A Journal of Lesbian and Gay Studies* 5, no. 4: 451–74.

———. 2007. *Desiring China: Experiments in Neoliberalism, Sexuality, and Public Culture.* Durham, N.C.: Duke University Press.

———. 2010. "The Traffic in Money Boys." *Positions* 18, no. 2: 425–58.

Rose, Nikolas. 1996. "Governing 'Advanced' Liberal Democracies." In *Foucault and Political Reason: Liberalism, Neo-liberalism and Rationalities of Government,* ed. Andrew Barry, Thomas Osborne, and Nikolas Rose, 37–64. London: UCL Press.

Ru, Zi. 2001. "Tongxinglian Yu Xingbing" (Homosexuality and STDs). *Yueguang Ruanjian* (Moon Soft), October 24. http://www.moon-soft.com/program/bbs/readelite309771.htm.

Ruan, Fang Fu. 1991. *Sex in China: Studies in Sexology in Chinese Culture.* New York: Plenum.

———. 1997. "China." In *Sociolegal Control of Homosexuality: A Multi-Nation Comparison,* ed. D. J. West and R. Green, 57–66. New York: Plenum.

Ruan, Fang Fu, and Yung-mei Tsai. 1987. "Male Homosexuality in Traditional Chinese Literature." *Journal of Homosexuality* 14, no. 3–4: 21–33.

Rubin, Gayle. 2002. "Studying Sexual Subcultures: Excavating the Ethnography of Gay Communities in Urban North America." In *Out in Theory: The Emergence of Lesbian and Gay Anthropology*, ed. Ellen Lewin and William L. Leap, 17–68. Urbana: University of Illinois Press.

Saich, Anthony. 2000. "Negotiating the State: The Development of Social Organizations in China." *China Quarterly* 161 (March): 124–41.

Sang, Deborah Tze-lan. 2003. *The Emerging Lesbian: Female Same-Sex Desire in Modern China*. Chicago: University of Chicago Press.

Sargent, Paul. 2001. *Real Men or Real Teachers? Contradictions in the Lives of Men Elementary School Teachers*. Harriman, Tenn.: Men's Studies Press.

Schifter, Jacobo. 1999. *From Toads to Queens: Transvestism in a Latin American Setting*. New York: Routledge.

Schmidt, Robert A. 2002. "The Iceman Cometh: Queering the Archaeological Past." In *Out in Theory: The Emergence of Lesbian and Gay Anthropology*, ed. Ellen Lewin and William L. Leap, 155–85. Chicago: University of Illinois Press.

Schoepf, Brooke. 1991. "Ethical, Methodological, and Political Issues of AIDS Research in Central Africa." *Social Science & Medicine* 33: 749–63.

———. 1995. "Culture, Sex Research, and AIDS Prevention in Africa." In *Culture and Sexual Risk: Anthropological Perspectives on AIDS*, ed. Han ten Brummelhuis and Gilbert Herdt, 29–51. Amsterdam: Gordon Breach.

———. 2001. "International AIDS Research in Anthropology: Taking a Critical Perspective on the Crisis." *Annual Reviews of Anthropology* 30: 335–61.

———. 2007. "Violence and the Politics of Remorse: Lessons from South Africa." In *Subjectivity: Ethnographic Investigations*, ed. Joao Biehl, Byron Good, and Arthur Kleinman, 179–233. Berkeley: University of California Press.

Scott, James. 1985. *Weapons of the Weak: Everyday Forms of Peasant Resistance*. New Haven, Conn.: Yale University Press.

———. 1990. *Domination and the Arts of Resistance: Hidden Transcripts*. New Haven, Conn.: Yale University Press.

Sears, James T. 2005a. *Gay, Lesbian, and Transgender Issues in Education: Programs, Policies, and Practices*. New York: Routledge.

———. 2005b. *Youth, Education, and Sexualities: An International Encyclopedia*. Westport, Conn.: Greenwood.

Sedgwick, Eve Kosofsky. 1990. *Epistemology of the Closet*. Los Angeles: University of California Press.

Seidman, Stephen. 1996. *Queer Theory/Sociology*. Oxford: Blackwell.

Serrant-Green, Laura, John McLuskey, and Alan White, eds. 2008. *The Sexual Health of Men*. Oxford: Radcliffe Publishing.

Shao, Jing. 2006. "Fluid Labor and Blood Money: The Economy of HIV/AIDS in Rural Central China." *Cultural Anthropology* 21, no. 4: 535–69.

Shen, Zhao. 2007. "Lun Woguo de Tongxinglian Lifa" (A discussion of the legislature of homosexuality in China). *Lilun Guancha* (Theory and Observation) 2: 20–45.

Sheng, Qi. 2009. "Ouyu Tongxinglian" (Running into homosexuals). *Zigui Luntan* (Zigui Forum), July 23. http://www.zigui.org/bbs/read.php?tid =28532.

Shi, Qing. 2007. "Tongxinglian Zhangfu Ranshang Aizi, Wo Xuanze Paita Zoudao Zuihou" (Homosexual husband was HIV positive and I chose to accompany him to the end). *Shehui Xinwen* (Society News), February 9. http://news.eastday .com/s/20070209/u1a2619978.html.

Shuai, Chi. 2005. "Shanghai Tongxinglian Saomiao: Sange Maishen Nanhai de Pirou Shengya" (A scan of Shanghai homosexuals: The life of three boy prostitutes). *Nanfang Renwu Zhoukan* (South Weekly), September 24, 4.

Sigley, Gary. 2001. "Keep It in the Family: Government, Marriage, and Sex in Contemporary China." In *Borders of Being: Citizenship, Fertility, and Sexuality in Asia and the Pacific*, ed. Margaret Jolly and Kalpana Ram, 118–53. Ann Arbor: University of Michigan Press.

Sina Blog. 2006. "Qianglie Kangyi Bandao Chenbao Fabu Qishi Tongxinglian de Wenzhang" (Strongly protesting *Bandao Morning Newspaper* for publishing prejudiced articles against gays). *Xinlang Boke* (Sina Blog), February 17. http:// blog.sina.com.cn/s/blog_48359f6101000265.html.

Sinnott, Megan. 2004. *Toms and Dees: Female Same Sex Sexuality and Transgender Identity in Thailand*. Honolulu: University of Hawai`i Press.

Siu, Helen. 2007. "Grounding Displacement: Uncivil Urban Spaces in South China." *American Ethnologist* 34, no. 2: 329–50.

Sobo, Elisa. 1995. *Choosing Unsafe Sex: AIDS-Risk Denial among Disadvantaged Women*. Philadelphia: University of Pennsylvania Press.

Solinger, Dorothy. 1995a. "The Chinese Work Unit and Transient Labor in the Transition from Socialism." *Modern China* 21, no. 2: 155–183.

———. 1995b. "The Floating Population in the Cities: Chances for Assimilation?" In *Urban Spaces in Contemporary China*, ed. Deborah Davis et al., 113–39. Washington, D.C.: Woodrow Wilson Center Press and Cambridge University Press.

———. 1999. *Contesting Citizenship*. Berkeley: University of California Press.

Sommer, Matthew. 2002. *Sex, Law, and Society in Late Imperial China*. Stanford: Stanford University Press.

Spires, Anthony. 2011. "Contingent Symbiosis and Civil Society in an Authoritarian State: Understanding the Survival of China's Grassroots NGOs." *American Journal of Sociology* 117, no. 1: 1–45.

Stein, Arlene, and Ken Plummer. 1994. "'I Can't Even Think Straight!' Queer Theory and the Missing Sexual Revolution in Sociology." *Sociological Theory* 12, no. 2: 178–87.

Stoler, Ann. 1995. *Race and the Education of Desire: Foucault's History of Sexuality and the Colonial Order of Things*. Durham, N.C.: Duke University Press.

Su, Su. 2009. "Kangyi Fuyang Aizibing Fangyi Bangongshi He CDC Dui Tongxinglian De Qishi" (Resisting Fuyang AIDS-prevention office and CDC's prejudice against homosexuality). *Gay Online Email List,* November 29.

Su, Xiong. 2009. "A Survey Revealed That More than Thirty Percent of 30 Million Tongzhi Desired to Commit Suicide." *Xinlang Boke* (Sina Blog), June 2. http://blog.sina.com.cn/s/blog_51ff48e30100d50m.html.

Sun, Peidong. 2012. *Shuilai Quwode Nuer? Shanghai Xiangqinjiao Yu Baifa Xiangqin* (Who will marry my daughter? Shanghai parental matchmaking corner and the sent-down youth). Zhongguo Shehui Kexue Chuban She (Chinese Social Science Publishing House).

Sun, Yunxiao. 2009. *Zhengjiu Nanhai* (Saving boys). Beijing: Zuojia Chubanshe.

Sun, Zhongxin, James Farrer, and Kyung-hee Choi. 2006. "Sexual Identity among Men Who Have Sex with Men in Shanghai." *China Perspectives* 64 (March–April): 2–12.

Tang, Ceng. 2007. "Tongxinglian Men, Shoulian Yixiaba" (Homosexuals, constrain yourselves!). *Fenghuang Wang* (Phoenix Net), August 17. http://bbs.ifeng.com/viewthread.php?tid=2730775###.

Tavory, Iddo, and Ann Swidler. 2009. "Condom Semiotics: Meaning and Condom Use in Rural Malawi." *American Sociological Review* 74, no. 2: 171–89.

Teh, Yik. 2002. *The Mak Nyahs: Malaysian Male to Female Transsexuals*. Singapore: Times Academic Press.

Thomson, Susan. 2011. "Whispering Truth to Power: The Everyday Resistance of Rwandan Peasants to Post-Genocide Reconciliation." *African Affairs* 110, no. 440: 439–56.

Tian, Faxuan. 2009. "Shoulei Tongxing Maiyin an Jingdong Quanguo Renda" (People's Congress is alarmed by the first same-sex prostitution case). *Xinxi Shibao* (Information Times), June 12, 5.

Tivers, Jacqueline. 2011. "'Not a Circus, Not a Freak Show': Masculinity, Performance and Place in a Sport for 'Extraordinary Men.'" *Gender, Place & Culture: A Journal of Feminist Geography* 18, no. 1: 45–63.

Tong, Ge. 1997. "Speech at the International AIDS Prevention Conference." Presented at the First International AIDS Prevention Conference in China, Beijing, June 27.

———. 2006. "Gay de Wenhua Chonggou" (The reconstruction of gay culture). In *Tongxinglian Jiankang Ganyu* (Intervention for the health of homosexuals), ed. Gao Yanning, 450–81. Shanghai: Fudan Daxue Chubanshe.

Tong, Xin. 2010. "QQ Qun Bei Guanbi Yiji Tongxinglian Wangzhan de Sheng-cun Xianzhuang" (The shut-down of QQ groups and survival status of gay websites). *Gay Online Email List,* January 11.

UNAIDS. 1997. China: Epidemiological Fact Sheet on HIV/AIDS.

———. 2010. *China's Epidemic and Response.* http://www.unaids.org/en/.

Unger, Jonathan. 1996. "'Bridges': Private Business, the Chinese Government, and the Rise of New Associations." *China Quarterly* 147: 795–819.

Unger, Jonathan, and Anita Chan. 1995. "China, Corporatism, and the East Asian Model." *Australian Journal of Chinese Affairs* 33: 29–53.

Van Gulik, Robert. 1961. *Sexual Life in Ancient China: A Preliminary Study of Sex and Society from ca. 1500 B.C. till 1644 A.D.* Leiden: Brill.

Vitiello, Giovanni. 1992. "The Dragon's Whim: Ming and Qing Homoerotic Tales from *The Cut Sleeve.*" *T'ung Pao* 77: 349–51.

———. 1996. "The Fantastic Journey of an Ugly Boy: Homosexuality and Salvation in Late Ming Pornography." *Positions: East Asia Cultures Critique* 4, no. 2: 291–320.

———. 2000. "Exemplary Sodomites: Chivalry and Love in Late Ming Culture." *Nan Nu* 2, no. 2: 207–57.

———. 2011. *The Libertine's Friend: Homosexuality and Masculinity in Late Imperial China.* Chicago: University of Chicago Press.

Wakeman, Frederic, Jr. 1993. "The Civil Society and Public Sphere Debate: Reflections on Chinese Political Culture." *Modern China* 19, no. 2: 108–38.

Wan, Yanhai. 2010. "Yanzhengkangyi Beijingshi Gonganbumen Xiji Tongxingli-an Shejiao Changsuo" (Protesting against the Beijing Public Security Department's attack on gay cruising areas). *Beijing Aizhixing Research Institute Email List,* September 28.

Wang, Andy. 2012. "HIV/AIDS Cases Rising in China." *Huffington Post,* November 28, 2.

Wang, David Der-wei. 1997. *Fin-de-siècle Splendor: Repressed Modernities of Late Qing Fiction, 1849–1911.* Stanford: Stanford University Press.

Wang, Fei-ling. 2010. "Renovating the Great Floodgate: The Reform of China's Hukou System." In *One Country, Two Societies: Rural-Urban Inequality in Contemporary China,* ed. Martin King Whyte, 335–64. Cambridge, Mass.: Harvard University Press.

Wang, Jichuan, Baofa Jiang, Harvey Siegal, Russel Falck, and Robert Carlson. 2001a. "Level of AIDS and HIV Knowledge and Sexual Practices among Sexually Transmitted Disease Patients in China." *Sexually Transmitted Disease* 28, no. 3: 171–75.

———. 2001b. "Sexual Behavior and Condom Use among Patients with Sexually Transmitted Diseases in Jinan, China." *American Journal of Public Health* 91, no. 4: 650–51.

Wang, Jun. 2010. "Cunzai de Liliang" (Power of existence). *Chinese Gay Men Health Forum,* May 22.

Wang, Junyong. 2008. "Guanyu F Cheng Tongzhi Yuchi Bei Jingcha Chafeng Shijian" (About police closedown of tongzhi bathhouse in F City). In *Nantongxing Lian Yuchi Kaizhan Yufang Aizibing Xingwei Ganyu* (AIDS intervention in male homosexual bathhouses), ed. Zhongguo Aizibing Gongzuo Minjian Zuzhi Lianxi Huiyi (Chinese Convention of AIDS Grassroots Organizations), 38–42. Beijing: Beijing Aizhixing Institute.

Wang, Liao. 2009. "Tongxinglian Nanzi Yin Nanyou Ti Fenshou Chi Xing Ai Guangdie Lesuo 6 Wan" (A homosexual man uses sex DVD to blackmail his boyfriend 60,000 yuan upon boyfriend's proposal of separation). *Jinjian Zaobao* (Jinjian Morning Newspaper), June 10, 7.

Wang, Long. 2009. "Guanyu Jinqi Henduo Tongxinglian Wangzhan Bei Wuduan Guanbi de Gongkaixin" (Open letter to the People's Republic of China's Industry and Information Ministry and Public Security Ministry about the shutdown of gay websites). *Chinese Gay Men Health Forum,* December 22.

———. 2010a. "Miqie Guanzhu Xi'an—Tongzhi Yushi Bei Minjing Wugu Daza Shijian" (Close focus on Xi'an—the incident of smashing gay bathhouse by the police). *Gay Online Email List,* April 20.

———. 2010b. "Mudanyuan de Daibu" (Arrests in Mudan Park). *Gay Online Email List,* September 27.

Wang, Pan. 2012. "Nanzi Zhongxue Dangbuzhu Nansheng Weiji" (Man's junior high school cannot block the crisis of manhood). *Dalian Ribao* (Dalian Daily), April 5, 13.

Wang, Quanyi, and Ross, Michael W. 2002. "Differences between Chat Room and E-Mail Sampling Approaches in Chinese Men Who Have Sex with Men." *AIDS Education and Prevention* 14, no. 5: 361–66.

Wang, Xiaobo. 2006. *Wang Xiaobo Quanji Di Er Juan: Wo De Jingshen Jiayuan* (My spiritual home: The second series of Wang Xiaobo's books). Yunnan: Yunnan Press.

Wang, You. 2008. "Tongxinglian Jiushi Biantai Yu Wuchi de Daimingci" (Homosexuality is synonymous with perversion and shameless). *39 Wang* (39 Net), May 10 http://news.39.net/xwzt/089/24/654574.html.

Wang, Yow-Juin. 2012. "Internet Dating Sites as Heterotopias of Gender Performance: A Case Study of Taiwanese Heterosexual Male Daters." *International Journal of Cultural Studies* 15, no. 5: 485–500.

Warner, Michael. 1993. *Fear of a Queer Planet.* Minneapolis: University of Minnesota Press.

———. 1999. *The Trouble with Normal: Sex, Politics, and the Ethics of Queer Life.* Cambridge, Mass.: Harvard University Press.

Watkins, Susan C. 2004. "Navigating the AIDS Epidemic in Rural Malawi." *Population and Development Review* 30, no. 4: 673–705.

Wei, Zhi. 2009. "Nantongxinglian Huazhe Gengyi Ganran Aizibing" (Male homosexual patients find it easy to get HIV/AIDS). *Jinyou Xinli Zixun* (Worry-Free Therapy), June 9. http://www.jieu.net/Article/life/homosex/200906/520.html.

Weinberg, Thomas. 1994. *S and M.* New York: Prometheus Books.

Weiss, Margot. 2011. *Techniques of Pleasure: BDSM and the Circuits of Sexuality.* Durham, N.C.: Duke University Press.

Weiss, Margot, and Naomi Greyser. 2012. "Introduction: Left Intellectuals and the Neoliberal University." *American Quarterly* 64, no. 4: 787–93.

Wen, Jiabao. 2006. *Aizibing Fangzhi Tiaoli* (Laws on AIDS prevention). Beijing: Office of State Council of China.

Willig, Carla. 1995. "'I Wouldn't Have Married the Guy If I'd Have to Do That.' Heterosexual Adults' Accounts of Condom Use and Their Implications for Sexual Practice." *Journal of Community and Applied Social Psychology* 5, no. 2: 75–87.

Wilson, Angelia. 2007. "With Friends like These: The Liberalization of Queer Family Policy." *Critical Social Policy* 27, no. 1: 50–76.

Wo, Shuo. 2006. "Da Er Nvsheng Yin Tongxinglianren Jiaren Xunqing, Zuida Yuanwang Zuo Bianxing Shoushu" (Sophomore female student commits suicide upon female lover's marriage, biggest wish is transgendered surgery). *Dongya Jingmao Xinwen* (East Asia Finance News), April 13. http://www.chinaren.com/20050718/n226355191.shtml.

Wong, Frank Y., Jennifer Huang, Weibing Wang, Na He, Jamie Marzzurco, Stephanie Frangos, Michelle E. Buchholz, Darwin Young, and Brian D. Smith. 2009. "STIs and HIV among Men Having Sex with Men in China: A Ticking Time Bomb?" *AIDS Education and Prevention* 21, no. 5: 430–46.

Wong, Linda, and Huen Wai-Po. 1998. "Reforming the Household Registration System: A Preliminary Glimpse of the Blue Chop Household Registration System in Shanghai and Shenzhen." *International Migration Review* 32, no. 4: 974–94.

Woon, Yuen-Fong. 1999. "Labor Migration in the 1990s." *Modern China* 25, no. 4: 475–512.

Worth, Dooley. 1989. "Sexual Decision-Making and AIDS: Why Condom Promotion among Vulnerable Women Is Likely to Fail." *Studies in Family Planning* 20: 297–307.

Wu, Cuncun. 2004. *Homoerotic Sensibilities in Late Imperial China.* London: RoutledgeCurzon.

Wu, Huimin. 2011. "Faxian Ziji You Tongxinglian Qingxiang, Zenmo Ban?" (What should you do when you find yourself a homosexual inclination?). *Zhongqing Wang* (Chinese Youth), May 16. http://xinli.9939.com/hlxl/txl/2011/0516/1424913.shtml.

Wu, Xiao. 2009. "Benzhoumo Kuer Yingxiang Zhan" (Queer movie exhibit this weekend). *Gay Online Email List,* October 20.

Wu, Yan. 2007. "Tongxinglian Yu Xingbing, Aizibing" (Homosexuality and STDs, AIDS). *Zhongguo Shengzhi Jiankang* (Chinese Biological Health), August 17, 3.

Wu, Yi-Li. 2010. *Reproducing Women: Medicine, Metaphor, and Childbirth in Late Imperial China.* Berkeley: University of California Press.

Wu, Zunyou. 2009. "Zhi Zhongguo Nantong Jiankang Luntan de Xin" (Letter to the Chinese Gay Men Health Forum). *Gay Online Email List,* December 4.

Xi, Si. 2012. "Qingchunqi Tongxinglian Ruhe Jiaozheng" (How to correct youth homosexuality). *Zhongguo Zhongxuesheng Lianmeng Wang* (Chinese Junior High Student Alliance Net), February 21.

Xi, Wang. 2007. "Shijie Aizibing Jie" (World AIDS Day). *Gay Online Email List,* December 1.

Xia, Jing. 2010. "Weiniang Shi Zenyang Liancheng de" (How are fake women formed?). *Chongqing Ribao* (Chongqing Daily), July 2, B7.

Xia, Pi. 2008. "Zuixin Daxuesheng Tongxinglian Duanbei Diaocha Baogao" (New reports about college homosexual students). *Bandao Shequ* (Peninsula Community), August 19. http://club.bandao.cn/thread-1020448-1-1.html.

Xin, Ling. 2009. "Xingquxiang Yantaohui Jizhe Zao Quzhu" (Reporter was driven out of sexual orientation symposium). *Xinling Kafei Wang* (Psychology Net), August 8. http://www.psycofe.com/read/readDetail_6808_1.htm.

Xin, Tong. 2009. "Zhongguo MB Zhong Jin 30% Shi Tongxinglian" (Only 30% of MBs in China are homosexuals). *Xintong Wang* (Xintong Net), February 14. http://www.1314xt.org/article/66/2395.html.

Xing, Fei. 2012. *Zhongguo Tongi Shengcun Diaocha Baogao* (An investigation report of Chinese wives of tongzhi). Chengdu: Chengdu Shidai Publishing House.

Xing, Kong. 2005. "Fang Ai: Cong Nan Tongzhi Zhua Qi" (AIDS prevention: Starting from male tongzhi). *Meiri Shangbao* (Daily Commercial Newspaper), August 22, 13.

Xu, Daozhen. 2005. "Tongxinglian Shi Ruhe Xingcheng de?" (How is homosexuality formed?). *Jingsheng Zaixian* (Spirit Online), June 7. http://www.xywy.com/xl/hlxl/200805/18-307319.html.

Xu, Qin. 2003. "Demanding Payment—Migrant Seek Suicide in Chongqing" (Wei Tao Gongqian—Chongqing Mingong Zisha). *Chongqing Shangbao* (Chongqing Business Newspaper), October 26. http://news.sohu.com/01/53/news214835301.shtml.

Xuan, Lu. 2006. "Nanjing Yi Tongxinglian Zhe Kanwan Huangdie Hou Fengkuang Weixi Shaonan Bei Panxing" (A Nanjing homosexual is sentenced for raping and molesting teenage boys after watching porn). *Yangzi Wanbao* (Yangzi Evening Newspaper), April 13, 6.

Xuan, Xuan. 2010. "Zhongguo Tongxinglian zhe Wunai de Xingshi Hunyin" (Chinese homosexuals' formula marriage). *Zhongguo Ribao* (China Daily), June 8, 18.

Yan, Hairong. 2008. *New Masters, New Servants: Migration, Development, and Women Workers in China*. Durham, N.C.: Duke University Press.

Yan, Xiaoguang. 2009. "Nanzi Zhaoshuaige Wei Tongxing Maiyin Tigong Shangmen Fuwu Beipan 5 Nian" (A man is sentenced to five years of prison for offering male prostitutes). *Xinxi Shibao* (Information Times), June 12, 3.

Yan, Yunxiang. 2010. *The Individualization of Chinese Society*. Oxford: Berg.

———. 2011. "The Changing Moral Landscape." In *Deep China: The Moral Life of the Person*, ed. Arthur Kleinman, Yunxiang Yan, Jing Jun, Sing Lee, and Everett Zhang, 36–77. Berkeley: University of California Press.

Yang, Li. 2011. *Huangdi Neijing Zhongde Paidu Yangsheng Quanji* (Complete works of detoxification and body cultivation in yellow emperor's inner canon). Shanghai: Shanghai Kexue Puji Chubanshe.

Yang, Mayfair Mei-hui. 1999. "From Gender Erasure to Gender Difference: State Feminism, Consumer Sexuality, and Women's Public Sphere in China." In *Spaces of Their Own: Women's Public Sphere in Transnational China*, ed. Mayfair Yang, 35–67. Minneapolis: University of Minnesota Press.

Yang, Yang. 2009. "Beijing Tongzhi Yingzhan Shihua" (History of Beijing queer film festival). *GS Spot*, June 9, 22.

Yeung, King-to, and Mindy Stombler. 2000. "Gay and Greek: The Identity Paradox of Gay Fraternities." *Social Problems* 47, no. 1: 134–52.

Yi, Ming. 2001. "Yige Tongxinglian Zhede Huayang Nianhua" (A homosexual's flowery youth). *Chongqing Fazhibao* (Chongqing Law Newspaper), July 19, 10.

———. 2008. "Muqin Shang Dianshi Gongkai Zhichi Tongxinglian Erzi" (Mother publicly supports homosexual son on TV). *Nanfang Zhou Kan* (Southern Weekly), January 17. http://news.163.com/08/0117/16/42E2MK7800011SM9 .html.

———. 2009. "Tongxinglian de Zhiliao Hen Kunnan" (Treatment of homosexuality is very difficult). *Senzhi Xinli Fuwu* (Senzhi Therapy Service), July 26. http://www.xl995.com/Article/xingxinli/xlcs/200907/19462.html.

Yi, Sheng. 2007. "Guangzhou Tongxinglian Kong Ai Guoban" (Over half of homosexuals are afraid of AIDS in Guangzhou). *39 Jiankang* (39 Health), April 8. http://www.39.net/aids/Souylm/zjaids/233943_2.html.

Ying, Zi. 2009. "Jiubali Tanfang Dalian Tongxinglian Qunti: Beijiaosheng Jiejie, Tamen Gaoxing Huile" (Visiting the Dalian homosexual group: They are ecstatic when you call them sisters). *Bandao Chenbao* (Bandao Morning Newspaper), June 18, B04.

Yip, Ray. 2006. "Opportunity for Effective Prevention of AIDS in China: The Strategy of Preventing Secondary Transmission of HIV." In *AIDS and Social Policy in China*, ed. Arthur Kleinman, Joan Kaufman, and Tony Saich, 177–89. Cambridge, Mass.: Harvard University Asia Center.

You, Haiyang. 2005. "Zhuanjia Guandian" (Experts' opinions). *Laodong Bao* (Labor Newspaper), September 8, 7.

You, Manni. 2005. "Tongxinglian Diaocha Liucheng Shoufangzhe Xingjiao Wubaohu" (Sixty percent of visited homosexuals do not use protection in sex). *Xinxi Shibao* (Information Times), November 18, 3.

You, Wen. 2012. "Tongxinglian Zhe Zuiyi Ganran Xingbing de Yuanyin" (The reasons that homosexuals are most easily affected by STDs). *Xingjiankang Wang* (Sex Health Net), August 20. http://c.120ask.com/xljkk/xqxyc/txl/10493516551 .html.

Young, Antonia. 2000. *Women Who Become Men: Albanian Sworn Virgins*. Oxford: Berg.

Yu, Yong. 2010. "Changsha Shiqu Nan Tongxinglian Renqun Shengcun Zhuang-kuang Yanjiu" (Study on gay men's living conditions in Changsha). Ph.D. dissertation, Public Health Department, Zhongnan University.

Yuan, Guoji. 2007. "Tongxinglian Sheji de Falv Wenti" (Legal problems associated with homosexuality). *39 Jiankang Wang Shequ* (30 Health Community), September 29. http://sex.39.net/xjy/079/29/132475.html.

Yue, Hao. 2012. "'Weiniang' Taiduo de Zhongguo Shi Weixiande" (A China with too many "fake women" is dangerous). *Dongfang Luntan* (Eastern Forum), April 10. http://bbs.eastday.com/viewthread.php?tid=1525432.

Zhang, Beichuan. 1994. *Tong Xing Ai* (Same-sex love). Jinan shi: Shandong kexue jishu chubanshe.

Zhang, Beichuan, Dianchang Liu, Xiufang Li, and Tiezhong Hu. 2000. "A Survey of Men Who Have Sex with Men: Mainland China." *American Journal of Public Health* 90, no. 12: 1949–50.

Zhang, Beichuan, and Yu Zengzhao. 2009. "Nantongxinglian Gengyi Ganran Aizibing Bingdu" (It is easy for male homosexuals to be infected with the HIV virus). *Jiankang Bao* (Health Newspaper), May 19, 3.

Zhang, Everett. 2011. "China's Sexual Revolution." In *Deep China: The Moral Life of the Person*, ed. Arthur Kleinman, Yunxiang Yan, Jun Jing, Lee Sing, and Everett Zhang, 106–51. Berkeley: University of California Press.

Zhang, Jun, and Peidong Sun. 2013. "'When Are You Going to Get Married?' Parental Matchmaking and Middle-Class Women in Contemporary Urban China." In *Wives, Husbands, and Lovers: Marriage and Sexuality in Hong Kong, Taiwan and Urban China*, ed. Deborah Davis and Sara Friedman, 118–46. Stanford: Stanford University Press.

Zhang, Li. 2002. *Strangers in the City: Reconfigurations of Space, Power, and Social Networks within China's Floating Population*. Stanford: Stanford University Press.

Zhang, Li, and Aihwa Ong, eds. 2008. *Privatizing China: Socialism from Afar.* Ithaca, N.Y.: Cornell University Press.

Zhang, Limei. 2012. "Weiniangtuan Shangyan Buduan Jiaju Xingbiecuowu Renzhi" (Fake women's incessant performance intensifies gender mistake). *Guangming Wang* (Guangming Net), April 11. http://news.ifeng.com/opinion /gundong/detail_2012_04/11/13810505_0.shtml.

Zhang, Liying, Xing Gao, Zhaowen Dong, Yongping Tan, and Zhenglai Wu. 2002. Premarital Sexual Activities among Students in a University in Beijing, China. *Sexually Transmitted Disease* 29, no. 4: 212–15.

Zhang, Yifei. 2010. "Yu Aizibing Huanzhe Yongbao, Zhangdama Diyige Zhanqi-lai" (Embracing HIV patients, Auntie Zhang stood up first). *Tongzhi (Gay) Online Email List,* December 1.

Zhang, Yuan. 1996. *Donggong Xigong* (East palace, west palace). Written by Xiaobo Wang. DVD. Amazon Entertainment Ltd. and Ocean Films.

Zhang, Zaizhou. 2001. *Aimei de Lichen—Zhongguo Gudai Tongxinglian Shi* (Ambiguous experience: An ancient history of Chinese homosexuals). Beijing: Zhongzhou Guji Publishing House.

Zhang, Zixuan. 2010. "Beijing Tongzhi Zhongxin-Tongzhimen de Jia" (Beijing Tongzhi Center—Home of Tongzhi). *Zhongguo Ribao* (China Daily Newspaper), June 7, 5.

Zhao, Xinxin. 2010. "Beijing Tongzhi Zhongxin" (Beijing Tongzhi Center). *Tongzhi Online Email List,* May 22.

Zheng, Lina. 2012. "Shanghai Nijian Nanzi Zhongxue Yingdui Nansheng Weiji" (Shanghai plans to establish men's junior high school to deal with crisis of manhood). *Xinhua Wang* (Xinhua Net), April 8. http://zt-hzrb.hangzhou.com .cn/system/2012/04/04/011847649.shtml.

Zheng, Nuo. 2003. "Tongxinglian Jiemi Dalian Tongzhi Wang, Yong Anyu Gong-kai Zhao Nanji" (Homosexuals disclose Dalian tongzhi net: Recruiting male prostitutes publicly with hidden language). *Yangzi Wanbao* (Yangzi Evening Newspaper), September 7, 6.

Zheng, Tiantian. 2006. "Cool Masculinity: Male Clients' Sex Consumption and Business Alliance in Urban China's Sex Industry." *Journal of Contemporary China* 15, no. 46: 161–82.

———. 2009a. *Red Lights: The Lives of Sex Workers in Postsocialist China.* Minneapolis: University of Minnesota Press.

———. 2009b. *Ethnographies of Prostitution in Contemporary China: Gender Relations, HIV/AIDS, and Nationalism.* New York: Palgrave Macmillan.

———. 2012. "Entrepreneurial Masculinity, Health, and the State in Post-Socialist China." *International Journal of Men's Health* 11, no. 1: 3–21.

———. 2013. "A Journey of Self-Discovery—From China to the U.S." In *Seeking the Common Dreams between the Worlds: Stories of Chinese Immigrant Fac-*

ulty in North America, ed. Yan Wang and Yali Zhao, 49–60. Charlotte, N.C.: Information Age Publishing.

"Zhengzhou 80hou Bailing Jingying" (Zhouzhou white-collar elite born after 1980). 2013. April 25. http://www.gayzx.com/gayqun/16288/detail/.

Zhong, Yuan. 2007. "Yidui Nvtongxinglianzhe de Beige" (A tragic song for a female homosexual couple). *Yuanju Zhongyuan* (Meet in Middle China), April 2. http://www.hntz.net/tzqg/tzqg/200704/670.html.

Zhong, Zhengyun. 2006. "Kuku Zhengzhang Zoubuchu Tongxinglian Ganga" (Unable to walk out of homosexuality despite bitter struggles). *Huaxi Dushi Bao* (West China Metropolitan Newspaper), November 18, 26.

Zhou, Dan. 2009. *Aiyue Yu Guixun* (Pleasure and regulations). Guilin: Guanxi Shifan Daxue Chubanshe.

Zhou, Huashan. 2000. *Tongzhi: Politics of Same-Sex Eroticism in Chinese Societies*. New York: Haworth.

Zhou, Lihang. 2014. "Zhongguo Shoulei Dianji Zhitongxinglian An Xuanpan, Xinli Zhongxin Peichang 3500 Yuan" (The first Chinese law case of shock therapy cure of homosexuality: Therapy center compensates 3500 yuan). *Jinghua Shibao* (Jinghua Times), December 21, 6.

Zhu, Yu. 2007. "China's Floating Population and Their Settlement in the Cities: Beyond the Hukou Reform." *Habitat International* 31, no. 1: 65–76.

Zhuan, Gao. 2004. "Fanggui Fuyou Fanmu Weichou" (Intimate friends become enemies). *Reading on QQ* (QQ Dushu), September 25. http://book.qq.com/a/20040925/000052.htm.

Zhuang, Liming. 2008. "Changchun Tongxinglian Shouci Gongkai Loumian" (The first homosexual man comes out in Changchun). *Dongya Jingmao Xinwen* (East Asian Finance News), April 18, 14.

Zi, Xun. 2010. "Tongxing Miyou Chansheng Haogan Bingfei Tongxinglian" (Good feeling between same-sex intimate friends is not homosexuality). *Shanghai Linghun Gongyuan Xinlizixun Zhongxin* (Shanghai Soul-Park Counseling Center), June 26. http://www.shjgz.net/txl/html/?211.html.

Zi, Yutang. 2013. "Beijing Fayuan Jianyi Tongxinglian Manhun Ke Chehun, Zhaogu Quxiang Zhengchangzhe" (The Beijing court recommends revocable marriage upon tongzhi's concealing tongzhi identity, favoring the party with normal sexual orientation). *XinJing Bao* (Xinjing Newspaper), January 11, 7.

Zuo, Feng. 2006. "Mangmu Fengsha Zaolian Zhi Tongxinglian" (Attacking early love leads to homosexuality). *Beijing Kejibao* (Beijing Technology Newspaper), March 17, 7.

Index

abnormality, 4, 28, 48, 205n3
activists, 128, 129, 136, 140, 159, 160, 205n3.
    See also health activism
AIDS Memorial Quilt, 5, 197n4
Altman, Dennis, 10, 76, 77

bars: entry into, 21, 107; hierarchy of, 29, 100,
    108–11; outreach in, 19; raided and closed
    down, 9, 106, 108, 134, 136, 166, 167; sexual
    services in, 106; venues for tongzhi, 9,
    10, 42, 58, 100, 105, 154, 160, 167
bathhouses: condom use in, 168–69, 180–81,
    183; drag show in, 21; entry into, 21, 107;
    hierarchy of, 108–9, 111; inside of, 167–69;
    outreach in, 206n5; owners, 22; raided
    and closed down, 9, 19, 59, 81, 134, 136,
    166, 167, 169, 207n2; sexual services in,
    105, 106, 108, 116
BDSM, 17
blackmail, 31, 58, 100, 101, 110, 133, 135, 160
blue-collar tongzhi, 97, 105–9, 121
boy actors, 35, 37–38, 40
boy servants, 37–38
brothels, 22, 102–3, 111, 115
Buddhism, 53, 161

catamites, 35–37, 199n5
chastity, 24, 38
child-rearing. *See* parenting
Chinese Tongzhi Health Forum, 128–31
Chinese traditional medicine, 32, 180–81, 183
civil law, 9
class: and homoeroticism, 35–39, 77; in
    postsocialist China, 9, 28; and sexuality,
    16; and tongzhi, 17–18, 29–30, 96–122
collective action, 31, 143–44, 159–60, 162
collective identity, 15, 129–30, 140
Communist Party: disciplinary sanctions,
    8, 41; founding generals of, 201n15;
    red-collar tongzhi, 99; the term of, 5
community building, 30, 125–27, 197n4

comrade. *See* tongzhi
condom use: and familiarity and love,
    175–78; and police harassment
    and cultural stigma, 166–70; and
    promiscuity, 173–75; and self-esteem,
    171–72; and tongzhi, 31–32, 163–83
conformity, 14, 74, 88, 93, 137, 139, 143, 190–91
Confucianism, 38, 45, 124, 153
consumerism, 13, 16, 18, 98, 115, 120, 122, 192
courtesans, 37
covert gayness, 12, 29, 101, 104, 111, 189–90
criminal law, 8, 41
criminals: homosexuals portrayed as, 45–46,
    57–59, 72; and money boys, 103, 110
cruising: benefits of, 107–8; hierarchy of,
    108–9; perils of, 106–7; spots (*see* bars;
    bathhouses)
cultural capital, 45
cure for homosexuality, lawsuit regarding,
    193–94

deviance: with condom use and STIs, 182;
    gender deviance and sexual deviance,
    12, 73; portray of homosexuality, 44,
    46, 52–57
discourse: of AIDS prevention, 136; of
    anti-feminized men, 62; of experts, 14,
    39, 46; of homosexuality, 4, 50–74; of
    the neoliberal polity, 16, 29, 97, 99, 104,
    109, 122, 124, 143; "quality discourse,"
    110; of rights, 11; theory of, 49–50, 73,
    139; of tongzhi, 5
discursive regime. *See* discourse
disorder, 56–59, 69
drag queens, 94–95
drug use, 32, 50, 181, 183, 200n6
duan xiu, 4, 34

economic normalization, 16, 190
effeminate men: gender confusion and
    gender misrecognition, 64–69;

241

TIANTIAN ZHENG is professor of anthropology at State University of New York, Cortland. Her book *Red Lights: The Lives of Sex Workers in Postsocialist China* (Minnesota, 2009) was awarded the 2010 Sara A. Whaley Book Prize from the National Women's Studies Association. Her book *Ethnographies of Prostitution in Contemporary China* received the 2011 Research Publication Book Award from the Association of Chinese Professors of Social Sciences in the United States. She is coauthor of *Ethical Research with Sex Workers: Anthropological Approaches* and *HIV/AIDS through an Anthropological Lens* and the editor of *Sex-Trafficking, Human Rights, and Social Justice* and *Cultural Politics of Gender and Sexuality in Contemporary Asia.*